COMPUTER SYSTEM ARCHITECTURE

COMPUTER SYSTEM ARCHITECTURE

Harsh Marwah

ANMOL PUBLICATIONS PVT. LTD.
NEW DELHI-110 002 (INDIA)

ANMOL PUBLICATIONS PVT. LTD.

Regd. Office: 4360/4, Ansari Road, Daryaganj,
New Delhi-110002 (India)
Tel.: 23278000, 23261597, 23286875, 23255577
Fax: 91-11-23280289
Email: anmolpub@gmail.com
Visit us at: www.anmolpublications.com

Branch Office: No. 1015, Ist Main Road, BSK IIIrd Stage
IIIrd Phase, IIIrd Block, Bangalore-560 085 (India)
Tel.: 080-41723429 • Fax: 080-26723604
Email: anmolpublicationsbangalore@gmail.com

Computer System Architecture

© Reserved

First Edition, 2010

ISBN 978-81-261-4607-9

PRINTED IN INDIA

Printed at Mehra Offset Press, Delhi.

Contents

Preface

This book is intended to be a guide and a textbook which helps in study and teaching of basic Computer and its Architecture. Its purpose is to assist the students and teacher to do the great work of every instructor in field of Computers. To this end, care has been taken to select and emphasize those facts and events, which illustrate the real character of the people, which shows the progressive development and explain the influence that exercised upon modern civilization.

The book has many aspects and interest in study of Computer and its related Peripherals, which becomes intensified to the extent that unity is perceived. The attempt has been made, therefore, to keep before the mind of the Computer students the real sequence of events. The early stages of Computer evolutions presented according to what we believe to be the most plausible and scientific views. The students should of course understand that the study of Computer and its Architecture that is based largely upon intelligence and inferences. For the purpose of encouraging the reading of this book, each chapter is supplemented by extra explanation, diagrams and illustrations.

Author

Chapter 1

Introduction to Design Technology

COMPUTER SYSTEMS

SYSTEMS

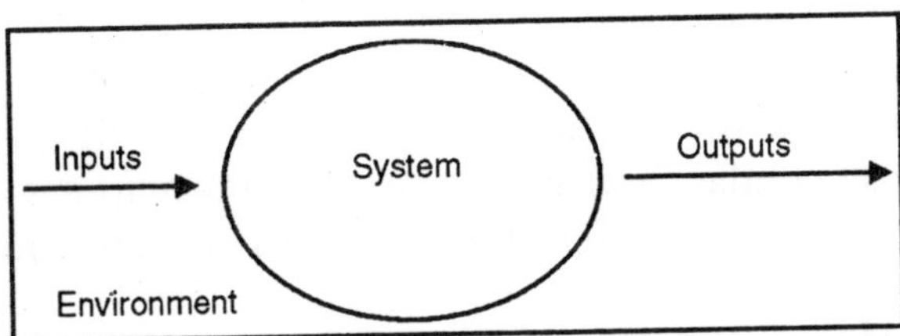

A system is contained within a boundary, either physical or logical. Outside the boundary is the environment, which the system interacts with via inputs and outputs. The system has no direct control over the environment, it can only control what happens inside the boundary.

The system receives inputs, but has no control over what these inputs are. It gives outputs but has no control over what then happens to them. Systems can be defined in many ways. They could have the same boundary, but a different way of looking at it. It could also have a different boundary.

For example, you could look at a computer system in the following ways:

- A tool that takes commands and returns data
- A collection of components that take in electrical signals and returns electrical signals

- A device for converting characters to binary code
- A component in an office workflow diagram
- A system is analogous to mathematical relations. A system maps inputs to outputs. This is an abstraction level which is sufficient for many purposes.

Systems are nested, therefore decomposition is normally a good way to study a system. Systems can "overlap" (at least logically). Definitions can be applied to all systems.

To design a system:

- Determine boundary
  - What can be changed
  - What is in the scope of design, what is outside
- Determine the interfaces/how it interacts with the environment
- Determine mapping relations
- Determine what internal data is required to support mappings
  - Data storage

To design a system to work into an existing system, you need to think of separate components. Each component contains a boundary and an interface, and I/O mappings. How the system works should be transparent to each other module.

All you need to know is:

- How to use the interfaces (I/O structures)
- What the mappings achieve
- How trustworthy the components are

HIERARCHIES

Systems are hierarchical structures. Each level is a component of a higher level, and each component also has components at lower levels. Some components and levels are logical. Each topic in Computer Science tries to deal with one level at a time. Mixing levels of hierarchy can lead to confusion.

SCIENCE AND ENGINEERING

Science explores the physics of computing, i.e., what happens in energy terms, what the components are and why they behave as they do and the theory underpinning hardware and software. Engineering studies ways to build systems. It looks at the hardware and software, and the network and systems architectures.

GENERALIZATION OF ENGINEERING

Engineering principles in one area usually apply in some form in other areas (one principle can be applied to, say, civil engineering, just as much as CS). For example, good practice in development, documentation and testing principles, the planning and management, dealing with cost effectiveness and professional oversight are all traits of engineers.

Students rarely meet reality, however engineering is based in reality. Reality is big, messy and imprecise. Reality changes goals and resources during projects, demands evidence of performance and wants things to last forever (but then discards them the following week).

As reality is often too much for engineers to conceive, they simplify it using models. Models are representations of reality. Programmes, diagrams, mathematical definitions, CAD, working scale models are all examples of models. Models are used to abstract away detail that is not relevant to the current purpose. Models can be static (diagrams, maths, etc) or dynamic (programmes, train layouts, animated CAD drawings, etc).

LIFECYCLES

All engineering projects can be characterized in general terms:

- Requirements
- Specifications
- Designs
- Implementations
- Testing
- Maintenance
- Decommission

We will briefly look at each. You should apply these principles in other modules. There are lots of lifecycle models (waterfall, spiral, etc) that can be used. Lifecycles are abstract summaries of a chaotic reality - don't expect models to be perfect, but they shouldn't be dismissed either. Development methods are different to lifecycles. The methods are practical help with the development based on expertise/experience of experts.

REQUIREMENTS

This is what the system is required to do. This is a constraint also - you should not be making the system do things that is beyond the requirements. Requirements are quite general, as this is looking at the system from a high level.

At lower levels, requirements are more specific to a particular architecture, platform, etc... Testing happens against the requirements, therefore the requirements need to be objective and clear.

Requirements also change, and these changes must be documented. Engineers aim to just meet the requirements; extras are not needed, or in some cases desired.

SPECIFICATION

A specification is a contact for a development. It meets the requirements and is an abstract description of the requirements - it is not how the requirements are going to be achieved. It could use diagrams, mathematics or logical analysis. It needs to be rigorous and unambiguous. It should be checked against the requirements.

VVC (Verification, Validation and Certification)

- *Verification*: This checks that the data is factually correct.
- *Validation:* This checks that the data fits in with it's intended use.
- *Certification*: The checks a system against external documentation and operational standards.

DESIGN

This is less abstract than a specification, however still does not contain any code. There may be different design at different levels. A design also adds more constraints.

IMPLEMENTATION

This must match the design. It also includes documentation - both of the development and for the users. Implementation is a trivial stage compared to the specification and designs, if they are done right.

Some tips for implementation are:

- Re-use code where ever possible
- Document the original or re-used code
- Document all change and the rationale behind those changes to re-used code.
- Write re-usable code
- Use a good style of coding and document your coding fully
- Document how procedures and packages are used
- Document what each component does and the conditions they take.

TESTING

This is the most important part. It is dependent on the earlier parts and consists of various parts.

- Unit tests - this tests the internal code
- Module, integration and system tests - testing the individual components and composition verification
- Acceptance or certification testing - validation that works as intended in context and within standards

Testing reveals errors, not correctness; it is impossible to show a programme is perfect.

Tests should be designed to break the system; you should always be testing for unexpected things (e.g., illegal inputs, out-of-range data). Testing should occur close to or on the boundary of the operational envelope.

MAINTAIN

Most systems change after delivery, perhaps a new platform is introduced, etc... Bug fixes may also need to be applied. Documentation and code needs to be maintained..

- Regression testing should be performed.
- Work out what tests should and should not still work

- Run all your tests again and check the results
- Don't just test the changed parts.

DECOMMISSION

Few systems are ever thrown away. If a system is used, it is likely to be replaced. You should try to reuse and recycle.

There could be lessons to be learnt from an old system, requirements and scenarios could be similar to the new system, components might need to be retained and each of these elements requires careful analysis.

COMPUTER HIERARCHY

A computer is a hierarchy of parts (a system). There are many overlapping hierarchies and views, logical and physical views are both hierarchical and you can look at things from both a functional and architectural point of view. ICS only covers some of the views and hierarchies that exist.

EVENTS

Any input is an event. A command or data sent may change the system state. How an event is determined depends on your view, for example from the view of the CPU only electrical pulses are valid. Logically this could be a single character, a signal, etc... From a human view, this could be a string of text, or a whole mouse movement (which relates to multiple signals).

KEYBOARD EVENTS

A keypress sends electrical signals to a keyboard transducer. The transducer converts the character pressed to an IRA (ASCII) bit value.

Mouse Event

Press, release, etc are all considered individual mouse events. The window manager interprets events and movements to commands. Commands are interpreted to machine instructions in the form of bits. Bits are transmitted to the I/O module and memory. Transmission of input is identical for all bits. In a window, a window manager interprets key presses and mouse movements to machine instructions or data.

A filename is a logical reference to a distributed set of addresses. Physically this is an index address and lots of separate data blocks. A computer takes well formed commands and then uses context to deduce what's intended.

VIEWS AND LEVELS

There are different ways you can look at things:

- Internals - above the hardware level but below the operating system
- Architecture - how the programmer sees the system
- Organisation - how features are laid out

Architecture

- Data representation
- Instruction set
- Addressing
- I/O mechanisms

Most of these are logical abstractions. Physical signals represent bits and they represent instructions and addresses.

Organisation

- Internal signals, clocks and controllers
- Memory addressing
- Instructions
- Hardware support

STRUCTURES AND FUNCTIONS

Structure	Functions
CPU	Storage
Memory	Processing
I/O	Movement
Communications	Control

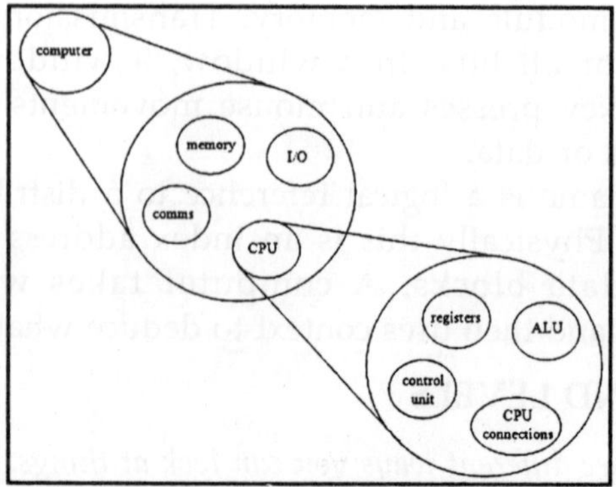

- *Control unit*: Controls execution cycle
- *ALU*: Computational core
- *Registers*: Internal memory
- *Connections*: Connections between other units

IAS

The first IAS machine was completed in 1952. Although this is later than Turing's efforts in the 1940's, the IAS system was public and open from inception so became more well known.

The IAS architecture stored data and instructions in a single read/write memory. The memory contents were addressable by locations and sequential execution from one instruction to the next occurred.

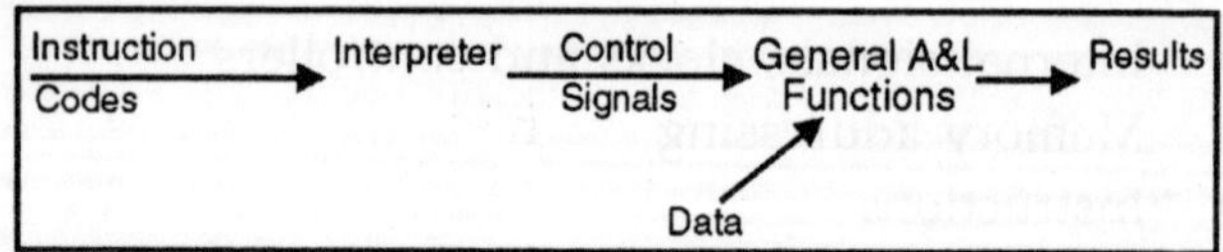

Main Memory

Main memory is a collection of locations, each holding a binary value. Instructions are stored and read sequentially in one set of addresses. A logical abstraction of this is a stack. All locations have sequential identities (addresses) which data is stored and accessed by.

Architecture functions and organisation are built round groups of addresses.

Instruction	0
Instruction	1
Instruction	2
Instruction	
Instruction	
Instruction	x
Data	x+1
Data	x+2
Data	
Data	
Data	n-1
Data	n

Main memory has n locations. Instructions are in locations 0-x. The instruction stack is a logical data structure with input at the top, and reads happen at the top too.

Words and Bits

Each memory location is 1 word. The IAS machine had 1000 words in memory. The Intel 8088 (1979) had 1 MB. The current Pentium 4 (IA32) architecture has 64 GB of words. Each word contains a fixed number of bits. The IAS had 40-bits words, but most modern systems have 2^n bits, for example, Intel processors until the 386 had 16 bit words. Early Pentium's had 32 bit words and the Pentium II onwards had 64 bit words.

There are many formats for a word. The simplest is the opcode followed by an operand. The opcode identifies one machine instruction (operation). The operand is the address of data to be operated on.

Fetch-Execute Cycle

Computer operations are in a series of cycles. For example, retrieve a word from main memory, execute instruction in a word, etc..

Instructions locations number logically from 0. When the computer systems, a programme counter (pc) is set (i.e., to 0). This causes the 0th instruction to be fetched. Instruction is then executed and the pc is incremented. The first instruction is executed next. The fetched instruction is written to the instruction register (ir) for execution. The pc and ir are CPU registers, like main memory, but fast and inside the CPU. pc and ir are CPU registers. The pc only needs to hold an address. CPU buffers are common, for example, between the pc, ir and main memory. Buffers could include the mar (memory address register) and the mbr (memory buffer register)

The CPU control unit determines when to fetch an instruction. The communication between the main memory and the CPU uses buses for addresses, control signals and data. The control uses a clock tick (this is a regular pulse signal). The control units ticks to start the next element of the F-E cycle.

Fetched instructions might need more memory interaction because an execution can take place - this is an indirect cycle. The execution that occurs depends on the instruction in the ir.

For example, it could be:

- Moving data among registers, from CPU to main memory, etc
- Modifying control
- I/O
- ALU invocation

INTERRUPTIONS

Assume end-to-end execution of stored programmes. The CPU is very efficient compared to other peripherals and the F-E cycle is faster than other devices. Rather than the CPU hanging and waiting for a device, interruptions allow the CPU to continue with another instruction and return to one that's waiting on a device when the interrupt is called.

Different types of interrupts exist:

- *Programme Interrupts*:- Illegal processing attempted (for example, a divide by 0, arithmetic overflow or an illegal memory call)
- *Timer Interrupts*: Allow regular functions to occur (housekeeping, polling for data, etc)

- *Device Interrupts:* Come from device controllers, such as I/O. These signals could be such as "ready", "error", etc.
- *Hardware Failure Interrupts*: Power out, memory parity error, etc.

DEVICE HANDLING

A processor fetches an instructiowww.n which involves a device call. The execution calls a set-up programme (I/O programme) which prepares buffers for data, etc... The device driver (an I/O command) is then called and the execution terminates.

Preparing for an Interrupt Cycle

This is a variant of the fetch cycle. The current pc is stored in a dedicated address. After the interrupt is completed, the control unit reads the stored pc value and resumes at that location. The CPU knows addresses to be used. The interrupt only starts when the previous instruction is fully executed.

Interrupt Handling

Any device may send an interrupt (signalling that it is ready for I/O, etc), however the handling details are specific - it might include the OS for example.

COMPUTER CONNECTIONS

Devices inside a computer are connected using buses, lines and interfaces. There are many different types of connections - point-to-point (a dedicated link) or a bus (a link shared by many components). A bus corresponds to a particular traffic type - data, addresses, etc...

Networking can be wired or wireless. Conceptually it is different to internal communications, but physically it is becoming similar to buses. Bus and network protocols are slowly converging. Internal and external communications have different emphases. Networking has an emphasis on security, whereas buses tend to emphasise robustness. Buses link at least two components, and traffic is available to all logical components connected to that bus. Logically, a bus is dedicated to either data, addresses or control signals. Physically, a bus comprises of a bundle of separate bus lines. Buses are things passing values - like a flow of communications.

In reality, it carries current, so has values at all points simultaneously - logically this is either 1 or 0. Unfortunately transfer isn't really instant (assuming that it is is a level of abstraction).

A pulse that is either on or off doesn't exist in the real world. There is a leading edge and a trailing edge as voltage rises or falls. These edges don't carry any data and signals are not relevant here.

Buses use serial communications, i.e., 1 bit at a time. There are 8 lines for an 8 bit bus. Parallel buses are buses of serial lines. Each bus still carries one thing, but a communication may be split over many buses. In theory, parallel is faster and more efficient, however serial buses tend to have higher data rates due to the overhead of parallel (assembly and disassembly of packets).

Early buses had separated, unsynchronised clocks - CPU time was wasted waiting for devices to catch up. Modern buses are controlled by a single CPU clock, however, variable speeds are being re-introduced according to application.

Data Bus and Lines

Data buses have one bus line per bit in a word (or multiples of this), e.g., 32-bit words have 32 (or a multiple of this) data lines, each requiring its own connection pin.

Address Bus and Lines

Buses may have a memory-I/O split. Most significant bit may say whether it's intended for memory or an I/O address.

Control Bus and Lines

These are normally sufficient with 1 bit. They carry things such as timing signals (clock/reset), command signals and interrupt signals.

Modules and Interfaces

Each computer component is a module with an interface. It is based on the engineering principle of each module being self-contained with minimal interfaces. This is true of modules in any other engineering (software, etc)

Memory Interface

The memory interface passes fixed length words to the memory. The memory doesn't care what it's storing, it could be an address or data, or anything.

Control signals (read signal, write signal) tell the memory module what to do, the address bus carries the address that's being considered, and the data bus will either carry the contents of the memory to or from the memory.

CPU Module

The CPU is "intelligent". It identifies the content of the data bus to be different types and deals with them accordingly. Coming in, it has control signals (interrupts) and data signals (instructions and data). Going out it gives out control signals, addresses and data.

DMA

To save CPU cycles, an architectural extension called Direct Memory Access allows the I/O module to read/write directly to memory. DMA modules control access between I/O and memory. It must avoid clashing with the CPU however - a common approach to solve this is cycle stealing.

Cycle stealing happens like this:

- The CPU is in the normal FE cycle
- It sends a write signal to the DMA
- Outputs to the data bus - the address of I/O and memory and the number of words to be written
- CPU resumes FE cycles

The DMA only has 1 data register. It only reads one word at a time and writes a word to the I/O device. The DMA also has a data count register. It holds the number of words it is supposed to transfer and it is decremented after each transfer.

When the data count register is 0, it sends an interrupt to the CPU to signal it is ready. This only works for memory to I/O. I/O to memory using DMA isn't implemented in most systems, but is essentially the same thing in reverse.

The DMA tends to interact with the FE cycle like this. The CPU and DMA module share control of devices. CPU cycles are suspended before bus access occurs and an interrupt is sent to the DMA. The DMA finishes transferring the current word and releases bus control, sending a signal to the CPU control unit. When the CPU finishes using the bus, it signals the DMA to resume.

CPU suspend is not the same as an interrupt - context is not saved and the CPU does nothing else whilst it is interrupted. The CPU simply waits one bus cycle then takes control.

DMA pause is also not an interrupt. The DMA has no other role in computation, so cannot defer tasks to a later date.

MODULE BUS ARRANGEMENTS

A very simple arrangement is as follows:

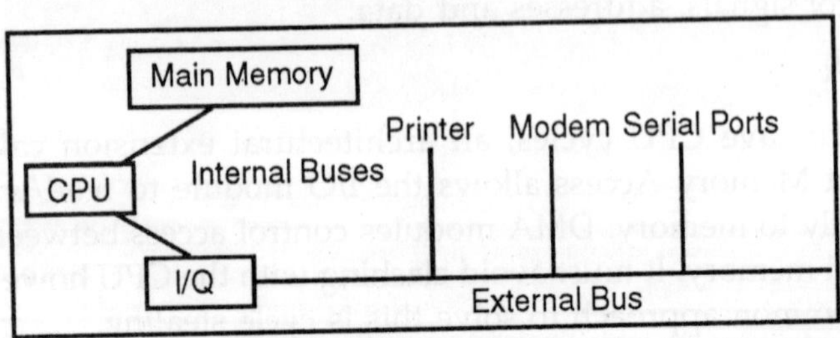

However, with external buses there are propagation delays. It takes time to co-ordinate bus use. More components or devices requite long buses, and this makes co-ordination slower.

Buses also tend to be bottlenecks, the classic example of this being the "von Neumann bottleneck". Ways to alleviate delays may involve deeper hierarchies (using caches and bridges), dedicated buses for high-volume traffic and separation of slow and fast devices. A more accurate bus diagram may look like this, for example:

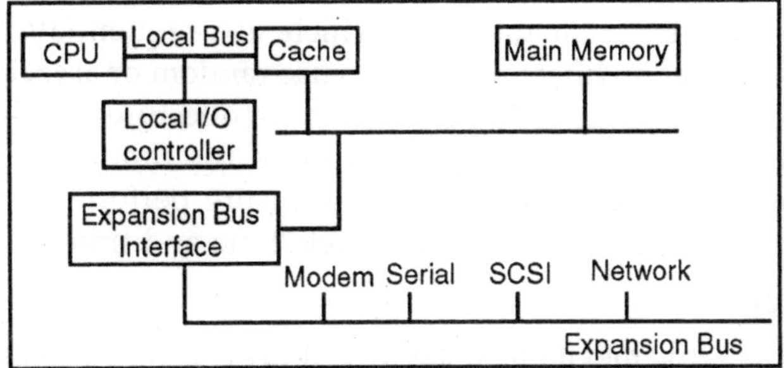

However this is still a gross simplification. In reality, there are many more layers than this.

MEMORY HIERARCHY

Memory can be simply split up into two forms, internal (registers, caches, main memory, etc) and external (hard disc drives, memory sticks, etc)... The focus in ICS is on internal. Total storage space is typically expressed in bytes. The size of a byte was variable in earlier architectures, but now is standardised on 8 bits. An alternative way of expressing memory is using words. A word is a "natural" unit of memory, and is architecture specific. Typically, a word is the length required to represent a number or instruction (commonly 8, 16, 32 bits, etc).

There are many exceptions to this though - variable/multiple word lengths, word lengths not in the form of 2^n, etc... Addressable units are the memory locations recognised. Each unit is a word length and the address range is built into the architecture. There are many exceptions, however, the most common being byte-level addressing within words. The number of addressable units is 2^n where n is the number of address bits. 16 bit addressing can cope with 2^{16} units, or 65536. These are number from 0 to 65535, for example. A unit of transfer is physically the number of data lines connected to memory. There are exceptions to this, for example partial words being read, etc. External transfer units are called a block.

MEMORY ACCESS AND PERFORMANCE

Different architectures have different methods. Older

forms used external memory, which use sequential/direct access. Newer architectures tend to use random or associative access. Access time is dependent on architecture, hardware and organisation. ICS considers these for random access memory. The parameters used to measure performance are access time)or latency), memory cycle time and transfer rate.

Latency

This is the inevitable delay whilst processing a command. For reads, the access time is the time from the request of an address to the memory until the data is ready to use. For writes, the access time is the time from presentation of the address and data until the write process is completed.

Cycle Time

Cycle time is the gap between memory access - for example waiting for memory to stabilise, buses to reset, etc...

Transfer Rate

This is the rate at which data can be transferred in and out of memory. It's the reciprocal of the cycle time.

Physical Media

This needs to be stable and hold two clearly distinct values, such as semiconductor, magnetic media, optical discs, etc.

Memory Volatility

Volatile memory requires a power source to maintain state. Memory such as cache is volatile.

Memory Hierarchy

Inboard Memory	Register
	Cache
	Main memory
Outboard Storage	Magnetic disc
	Optical
Off-line Storage	Magnetic Tape
	Magnetoptical
	Write Once Read Many

As you move down the hierarchy, you get a lower cost per bit, greater capacity, slower access and rarer use by the CPU.

ERRORS AND ERROR CORRECTION

Errors can occur in the semi-conductor. Hard errors are permanent errors where a cell is always stuck at 0 or 1, or a random value. Soft errors are unintended events changing cell values, physical causes, power surges, alpha particles, etc. Error detection works on the principle of storing two values, m - the data - and k, which is a function of m.

If m has M bits and k has K bits, then the stored word is M + K bits. When m is read, f(m) is calculated again, giving k', which is compared to the stored value of k. If k' and k are the same, no error has been detected, however if they're different, two things can occur. m gets sent to the corrector and corrected, if it's correctable, and if not, an error is reported.

This gives three various levels of detection: no detection, uncorrectable detected error, or correctable detected error. However, this is not always accurate. An error could have gone undetected, or a corrected error may not still give the right value. An early method of detection was parity, which was 1 bit long. If the stored number is even, parity is 0, otherwise if it's odd it's 1. If a double bit flip occurs, no error is detected, so it is limited. Also, it can not correct detected errors.

Hamming Error Detection

This improves detectiblity (known as Hamming distance) and also maximises the data:parity bit ratio (the information rate).The Hamming distance is the minimum number of bit flips that cannot be detected. For parity, this is 2.0 Because there is also the chance that parity is incorrect, embedding parity in the data increases the chance of it being accurate. Only one error in parity gives a parity error.

If two bits are flipped, but corrections applied then an even more wrong number will be extracted. Combining old style parity with Hamming allows you to check between single bit flips and two-bit flips. If parity is right, but Hamming is wrong, you know 2 bit flips have occurred, so no correction is possible. This type of method is known as SEC-DED (single error correction, double error detection) and it is considered adequate for most modern systems. The probability of error is quite low.

CACHE MEMORY AND MEMORY ADDRESSING

Caching works on block of memory contents, rather than single words. For example, a 16-bit main memory address may identify a block of data (where a block is 4 words in this example). In this case, this make 0000_{16} the start of the first block, 0004_{16} the start of the second, etc... A word is then identified by its offset from the start.

Caching is used to improve memory performance (it was first introduced in 1968 on the IBM S/360-85) and has become a feature of all modern computing. Cache is typically the fastest memory available and behaves like a module in the CPU. All information is still held in main memory. The cache holds copies of some memory blocks (recently accessed data). CPU reads are initiated as normal, the cache is checked for that word, and if it's not cached, the block is fetched into cache and the CPU gets served directly from cache.

Main memory consists of 2^n words with unique addresses 0 to $2^n - 1$ assigned to blocks of K words. This makes $2^n / K$ blocks. Cache consists of C lines of K words, where C holds a block. $C < M$. There are many different ways of implementing cache. The most common is that all buses lead to cache and the CPU has no direct memory access (logically). The cache needs to know which memory block contains which word. Two ways of accomplishing this is with direct mapping and associative mapping.

DIRECT MAPPING

A section of memory is mapped to one line in cache. This is simple and cheap. However, swapping could happen a lot. Two blocks which are accessed a lot by a programme are mapped to the same cache line. The programme causes these lines to be constantly swapped in and out, this is called "thrashing" and wastes CPU time.

ASSOCIATIVE MAPPING

Here, any memory block can map to any cache line. The main memory needs a block tag and word, the cache just needs a block tag.

This isn't as fast to look up, as more lines need to be checked for a particular word. There are further cache issues to consider, for example, what happens when a cache line is overwritten. A delete/write policy needs to be defined, the block and line size needs to be considered, and there could be multiple caches.

CPU

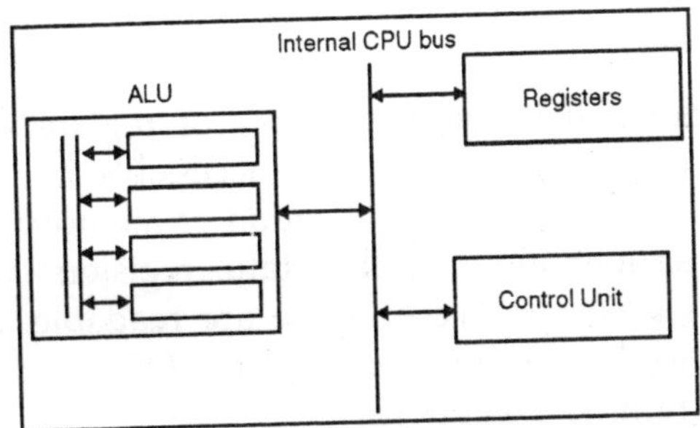

The ALU performs computation and the other CPU units exist to service the ALU. The ALU is made of simple digital hardware components. It stores bits and performs Boolean logic operations. All data comes to and from registers, input is from the control unit and outputs goes to registers, with status flags going to the control unit. As a module, the ALU may be made up of more modules (4 common ones are the status flag, the shifter, the complementer and the boolean logic unit).

Status Flag

This is linked to the status register, or programme status word. All CPUs have at least one.

Condition codes and other status information may consist of:

- The sign of the result of the last operation

- A 'zero' flag (if the last operation returned 0)
- Carry (for multi-word arithmetic operations)
- Equal (a logical operation result)
- Overflow
- Interrupt

Shift and Complement

This is a very common ALU component and is a computational function that occurs frequently. It can be solved using addition, but it normally more efficient to use shifts. Shifting multiplies or divides by 2. 11111111 may become 11111110 if multiplied or 01111111 if divided.

There are also circuits for boolean logic and arithmetic, but the implementation details vary from architecture to architecture.

Registers

CPUs normally have two types of registers, general-purpose (or user-visible), which are accessible from low level languages and allows for optimisation of memory references by the programmer and control & status registers - the control unit controls access to these. Some are readable, and some are also allowed to be written to by the OS, for example, to control programme execution.

Instructions

A computer operates in response to instructions. The lowest representable form is machine code (binary). This is normally represented in hex, however, as it is easier to read. The first human-readable form of the code is assembly, which is a textual representation of machine code.

Instructions have an opcode and an operand(s). The opcode names a particular CPU operation. The operand is either data, or related to the data (an address, for example), or a number, etc... In some cases, operands may be implicit. Many simple operations combine to form fetch-executions, etc. Sometimes these are called micro-instructions. Normally, there is 1 opcode and up to 4 operands. The format of the instruction is architecture dependent. Architecture designs have different representations for data types and how the CPU distinguishes them.

REPRESENTATIONS

REPRESENTING INTEGERS

Binary natural numbers aren't a problem for computers, however, integers are signed (can be positive or negative) and normally the msb represents the sign (-ve is binary 1 and +ve is binary 0). Therefore, a binary representation of an integer must contain the sign and the magnitude. The advantage to this method is that negation can happen due to a single bit flip, however, there are now two different representations of 0 and arithmetic must consider both sign and magnitude.

Another method of representing integers is the two's complement method. Here, a positive number has msb 0. In 4 bits, 1111 is the largest representable negative and 0111 is the largest representable positive. The range of representable numbers is -2n-1 to 2n - 1 - 1. For 4 bits, this gives us +7 to -8. 0 is always positive. The main advantages to this method of representation is that there is a single representation of 0, and the arithmetic is simpler (for a computer).

REPRESENTING REAL NUMBERS

Real numbers are identified by a 32-bit word. There is a 1 bit sign, 8 bit exponent and 23 bits for the significand. This is defined by the IEEE 754 floating point standard. IEEE 754 also defines the 1,11,52-bit standard for 64 bit systems and extended standards which can be used in the internals of a CPU only.

The standard also gives standard meanings for extreme values, e.g., 0 is represented by all 0s, infinity is represented by all 1s in exponent and 0s in the significand, etc... A de-normalised number should have an all-0 exponent, whereas all 1s in the exponent and a non-0 significand represents 'NaN' - not a number. Underflow (the numbers get too close to 0 - i.e., too precise for the 32-bit word to represent) and overflow (numbers get too large) occurs when the exponent can't represent all bits. 0 can not be represented as a floating point. For integers, a normalised floating point 32-bit word can hold one of 2^{32} values. Some values are too precise to represent so they get rounded to the nearest one - in the case of underflow errors this is 0. There is a trade off between precision and range by changing the number of exponent and significand bits. Exceptions are errors - where something different happens from normal expectations. Exceptions tend to be raised by a programme and can occur at any level - exception handling is an essential part of good programming at all levels.

REPRESENTING CHARACTERS

Text is a thing that you don't do arithmetic on. It consists of printable characters (such as this text) and non-printing characters (newline, escape, bell, etc). Characters are coded in an order and this can be exploited for inequality and mathematical ordering (1 < A < a < }) Computers store binary values, so text must be encoded.

The most standard encoding (until recently) was ASCII, but others existed such as the International Reference Alphabet (IRA, IA5), EBCDIC, etc... These traditionally used 7-bits, but extended forms were available. Normally, a parity bit was added to pad it to 8 bits for storage. International standards have taken longer to develop, and have only recently come to dominate. Most of these standards are derived from ASCII. The modern international standard is Unicode, which was developed by ISO. Unicode was originally 16-bit, but nowadays can be up to 32.

REPRESENTING OTHER OBJECTS

There are far too many to discuss in detail, but other items, such as images, sound, video, etc... needs to be represented also. These are traditionally done using large data structures with special handling procedures.

ADDRESSING MODES

Addresses have several modes, identified by operand types, special flag bits, etc. Address (A) is the contents of the instructions' address field. Register (R) is used in specialised addressing modes where contents of the address field refers to a register. Effective Address (EA) is address of an actual operand location. (X) means the contents of memory location X.

IMMEDIATE

A = Operand. There is no separate memory reference and this can be used to set constants or initialise variables. e.g., LOAD 11111001. Loads a two's complement value in an 8-bit address field. When stored, it is padded to word or address size. This mode is not very common due to capacity limitations

DIRECT ADDRESSING

The operand holds the effective address. EA = A. This means there is one memory reference per operand, however there is still limited address space and for this reason it is not used much.

INDIRECT ADDRESSING

Operand points to a memory location, which points to EA. EA = (A). The operand is smaller than a memory word - but the possible addresses are still limited. The memory location is a full word, and any address is possible. This method of addressing is used in virtual memories.

REGISTER ADDRESSING

The address directly refers to a CPU register.

REGISTER INDIRECT ADDRESSING

The address is in a register, not main memory, otherwise it's the same as indirect.

DISPLACEMENT ADDRESSING

This combines direct and register indirect.

$$EA = A + (R)$$

There are three common variants to this:

- *Relative addressin:* Programme counter is the displacement

- *Base-register addressing:* The register is implicit
- *Indexing-the reverse of base-register:* This is fast for iteration.

STACK MEMORIES

Stacks are standard computer data structures. A sequence of memory locations are applied to for a stack memory. Stacks operate as FILO, so access is only to the top item in memory. You "push" to an empty address above the current top and "pull" to get the current top address.An area of memory is reserved for stack.

A pointer is directed to the current top address in a dedicated stack pointer register, because of this, stacks use register indirect-addressing. The top few items in a stack may be in a register or cache for fast access. With stacks, instructions don't need addresses. The opcode always operates on the top value.

ASSEMBLER AND MACHINE CODE

To execute an instruction, each element is read and decoded in turn. Micro-operations occur for decoding addresses and data and then the instruction cycle is a sub-unit of the execution.

The CPU and instructions should be designed to remove any ambiguity.

The instruction cycle works like this:

- *CPU:* Calculate next instruction address
- *Memory:* Fetch next instruction
- *CPU:* Decode instructions (using micro-instructions, where are arch dependant) and get input operands, opcodes and output operands.
- *CPU:* Calculate address of input operands
- *Memory:* Fetch the address and return the data
- Perform the operation (determined by the opcode) on the data.
- *CPU:* Calculate the output address
- *Memory:* Store the output
- *CPU:* Loop to the next item in the F-E cycle.

The exact instruction cycle varies according to the architecture (there may be multiple operands, implicit operands, etc). The maximum amount of operands any instruction needs is 4 - two input, 1 result and the next instruction reference. However, due to implicitness, a 4 operand instruction set is rare. 1 or 2 operands instruction sets are common.

REVERSE POLISH NOTATION

Reverse Polish Notation is useful when coding for a 1 operand instruction set. The format always gives correct precedence and it is most easily envisaged as a graph.

There are different ways of representing machine code:

- *Machine code:* Binary codes that map directly to electrical signals.
- *Symbolic instructions:* Assembler - mnemonic codes and addresses (normally hexadecimal). This needs to be "assembled" in machine code.
- *High-level programming language:* Needs to be compiled and assembled.

The instruction set determines functionality and capabilities, and also how easy programming is. More instructions require more opcodes, and therefore more space, but it makes coding easier. There are many issues in dispute about instruction set design, the hardware has never been stable enough for consensus to occur.

TYPES OF OPERATION

In 1998, J Hayes said there were 7 types of operation which instructions can be grouped into.

- *Data Transfer:* apply to transfer chunks of data (e.g., MOVE, LOAD, STORE, SET, CLEAR, RESET, PUSH, POP). These are usually the simplest operations to build.
- *Arithmetic:*ADD, SUB, MULT, etc...
- *Logic:*- like arithmetic, but for any value, for example NOT (bit flipping/twiddling), AND, EQUAL, bit shifting, etc...

- *Conversion:* Translation between numeric formats (floating point/integer, normalised/denormalised), length translations, etc.
- *I/O:* Can either be memory mapped (the I/O addresses are in memory address space, so only one set of instructions is needed for both I/O and memory) or isolated (separate addresses and opcodes for I/O and memory)
- *System Control:* Usually only available to CPU and OS, allows access to privileged states and instructions, e.g., modifying special registers.
- *Transfer of Control:* Breaking the normal F-E cycle, essentially overriding the programme counter. Using these instructions you can implement thinks like loops (JMP), conditionals (Branch if). You can call procedures with a CALL command, which runs a new programme in the F-E cycle. RETURN then goes back to where you CALLed from to continue. A stack of CALL locations allows you to implement multiple levels of procedures.

GATE-LEVEL COMPONENTS

The Hades framework includes a large library of simulation models for digital systems. All gate-level simulation models are based on the industry-standard VHDL std_logic_1164 multilevel logic system. While std_logic_1164 is slightly more complex than the simple 01X- or 01XZ-logic models, the option to model bus systems with floating ('Z') and weak ('H') values is a clear advantage. The use of std_logic_1164 also means that students will already be trained in a multilevel logic model from the beginnning. The thumbnails below show three simple circuits built from Hades gate-level simulation models. Check the applet collection for the interactive versions of these circuits.

From left to right:

- Parity generator (8+2 bits).
- JK-flipflop.
- Array multiplier (4x4 bits).

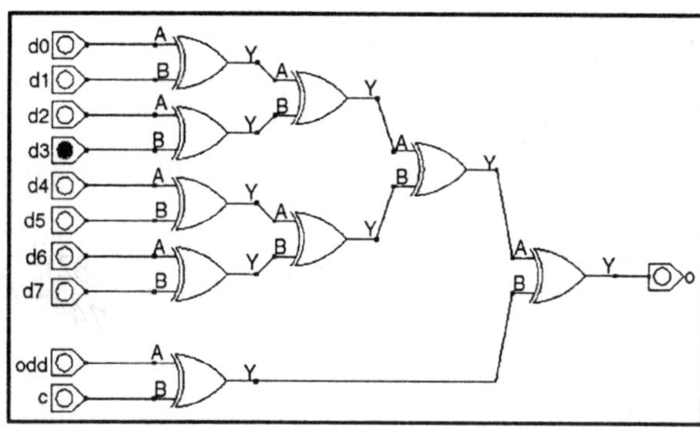

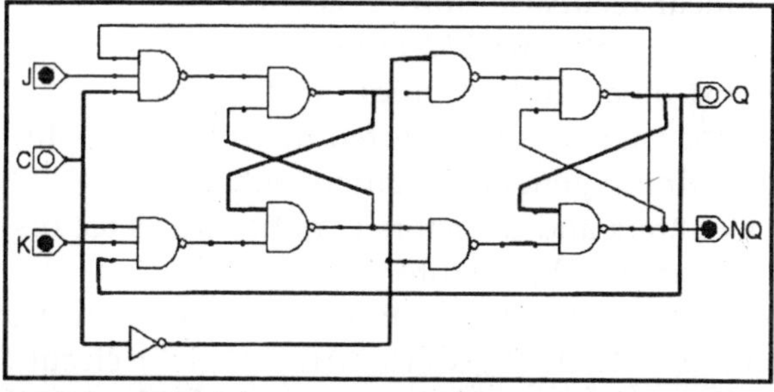

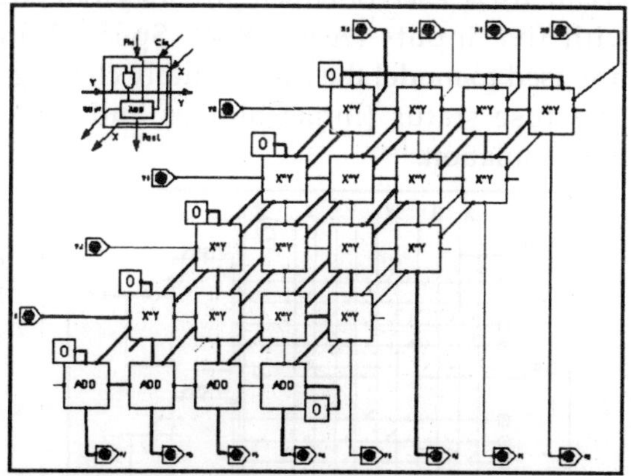

So far, the Hades simulation model library includes:

All basic gates with up to four inputs (buffer, inverter, AND, OR, NAND, NOR, XOR).

- Complex gates (AOI and OAI).
- Multiplexers and tri-state buffers.

- All standard latches and flipflops.
- A variety of interactive switches and displays.
- Variants of all the above with DIN-style (German) symbols.
- TTL-series combinational components (e.g. 7400/7449/74154).
- TTL-series arithmetic (e.g. 7483/74181/74182).
- TTL-series registers and counters (e.g. 7447/74390/74590).
- Registers and memories (RAM, ROM, e.g. 74219, 6116).
- Linear-feedback shift-registers.
- Configurable RS-232 terminal.
- Text-mode and graphics LC displays.
- Subdesigns (can be nested to arbitrary depth).
- A stimuli-generator component.
- Counters and detectors (e.g. hazard-detectors).
- A state-machine editor.

The following image shows the demonstration of a programmable GAL ("generic array logic") circuit. Three output cells are used, each of which provides four AND-gates (terms) with five inputs (A,B,X,Y,Z). Special interactive switches are used to model the fuses; simply clicking a switch changes the fuse status (intact/blown) and immediately updates the simulation.

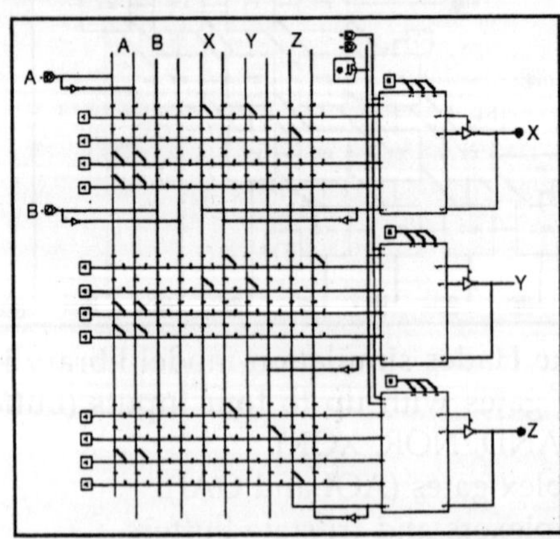

DESIGN ENVIRONMENTS

INTRODUCTION

Primitives and Environments

Design has two fundamental aspects: its methods and its materials. Methods are the techniques that when used creatively, achieve a result, and materials are the medium on which the methods are used. For example, writers design literature by applying the methods of syntax, grammar, and semantics to the materials called words, letters, and punctuation. Sculptors apply the methods of marker, hammer, and chisel to the materials wood, marble, and ice. Closer to home, engineers design circuits by applying the methods of synthesis and analysis to the materials called gates, wires, and silicon layers. Although most of this book is concerned with the automation of VLSI design methods, this chapter focuses on the materials.

There are many different ways to construct a circuit, and each has a somewhat different collection of materials. The collection, for a particular type of circuit, forms a semiconductor process technology. In addition, there are many styles of circuit design and many variations of fabrication techniques, all within a given technology. These variations of style and manufacturing methodology give rise to a large number of environments for VLSI design. Each environment has its own set of materials, called primitive components.

This chapter describes a number of environments for VLSI design and illustrates the primitives in each. One might think that the two-dimensional nature of circuits allows all environments to be described simply with points, lines, and polygons. However, good design systems extend this limited set so that more useful layout can be done. Given a good set of primitives for a particular style of design, any circuit can be built, usually by aggregating the components hierarchically. With a weak set of primitives, the resulting circuits are limited in complexity and clarity. Therefore the proper selection of design primitives is a significant aspect of the programming of a design system. One effect that the selection of primitive components has on the design style is that it establishes the granularity of the lowest levels of the circuit. Given that objects can be infinitely subdivided, it is not interesting to select very tiny objects as primitives. A design made of components that are too elemental will have great complexity, possibly characterized by a very deep hierarchical description. For example, it is nonsensical to design an IC chip by using protons, neutrons, and electrons as the primitive components. Instead, areas of semiconducting material make more sense.

Even better than that would be to use higher-level combinations of the semiconducting material that perform specific circuit operations. However, a selection of components at too high a level will restrict design flexibility. If the primitives are too complex, the designer will be forced to tailor special ones whenever the existing components are inappropriate for a given task. An optimal set of primitives allows easy and unrestricted design without introducing distracting detail.

In addition to providing sensible building blocks for design, the selection of primitive components determines the nature of the interaction between the designer and the design. When a circuit is specified, it is the primitive components that provide the fundamental interface. If the components do not match the designer's notions of the circuit being built, the interaction will become strained.

To provide properly for the designer's expectations, it should be understood that there are several different kinds of designers. Each designer requires a somewhat different set of primitives in order to match his or her mental model. For example, a circuit designer is usually concerned with the logical interactions of a circuit and is less concerned with its physical layout. A mask designer, on the other hand, is responsible for the physical layout and may be unaware of the overall nature of the circuit. A machine architect is a designer who is not concerned with the details of logical or physical layout. This person is interested in only the abstract floor-plan of large systems. Modern VLSI tools and techniques have merged all these design functions so that one person can specify a machine, its structure, and its layout. This person is the VLSI designer. It is important that each type of designer feel comfortable with the primitives of the design environment.

As an example, assume that the primitive components of MOS design are rectangular areas of metal, polysilicon, and diffusion. Then, a MOS transistor can be viewed as the overlap of a diffusion primitive and a polysilicon primitive. Given such an environment, a VLSI or circuit designer may not notice that a change to one primitive affects the whole device. These designers need a single, indivisible component that implements a transistor, because they think of the circuit in terms of such transistors.

Mask designers can use the polysilicon and diffusion primitives because their view of a circuit is one of polygons on different material layers. However, even mask designers can benefit from a single transistor primitive, provided that it is flexible enough to describe all the necessary geometries.

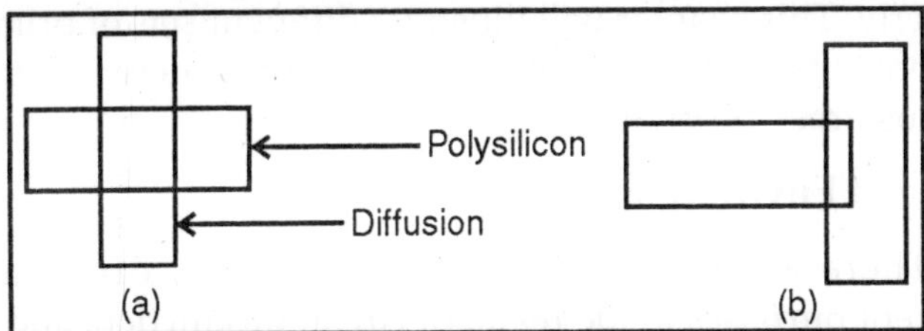

Figure Incorrect primitives make design difficult: (a) MOS transistor composed of two primitive components (b) Motion of one primitive destroys the implicit transistor.

Another example of primitive components that fail to match a VLSI or circuit designer's mental model are ones that make no use of connectivity. It has already been established that circuits are always interconnected, so the primitive components for VLSI design should reflect this fact. A system that provides unconnected regions of layout material is not as intuitive as one that distinguishes between components and connecting wires. The former system will not be able to capture networks as well as the latter system and will be less easy to use for many designers. Thus the set of primitives must match the designer's own ideas of the proper way to build a circuit.

As a final consideration, the number of primitive components should be kept small. This allows the entire set to be learned and used effectively by the designer. Any collection of primitives that is too large will not be used uniformly, which can degrade the quality of designs. Also, the pieces of multidesigner circuits will not match well if each designer has become familiar with, and used, a different subset of the primitive components.

In summary, a good collection of primitives must satisfy a number of conditions. For circuit design, there must be primitive components that can connect. The set of components must be flexible enough to generate any circuit without being so general that the layout has distracting detail. The components must also express the nature of the circuit in terms understandable to the designer. Finally, the collection must be small enough to be learned completely and used properly. This chapter will illustrate different sets of primitive components that were developed to meet these criteria in various areas of VLSI design.

Space of Environments

There are many design environments, each having different purposes in the realm of circuit production, and each making different demands on the necessary set of primitives. Some environments are considered to be very high level because their primitives are further defined by lower-level environments. Sometimes there are families of similar but not identical environments.

The proliferation of environments within a family can be caused by new design methodologies, commonalities of some components, or variations in manufacturing processes. All the different circuit design environments form a space that can be organized in many ways. There is no correct ordering of design environments, but there is a general idea that the higher levels are more abstract and the lowest levels are more manufacturing-specific. Algorithmic environments are arbitrarily located between system and component environments, but they represent a different class that really spans all levels. Environment families also appear in this chart. For example, the MOS (metal oxide semiconductor) family includes nMOS (*n*-channel MOS) and CMOS (complementary MOS), which function differently but share many design attributes.

Level	Environment	Parts
System	PMS	Processors, memories, links
Algorithm	Schematics	And, or, negation
	Temporal logic	Henceforth, eventually
	Flowchart	Test, compute, I/O
	Dataflow	Select, merge, function
Component	Register Transfer	Control, arithmetic, memory
	ISP	Registers, ALUs
Layout	MOS	Metal, polysilicon, diffusion, transistor
	Bipolar	Base, emitter, collector
	Packages	SSI, MSI, LSI
	Artwork	Rectangle, line, spline

SYSTEM LEVEL

The environments with the greatest abstraction are at the system level. These environments view designs as collections of large functional units. The units can be arbitrarily complex, and they typically form the major components of a computer system (see Fig.). Connections in these designs also can be arbitrarily complex, carrying unspecified numbers of signals that use unspecified protocols. The reason for this is that, at a system level, the design is done by machine architects, so the precise method of communication is not important. All that matters is whether or not a particular function block connects to another. Sometimes the abstract nature of a connection is specified, such as whether it carries data or control. Often, however, a system-level environment exists only to show design topology without providing excessive detail.

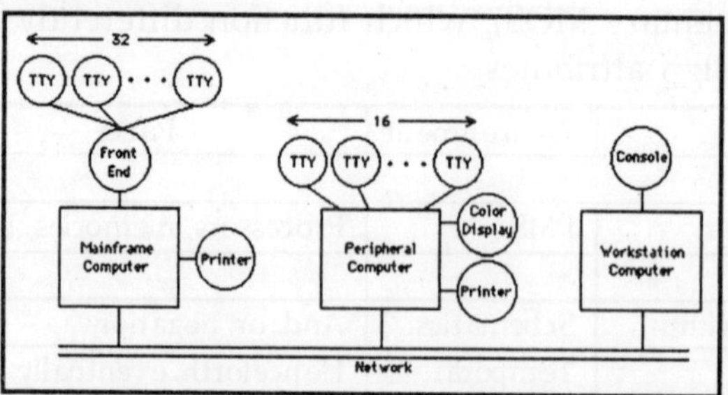

Figure System design. Major components are informally drawn and connected.

PMS Environment

The best example of a system-level environment is PMS [Bell and Newell]. PMS stands for "processor-memory-switch," three of the components in this environment. In addition to processors, memories, and switches, this environment has components for links, data operations, transducers, and control units. Solid lines are used to connect two components tightly, whereas dashed lines indicate secondary, control connections. Hierarchy can be used by defining new components that are collections of existing ones. The following paragraphs describe the seven primitives of the PMS environment.

P_t	Processor, name is "t"
M_t	Memory, nature is "t"
S	Switch
L	Link
D	Data operation
T_t	Transducer, nature is "t"
K	Control

Fig. PMS Components

The processor component (P) is used to represent the central processing element of a computer. This includes the instruction fetch, decode, and execution but does not include the instruction or data memory, nor any of the input/output (I/O) devices. This distinction can be difficult because some processors have built-in memory for stacks, caches, or microinstruction sets and, in these cases, the memory is considered to be part of the processor component. Also, all internal state such as machine registers and status bits are part of the processor. The intention is to encapsulate a component that is typically indivisible and the same in any less abstract environment.

Memory components (M) are generally connected to processors. Although the precise amount of memory need not be specified, the nature of the memory is given as a subscript on the component letter. For example, M_p indicates primary memory, which might distinguish it from secondary memory, fast memory, double-ported memory, or any other scheme in a given PMS diagram. A switch (S) is a general component for joining multiple objects in a controllable fashion. Switches can be used to select among multiple I/O devices on a processor, multiple memories, or even multiple processor components. Their presence in a PMS diagram indicates that there is a choice in the use of the connecting components.

The link (L) is used to indicate an unusual connection configuration. For example, the connection of two separate processors is frequently done with some sort of link that moves information across physical distances. Buses, networks, and telephone lines are all links. Some processors do not need links to communicate if, for example, they share memory or are directly connected with common internal state. A data operation (D) is any functional block that generates data. The category includes processors but is really meant to cover those devices that perform input, such as digitizers and keypads. The opposite of a data operation is a transducer (T), which takes data and transforms them for some other use. All output devices are transducers, including printers, displays, and robots. The final primitive component of the PMS environment is the control unit (K). A control unit is one that causes another component to function. Thus, to make a transducer or data operation work, a control unit is needed. Processors are the only other components that have control and so they can replace these control units in situations that demand more intelligence. The PMS notation has been used to describe the configuration of computer systems [Bell and Newell; Siewiorek, Bell and Newell]. It is particularly useful in describing computer networks because it shows the components concisely. A PMS diagram for the computer network. Notice the informal use of subscripts to qualify components and superscripts to indicate repetition.

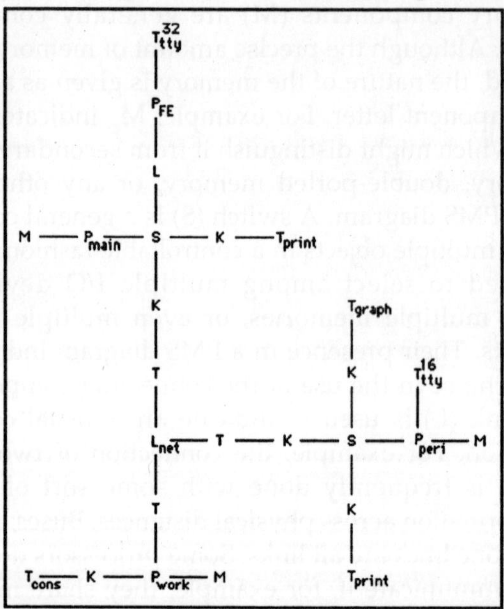

Figure PMS description of the computer network in shown. Subscripts indicate component attributes and superscripts indicate repetition.

ALGORITHM LEVEL

Somewhere in the continuum of environments that ranges from layout-specific to system-general are a set of environments that are more detailed than are the previously described machine architectures, but that have no circuit layout associated with them. These environments specify the precise function or algorithm of a design without providing an indication of how the algorithm is realised. The most popular algorithm-level environment is the schematic, which uses logic components to implement Boolean functions. Temporal logic is an extension of standard logic that is particularly well suited to electronic circuit specification.

Another way to specify an algorithm is with a flowchart that passes either flow of control or flow of data. Of course, the most common way of specifying algorithms is with programming languages. However, textual languages can always be implemented graphically by flowcharting them. Therefore, for the purposes of this discussion, programming languages will not be considered separately from the control-flow and dataflow environments.

Schematic Environment

A schematic is a stick-figure drawing of an electronic circuit. The process of drawing a schematic is sometimes called schematic capture because it graphically represents the circuit. It is so flexible and abstract that many circuit designs start this way and are subsequently translated into some other layout-specific environment for manufacturing.

Synthesis tools can translate a schematic into layout, producing printed circuits, integrated circuits, and more. Eventually, these tools will be able to translate reliably from higher-level input (for example system-level environments) into lower-level layout (optimized circuitry as opposed to highly regular layout). Until such time, the schematic environment will be very popular. In digital electronic design, the schematic components are strictly Boolean and the wires that connect these logical elements carry truth values. For every CAD system that can do schematic design, there is a different set of logic gates available to the designer. In pure logic there are four operations: NOT (¬), AND (∧), OR (∨), and IMPLICATION (E), but common practice also includes EXCLUSIVE OR (→). These operations are presented in a truth table.

		And	Or	Implication	Negation	Exclusive Or
A	B	A∧B	A∨B	A→B	¬A	A⊕B
F	F	F	F	T	T	F
F	T	F	T	T	T	T
T	F	F	T	F	F	T
T	T	T	T	T	F	F

Fig. Truth Tables

Designers often combine these functions into more complex symbols that are treated like primitive components. For example, NAND ($\overline{\wedge}$) is simply the not of and (the result is negated, not the input terms). Some typical logic symbols and their variations. Notice that there is only one connection in the schematic environment: the Boolean that carries either *true* or *false*.

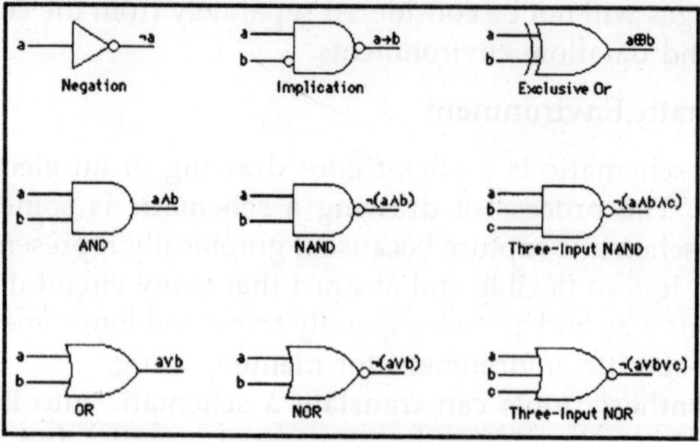

Fig. Logic Gates

In some situations, the number of different logic gates is too great and it is desirable to reduce the number of components by expressing all of them in terms of a few. For example with just one component, the NAND gate, all the previous logical operations can be derived.

$\neg a$	$\equiv$	$a \overline{\wedge} a$
$a \wedge b$	$\equiv$	$(a \overline{\wedge} b) \overline{\wedge} (a \overline{\wedge} b)$
$a \vee b$	$\equiv$	$(a \overline{\wedge} a) \overline{\wedge} (b \overline{\wedge} b)$
$a \rightarrow b$	$\equiv$	$a \overline{\wedge} (b \overline{\wedge} b)$
$a \oplus b$	$\equiv$	$(a \overline{\wedge} (a \overline{\wedge} b)) \overline{\wedge} (b \overline{\wedge} (a \overline{\wedge} b))$

These manipulations are aided by sets of equivalence rules that explain how one logic symbol can be expressed in terms of another. To prove these logical equivalences, mathematicians have developed sets of axioms. Given these axioms as truths, any logical manipulations can be done. For example, the following nine axioms are always true, regardless of the values of *a*, *b*, or *c* [Bell and Slomson].

a	$\rightarrow$	$(b \rightarrow a)$
$(a \rightarrow (b \rightarrow c))$	$\rightarrow$	$((a \rightarrow b) \rightarrow (a \rightarrow c))$
$(\neg a \rightarrow \neg b)$	$\rightarrow$	$(b \rightarrow a)$
$(a \wedge b)$	$\rightarrow$	a
$(a \wedge b)$	$\rightarrow$	b
$(a \rightarrow b)$	$\rightarrow$	$((a \rightarrow c) \rightarrow (a \rightarrow (b \rightarrow c)))$
a	$\rightarrow$	$(a \vee b)$
b	$\rightarrow$	$(a \vee b)$
$(a \rightarrow b)$	$\rightarrow$	$((c \rightarrow b) \rightarrow ((a \vee c) \rightarrow b))$

These expressions are sufficient to define all logic because any true statement can be manipulated into one of them. In addition to logic gates, there must be some accommodation for storage of data. (b) shows the design of a flip-flop using AND, OR, NOT, and NAND gates. This circuit can be built electronically so that it correctly stores a single bit of data. With the addition of such a memory facility, any functional design can be done.

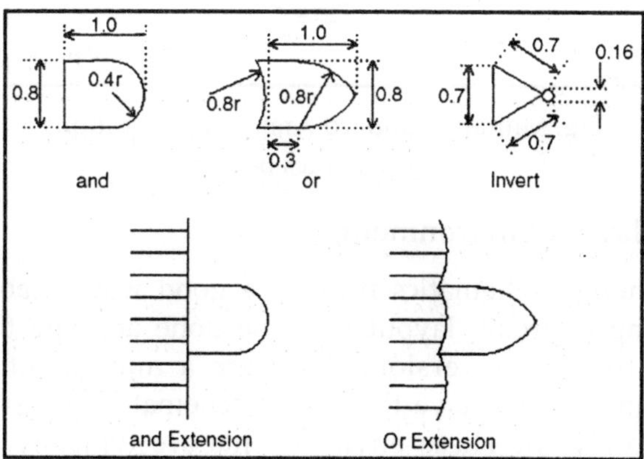

Fig. Military Standard Graphics for Schematics

For the builder of CAD tools, it is useful to know how to draw all these schematic elements. The U. S. government has standardized the drawing style in a document called Military Standard 806B [Department of Defence]. The standard provides proper ratios for graphics and explains how to extend symbols when there are many input lines .

In addition, the standard provides the meaning of abbreviations (C is "clear," FF is "flip flop," RG is "register," and so on) and the proper location of annotation on bodies (top line is the function, middle line is the type of hardware, lower line is the physical location; see Fig.). Although this standard is not followed rigorously and is incomplete in some areas, it does provide a starting point for the programmer of schematics systems.

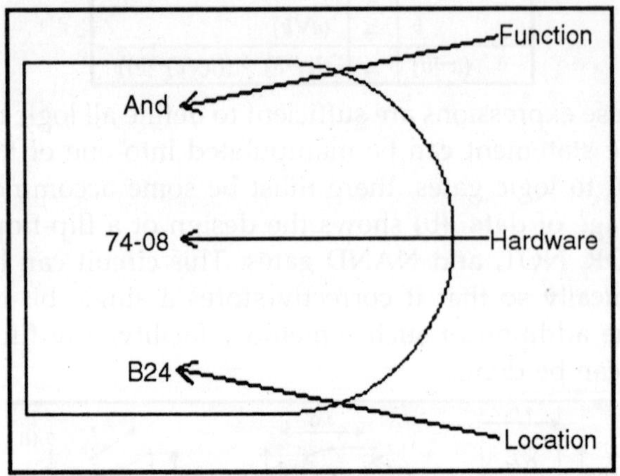

Fig. Military Standard Annotation Locations on Schematics Bodies.

Pseudolayout Environments

Although schematics provide a good way of abstractly specifying a circuit, layout must be done at some time. To help with the conversion, there are a number of design environments that have the feel of schematics yet are much closer to layout. These environments are typically specific about some aspect of layout while abstract about the rest. The sticks environment is specific about the relative placement of components but abstract about their size and exact dimensions [Williams]. Transistors are drawn as stick figures with connecting wires that have no dimension.

This design is much more specific than a schematic because abstract logic gates are not allowed. Rather, only those components that can be implemented directly in silicon are present. To convert this environment into actual layout, the components are expanded to their proper size, wires are given actual silicon layers, and the distances are adjusted to be design-rule correct. Sticks environments must be tailored to a particular type of layout. Although most are for MOS layout, there are some for bipolar design

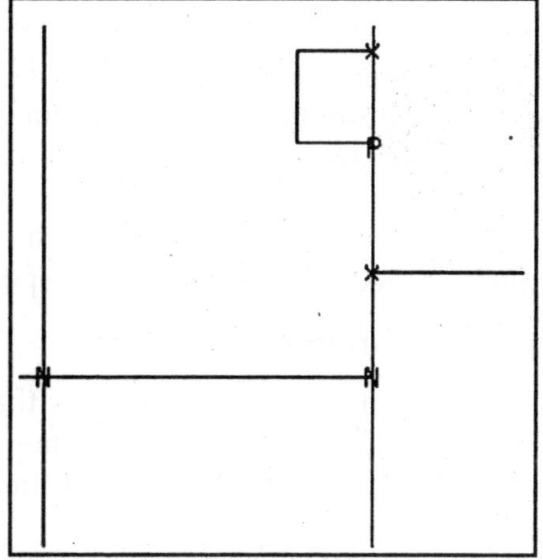

Figure Sticks nMOS inverter layout. The "N" is a pulldown transistor, the "P" is a depletion transistor; and the "X" is a contact. Another abstract environment used to approach layout is virtual grid. As with sticks, only those components that will appear in the final layout may be used. Virtual grid, however, draws all components with a nominal size that, although not true to the final dimensions, do impart a feeling for the geometry. Another important feature of virtual grid design is that the relative spacings are preserved when true layout is produced. Thus two transistors that line up horizontally or vertically will stay in line, even if they are not connected. This is because the conversion to layout is simply a process that assigns actual coordinates to the virtual grid coordinates. This makes conversion quite simple yet retains the abstract nature of the design environment.

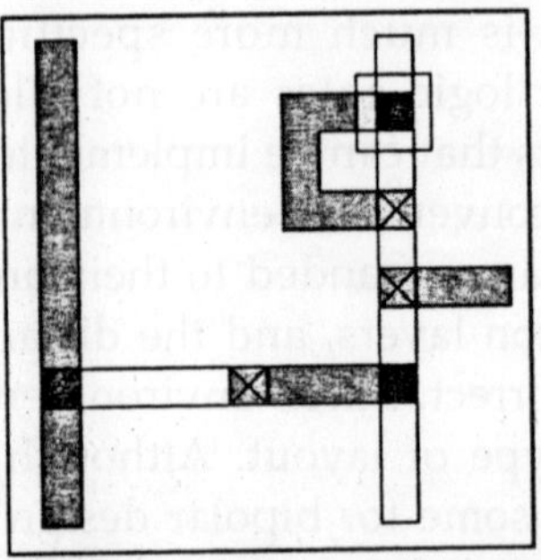

Fig. Virtual Grid nMOS Inverter Layout

Yet another pseudolayout environment is SLIC [Gibson and Nance], which describes layout component placement using text letters. An array of these letters, displayed on a video terminal, shows component placement and connecting wires. Special letters distinguish horizontal from vertical wires, and allow correct connectivity to be specified.

Temporal Logic Environment

One problem with traditional logic is that it does not inherently deal with time in any way. One solution is to parameterize logic values with the current time, resulting in expressions like:

$$W(t)\wedge(t)\rightarrow(t + 1)$$

which means "if working at time t, and inputs are available at time t, then there will be outputs at time t + 1." However, because this structure can be awkward to use, recent work has turned to using temporal logic, a modal logic that has operators applying to sequences of states over time. Although many formulations of temporal logic have been used, this xhapter will discuss one method that has been applied to electronic circuit descriptions. Four basic operators can be used to describe state properties over time. The symbol means "eventually" and its use in the expression " p" means that p will be true at some future time (or is true in the present). The symbol means "henceforth" and indicates that its operand is true now and at all future times. The symbol means "next" and indicates that its operand will be true in the very next moment of time.

Finally, the symbol U means "until" and is used in a two-operand sense "p U q" to mean that p is true at all times from now until the first instance that q is true. As with pure logic, a set of axioms relate these operators and show how they are used to define each other. For example,

$$p \rightarrow p \wedge OpOp$$

states that "henceforth" *p* implies that *p* must be true now, at the next interval, and henceforth beyond that interval. A simpler tautology of temporal logic is:

$$p \rightarrow pUq$$

In addition to basic operators, it is common to define new operators that are derived from the original set. These new operators are better suited to circuit design because they behave in ways that are more intuitive to designers. Thus the "latched while" operator is defined as:

$$pLWq \equiv p \rightarrow (pU \neg q)$$

meaning that, when *p* is true, it will remain that way as long as *q* remains true. Another derived operator that is important in defining the liveness of a system is "entails" ($\rightsquigarrow$):

$$p \rightsquigarrow q \equiv p \rightarrow \Diamond q$$

meaning that the truth of *p* demands the eventual truth of *q*. Temporal logic is well suited to the description of digital circuits over time. This is because it can describe the behaviour of a single component or a collection of parallel activities. In fact, some form of temporal logic can be found wherever the behaviour of circuits is specified. Variations on basic temporal logic exist to improve its expressiveness. For example interval temporal logic generalizes the basic scheme so that subintervals of time can be conveniently described.

Flowcharting Environment

Flowcharting is a general-purpose algorithm environment that is often used to represent textual languages graphically.

Typically, the components of a flowchart operate on data and the connections in a flowchart indicate flow of control. Each component in a flowchart can be arbitrarily complex because it contains an English-language description of its operation. Typically, however, there are a limited set of components that perform distinct classes of operations.

The four basic primitives that are most often used to do control-based flowcharting. The computation component is used for all data manipulations, with the actual function written in the box. The decision component is used to make arbitrary tests and modify the flow of control. The I/O component indicates control of devices. The connector component is used for special control flow cases such as are necessary in multipage designs or for programme termination. The layout in Fig. is an example of a control-based flowchart specification, but it does not differentiate the component types because it is a different environment (register transfer).

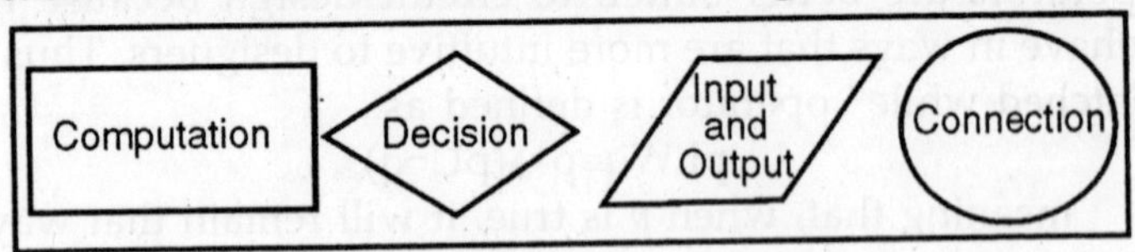

Fig. Control-Flow Components

A somewhat different style of control-flow specification is the use of state diagrams. The components of a state diagram perform actions that may alter a global state. The connections between components are each labeled with a state, such that only one connection will match and direct the control to another component. State diagrams are a very formal way of expressing an algorithm, as opposed to flowcharting, which has imprecise rules for actions and tests.

Dataflow Environment

Dataflow programming is a twist on the commonly used flowcharting technique because the connections between components carry data values rather than control invocation. This means that parallel activity is easier to specify and that the operation of an algorithm is driven by the presence of data rather than a "start" signal. The components of a dataflow programme are called actors [Dennis] and there are many possible sets that can be used. One typical set of dataflow actors. Dataflow actors function only when a predetermined set of input lines have data values waiting on them. This set of inputs is called the firing set. When the firing set becomes available, the actor executes and produces output values for other actors. A dataflow network that guarantees no more than one data value will be pending on any input line is safe.

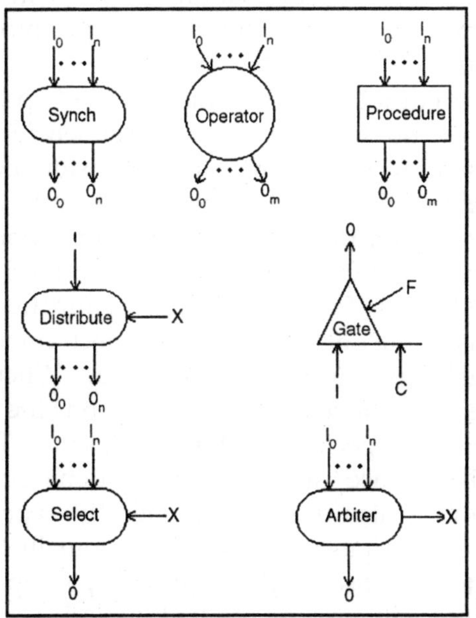

Fig. Dataflow Primitives Activity Occurs when Data are Ready on the Proper Input Lines

The seven actors outlined in the following paragraphs are sufficient to describe any computation. In fact, some of them are redundant and exist purely for convenience. The initiation of parallel computation is done simply by having one actor's output go to the input of multiple other actors. Then all the actors that receive input data begin operation, creating parallel execution sequences. Synchronization of these parallel paths is done with the "synch" actor that waits for all of its inputs to have data and then passes each input value to an output value at the same time. Therefore this actor synchronizes parallel data paths that complete at different times. The "operator" actor is a general-purpose function primitive that can perform any arithmetic or logical operation. When the operation name is placed inside the actor symbol and the correct number of inputs and outputs are used, the operator functions in the proper manner. For example, the "+" actor with three inputs and one output will wait for all three data values to be present and then produce their sum on the output.

The "procedure" actor is similar to the "operator" actor except that it is used for programmer-defined functions. The name of a dataflow subroutine is placed inside the symbol as an indication that this code is to be run when the appropriate inputs appear. Both this actor and the "operator" actor are subroutine calls, but the former is for higher-level procedures whereas the latter is for low-level library functions.

The "distribute" actor is used to select among multiple output paths according to an index value. When the input and the index lines have data, this actor sends the input value to the output line specified by the index value. This actor is somewhat like a "case" statement in traditional programming languages and is also used for simpler "if"-type branching. The "select" and "arbiter" actors are conceptually the opposite of "distribute" because they reduce multiple input values to a single output value in a controlled manner.

In the case of the "select" actor, an index is used to determine which input will be used. When the index and the indexed input are present, that input is passed to the output. The "arbiter" does not need any particular input; rather, it executes as soon as any input appears, generating both the input and its index as outputs. Both "select" and "arbiter" reduce many inputs to a single output: One requires a predetermined choice of inputs and the other reports its own choice. The final actor of this particular dataflow environment is the "gate," which is used for loop control. This actor has three inputs and an output. The condition input acts as a switch to select between the initial input and the feedback input. When the loop is not active, the condition is false, which causes the initial value to be passed to the output. Once this initial value is passed to the output, the loop is activated. Active "gate" actors ignore the initial value and pass the feedback value to the output. This continues while the condition input is true. When this condition becomes false, the loop terminates, the feedback values are ignored, and a new initial value is awaited to restart the loop. The dataflow actors described here can be used to write arbitrarily complex algorithms. The design in the computation of Fibonacci numbers in a recursive and parallel style. Notice that this subroutine starts at the bottom with its input parameters and filters up to the top where the function value is returned. This layout uses only the "operator," "procedure," "select," and "distribute" actors and thus does not make use of the powerful concurrency control available in the environment. Nevertheless, graphically specified dataflow is a useful environment for the design of algorithms, both serial and parallel.

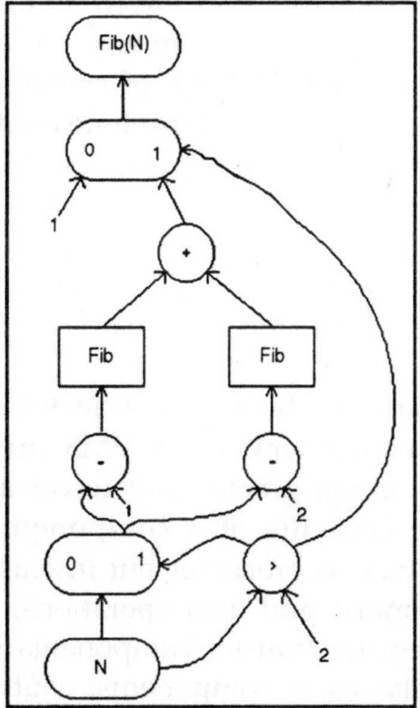

Fig. Dataflow Layout for Fibonacci Numbers. Flow Begins at the Bottom and Filters Upward

COMPONENT LEVEL

The next level of abstraction that defines a class of design environments is the component level. Environments of this type are usually composed of primitives that perform a small number of arithmetic or logical operations. For example, an adder or a small block of memory are acceptable component-level primitives, but an entire processor or a fully interfaced bank of memory are generally not.

A number of different environments exist at the component level. Register transfer is an environment that is used to describe the design of processors.

ISP is a language that is used to describe the instruction set of a computer and how those instructions are implemented. Even integrated-circuit packages, although quite variable in their functionality, form a component-level environment in common use.

Register-Transfer Environment

The first component-level environment of interest is register transfer. In this environment, the components are specific hardware manipulations of control and data with connections showing the flow for the desired algorithm.

This environment can be used to describe the instruction set of computers because it shows the flow of control in a processor that effects the machine's operation. It is also useful in the design of algorithms. Actual implementations of these components were used to teach hardware design to university students.

The components of the register-transfer environment are named after the components of the PMS environment. Their level of detail is much greater and fewer assumptions are made about the contents of a component. For example, register transfer has no processor but instead constructs one from control, memory, and data operations.

The set of register transfer components is shown in Fig. There are four classes of components: control (K), memory (M), data/memory (DM), and transducers (T). The control and memory components are similar to their counterparts in the

PMS environment. The data/memory component is similar to the PMS processor, although much less powerful. The transducer component combines the functions of the PMS transducer and the PMS data operation.

Two PMS components are missing from this list: the switch and the link. The switch is a type of control component in register transfer, as will be discussed. The link does not appear in the register-transfer environment because of the connection distinctions. Rather than describe a connection in terms of physical distance, register transfer distinguishes connections by their contents.

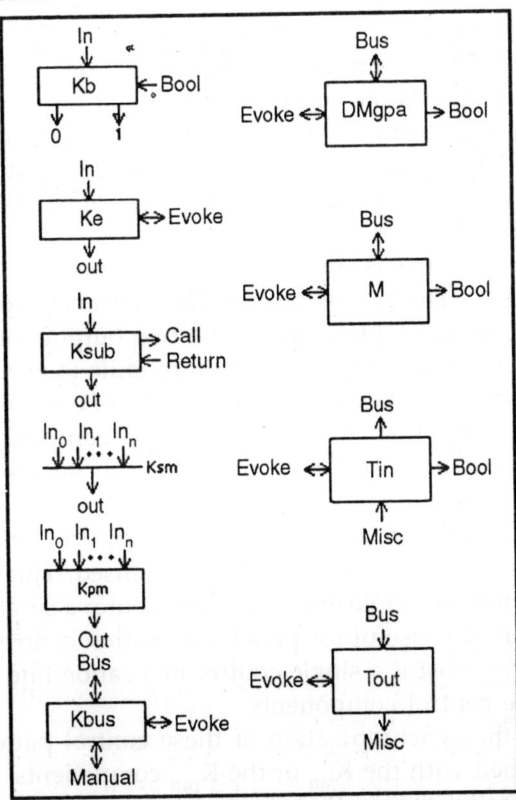

The components of the register-transfer environment. "K" is control; "D" is data; "M" is memory, and "T" is input/output. Register transfer has four types of connections between components: bus, control, Boolean, and miscellaneous. The bus is a general-purpose data and control connection that passes synchronized information between components.

Control connections are used to link the control components and also to invoke activity in other components. Boolean connections are special-purpose signals that aid the flow of execution by linking conditions with decision-making control components. Finally, miscellaneous connections exist to link these register-transfer components with external devices.

Every register-transfer design has exactly one K_{bus} component. This controls the bus connections for all other components and is the source of initial and terminal control that links the design with the outside world. In student hardware laboratories, where register-transfer modules were used most, this component provides the manual interface to the running circuit.

Flow of control is done with four components: K_b, K_{sub}, K_{sm}, and K_{pm}. The K_b component does a branch, conditional on a Boolean input. Only one of the two output connections will be invoked, causing that control module to execute next. The K_{sub} component executes a subroutine of control modules by invoking the first module, awaiting a completion signal on the return line, and then invoking the next sequential control component.

The K_{sm} does a serial merge, invoking the next control component when any one input line is raised. This is useful in loops where multiple execution paths enter a single control stream. It is also useful for parallel execution control. Such a situation can exist if a single control-invocation line connects to multiple control components.

Then the synchronization of these control paths can be accomplished with the K_{sm} or the K_{pm} components. The K_{pm} does a parallel mergc that waits for all input lines to be invoked before it generates its own output. All of these control components are used to construct a flow of execution in a register-transfer design. However, none of them cause any data to be manipulated. All data operations are controlled with the evoke component, K_e. The K_e acts like a subroutine call to a data component: It initiates the data operation, awaits completion, and then invokes the next sequential control component. All data components communicate between each other on the bus and communicate back to the control components via Boolean connections. There are two internal data components: the DM_{gpa} and the M.

The DM_{gpa}, or "general-purpose-arithmetic" component, is able to perform the simplest of arithmetic and logical operations. It holds two registers that it can move, add, subtract, complement, logically AND, logically OR, and shift. It generates Boolean signals that indicate numeric test results. This component is the workhorse of any algorithm done in the register-transfer environment.

The M is the other internal component and it stores memory. To use it, both a memory address and a data value must pass across the bus on separate control cycles. The Boolean output signal is used in slower memories to indicate the completion of the operation. This allows other work to proceed in parallel with the memory access. The size and speed of the memory varies, yielding a subclass of these components.

Transducer components are used to convert between bus data and analog signals for external use. Input transducers can handle analog input, switch bank sensing, and keyboards. Output transducers can print, plot, and produce general analog signals. An example of register-transfer layout that normalizes a floating point number.

The two DM_{gpa} components store and manipulate three values: a sign flag called Flag, the mantissa (Man) and the exponent (Exp). The top six components set the sign flag and ensure a positive mantissa. Following that, the mantissa is shifted until there is a "1" in its high bit (a normalized fraction is between one-half and one). Each shift of the mantissa requires an increment of the exponent to keep the overall value correct. When the number has been normalized, the sign flag is used to restore negative values.

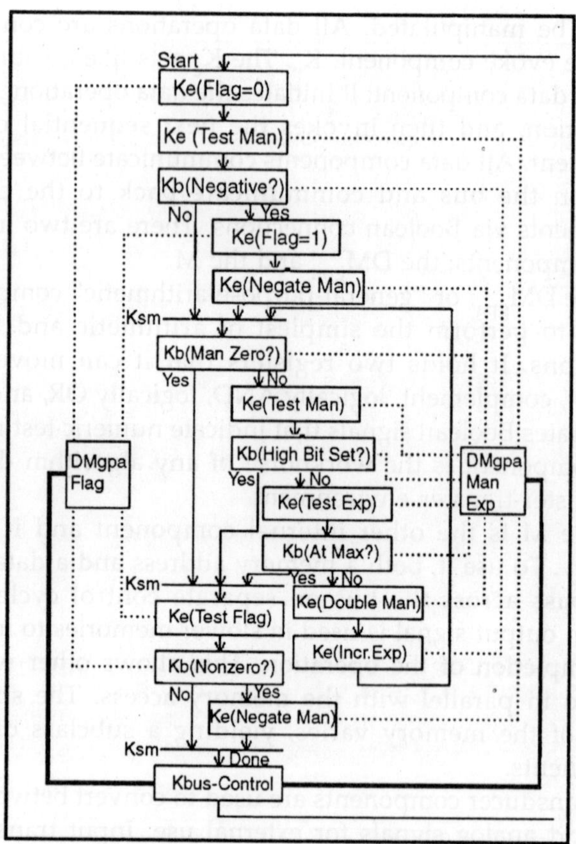

Fig. Register-Transfer Layout to Normalize a Floating-Point Number

Shown complete with bus connections (thick) and data-evocation lines (dotted). The bus-control component links the data buses and controls the execution of the algorithm.

Many register-transfer designs are done without explicitly showing the data and K_{bus} components or any bus connections. The same algorithm without these datapath complexities. This makes the design simpler without sacrificing the detail of this environment, because the data components and their connectivity can be inferred from the control components.

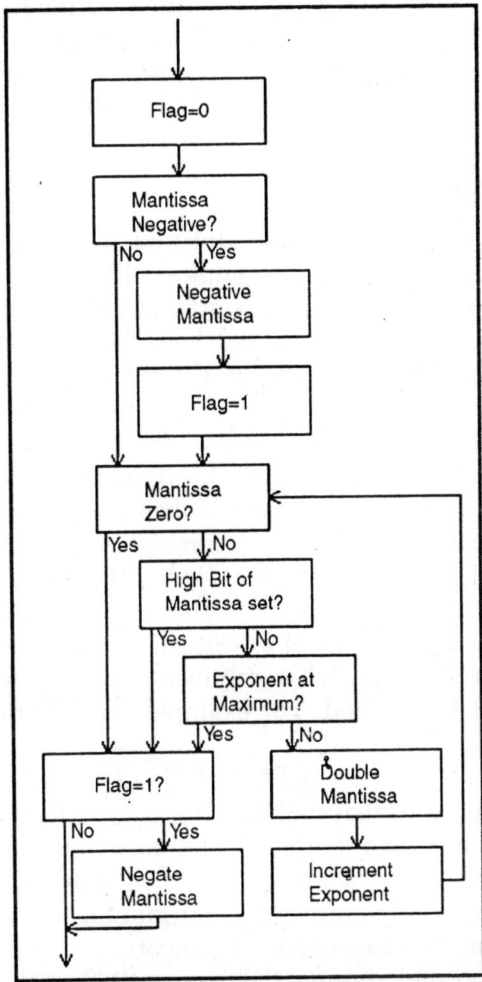

Shown without bus or data-evocation connections. In addition to being a useful environment for algorithm specification, register-transfer designs are able to be built in hardware. Every component in the environment has associated electronic modules that can be wired together.

Thus a working register-transfer machine can be built directly from these designs. Although these register-transfer modules are no longer used, the concepts in this environment are still valid and can be realised with other implementation methods. Many hardware-description languages textually capture the same information as the register-transfer environment does. One language separates data structure from control [Baray and Su], similar to the distinction made in register transfer.

ISP Environment

Bell and Newell also defined a component-level environment for describing computers [Bell and Newell]. ISP, or instruction-set processor, is a language for describing the instructions in a processor and how they are implemented. Notation is provided to specify the machine organization, to manipulate machine registers, and to specify parallel or pipelined execution. For example, the statement:

(OP = 1)→(M[OPERAND]←AC; AC←0);

states that if OP is equal to 1 then two actions will occur in parallel: The value of the accumulator register AC will be deposited at memory location OPERAND and the accumulator will be cleared. This statement handles the decoding and execution of a "deposit and clear accumulator" instruction. Prior to such a statement, the meanings of every term must be defined. For example, the OP field may be defined as:

OP:= M[PC]<0:2>

which means that the three high bits of memory-location PC define this field. Similarly, the meaning of PC, AC, and even the memory M must be explicitly defined. Thus ISP resembles a programming language, complete with declarations and executable statements.

Nonparallel sequencing is specified with the "next" clause, as in the following example:

(AC←AC + T; next M[D]←AC)

This ensures that the addition of T to AC is completed before the result is stored at memory location D. Determination of when an operation can be done in parallel is dependent on the architecture of the processor. This architecture is specified implicitly by the various ISP components and the operations that can be performed on them. ISP is often used to describe computer instruction sets. It is a highly algorithmic environment, which leads one to believe that it should not be a component-level environment. However, there are direct associations between ISP statements and the machine registers that implement them because the text can be used to infer a diagram of the target machine. Thus ISP is another example of a component-level environment. These environments illustrate detailed electronic design without completely precise specification.

Chapter 2

Processor Level Components

THE PROCESSOR

The processor (really a short form for *microprocessor* and also often called the *CPU* or*central processing unit*) is the central component of the PC. It is the brain that runs the show inside the PC. All work that you do on your computer is performed directly or indirectly by the processor. Obviously, it is one of the most important components of the PC, if not the most important. It is also, scientifically, not only one of the most amazing parts of the PC, but one of the most amazing devices in the world of technology. The processor plays a significant role in the following important aspects of your computer system:

PERFORMANCE

The processor is probably the most important single determinant of system performance in the PC. While other components also play a key role in determining performance, the processor's capabilities dictate the maximum performance of a system. The other devices only allow the processor to reach its full potential.

SOFTWARE SUPPORT

Newer, faster processors enable the use of the latest software. In addition, new processors such as the Pentium with MMX Technology, enable the use of specialized software not usable on earlier machines.

RELIABILITY AND STABILITY

The quality of the processor is one factor that determines

how reliably your system will run. While most processors are very dependable, some are not. This also depends to some extent on the age of the processor and how much energy it consumes.

ENERGY CONSUMPTION AND COOLING

Originally processors consumed relatively little power compared to other system devices. Newer processors can consume a great deal of power. Power consumption has an impact on everything from cooling method selection to overall system reliability.

MOTHERBOARD SUPPORT

The processor you decide to use in your system will be a major determining factor in what sort of chipset you must use, and hence what motherboard you buy. The motherboard in turn dictates many facets of your system's capabilities and performance.

The processor (CPU, for *Central Processing Unit*) is the computer's brain. It allows the processing of numeric data, meaning information entered in binary form, and the execution of instructions stored in memory. The first microprocessor (Intel 4004) was invented in 1971.

It was a 4-bit calculation device with a speed of 108 kHz. Since then, microprocessor power has grown exponentially. So what exactly are these little pieces of silicone that run our computers?

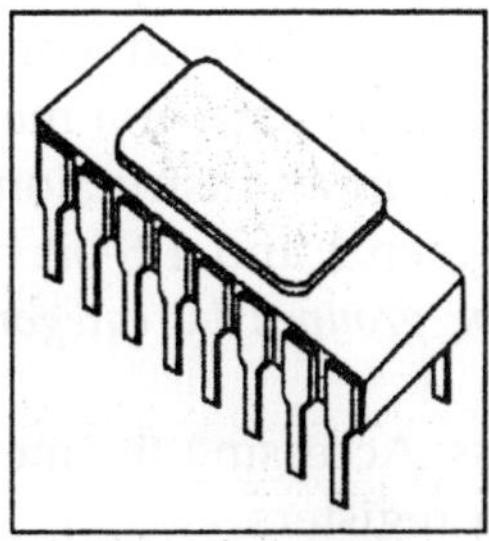

OPERATION

The processor (called CPU, for *Central Processing Unit*) is an electronic circuit that operates at the speed of an internal clock thanks to a quartz crystal that, when subjected to an electrical currant, send pulses, called "peaks". The clock speed (also called cycle), corresponds to the number of pulses per second, written in Hertz (Hz). Thus, a 200 MHz computer has a clock that sends 200,000,000 pulses per second. Clock frequency is generally a multiple of the system frequency (*FSB, Front-Side Bus*), meaning a multiple of the motherboard frequency. With each clock peak, the processor performs an action that corresponds to an instruction or a part thereof. A measure called CPI (*Cycles Per Instruction*) gives a representation of the average number of clock cycles required for a microprocessor to execute an instruction.

A microprocessorâ€™s power can thus be characterized by the number of instructions per second that it is capable of processing. MIPS(millions of instructions per second) is the unit used and corresponds to the processor frequency divided by the *CPI*.

INSTRUCTIONS

An instruction is an elementary operation that the processor can accomplish. Instructions are stored in the main memory, waiting to be processed by the processor.

An instruction has two fields:

- The operation code, which represents the action that the processor must execute;
- The operand code, which defines the parameters of the action. The operand code depends on the operation. It can be data or a memory address.

The number of bits in an instruction varies according to the type of data (between 1 and 4 8-bit bytes).

Instructions can be grouped by category, of which the main ones are:

- *Memory Access:* Accessing the memory or transferring data between registers.
- *Arithmetic Operations:* Operations such as addition, subtraction, division or multiplication.
- *Logic Operations:* Operations such as and, or, not, exclusive not, etc.

- *Control:* Sequence controls, conditional connections, etc.

REGISTERS

When the processor executes instructions, data is temporarily stored in small, local memory locations of 8, 16, 32 or 64 bits called registers. Depending on the type of processor, the overall number of registers can vary from about ten to many hundreds.

The main registers are:

- The accumulator register (*ACC*), which stores the results of arithmetic and logical operations;
- The status register (*PSW, Processor Status Word*), which holds system status indicators (carry digits, overflow, etc.);
- The instruction register (*RI*), which contains the current instruction being processed;
- The ordinal counter (*OC* or *PC* for *Programme Counter*), which contains the address of the next instruction to process;
- The buffer register, which temporarily stores data from the memory.

CACHE MEMORY

Cache memory (also called *buffer memory*) is local memory that reduces waiting times for information stored in the RAM (Random Access Memory). In effect, the computer's main memory is slower than that of the processor. There are, however, types of memory that are much faster, but which have a greatly increased cost.

The solution is therefore to include this type of local memory close to the processor and to temporarily store the primary data to be processed in it. Recent model computers have many different levels of cache memory:

- Level one cache memory (called L1 Cache, for Level 1 Cache) is directly integrated into the processor. It is subdivided into two parts:
- The first part is the instruction cache, which contains

instructions from the RAM that have been decoded as they came across the pipelines.

- The second part is the data cache, which contains data from the RAM and data recently used during processor operations. Level 1 caches can be accessed very rapidly. Access waiting time approaches that of internal processor registers.
- Level two cache memory (called L2 Cache, for Level 2 Cache) is located in the case along with the processor (in the chip). The level two cache is an intermediary between the processor, with its internal cache, and the RAM. It can be accessed more rapidly than the RAM, but less rapidly than the level one cache.
- Level three cache memory (called L3 Cache, for Level 3 Cache) is located on the motherboard.

All these levels of cache reduce the latency time of various memory types when processing or transferring information. While the processor works, the level one cache controller can interface with the level two controller to transfer information without impeding the processor. As well, the level two cache interfaces with the RAM (level three cache) to allow transfers without impeding normal processor operation.

CONTROL SIGNALS

Control signals are electronic signals that orchestrate the various processor units participating in the execution of an instruction. Control signals are sent using an element called a *sequencer*. For example, the *Read / Write* signal allows the memory to be told that the processor wants to read or write information.

FUNCTIONAL UNITS

The processor is made up of a group of interrelated units (or control units). Microprocessor architecture varies considerably from one design to another, but the main elements of a microprocessor are as follows:

- A control unit that links the incoming data, decodes

it, and sends it to the execution unit:The control unit is made up of the following elements:

- Sequencer (or *monitor and logic unit*) that synchronizes instruction execution with the clock speed. It also sends control signals;
- Ordinal counter that contains the address of the instruction currently being executed;
- Instruction register that contains the following instruction.

- An execution unit (or *processing unit*) that accomplishes tasks assigned to it by the instruction unit.

The execution unit is made of the following elements:

- The arithmetical and logic unit (written ALU). The ALU performs basic arithmetical calculations and logic functions (AND, OR, EXCLUSIVE OR, etc.);
- The floating point unit (written FPU) that performs partial complex calculations which cannot be done by the arithmetical and logic unit.
- The status register;
- The accumulator register.
- A bus management unit (or *input-output unit*) that manages the flow of incoming and outgoing information and that interfaces with system RAM.

The diagram below gives a simplified representation of the elements that make up the processor (the physical layout of the elements is different than their actual layout):

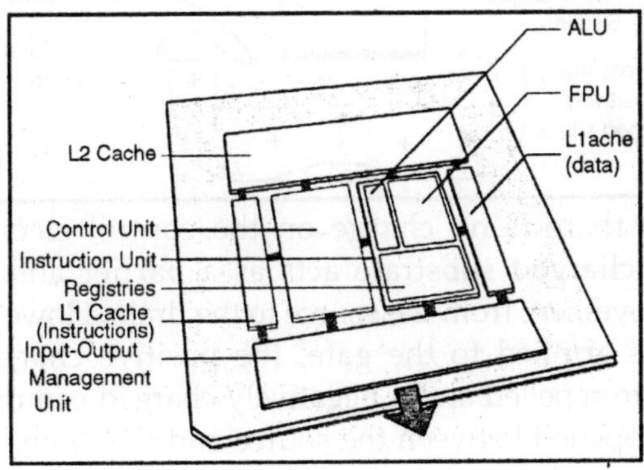

TRANSISTOR

To process information, the microprocessor has a group of instructions, called the "instruction set", made possible by electronic circuits. More precisely, the instruction set is made with the help of semiconductors, little "circuit switches" that use the transistor effect, discovered in 1947 by *John Barden, Walter H. Brattain* and *William Shockley* who received a Nobel Prize in 1956 for it.

A transistor (the contraction of *transfer resistor*) is an electronic semi-conductor component that has three electrodes and is capable of modifying current passing through it using one of its electrodes (called control electrode). These are referred to as "active components", in contrast to "passive components", such as resistance or capacitors which only have two electrodes (referred to as being "bipolar").

A MOS (*metal, oxide, silicone*) transistor is the most common type of transistor used to design integrated circuits. MOS transistors have two negatively charged areas, respectively called source (which has an almost zero charge) and drain (which has a 5V charge), separated by a positively charged region, called a substrate). The substrate has a control electrode overlaid, called a gate, that allows a charge to be applied to the substrate.

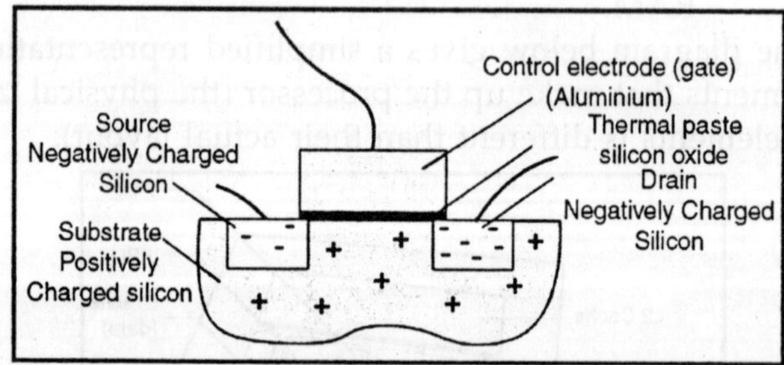

When there is no charge on the control electrode, the positively charged substrate acts as a barrier and prevents electron movement from the source to the drain. However, when a charge is applied to the gate, the positive charges of the substrate are repelled and a negatively charged communication channel is opened between the source and the drain.

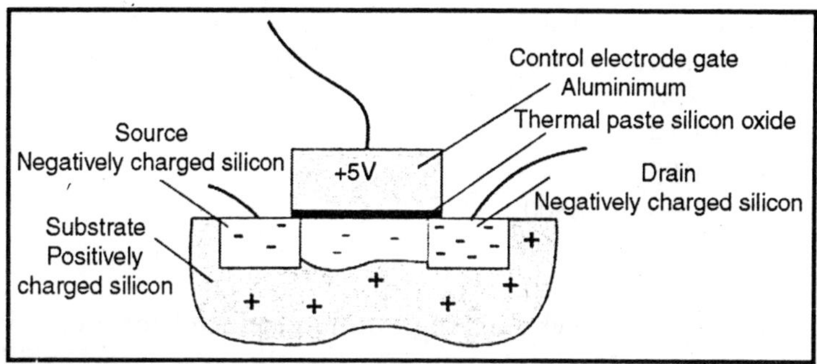

The transistor therefore acts as a programmable switch, thanks to the control electrode. When a charge is applied to the control electrode, it acts as a closed interrupter and, when there is no charge, it acts as an open interrupter.

INTEGRATED CIRCUITS

Once combined, transistors can make logic circuits, that, when combined, form processors. The first integrated circuit dates back to 1958 and was built by *Texas Instruments*. MOS transistors are therefore made of slices of silicone (called *wafers*) obtained after multiple processes. These slices of silicone are cut into rectangular elements to form a "circuit". Circuits are then placed in cases with input-output connectors and the sum of these parts makes an "integrated circuit".

The minuteness of the engraving, written in microns (micrometers, written *Âμm*) defines the number of transistors per surface unit. There can be millions of transistors on one single processor. Moore's Law, penned in 1965 by Gordon E. Moore, cofounder of Intel, predicted that processor performance (by extension of the number of transistors integrated in the silicone) would double every twelve months. Because the rectangular case contains input-output pins that resemble legs, the term "electronic flea" is used in French to refer to integrated circuits.

FAMILIES

Each type of processor has its own instruction set. Processors are grouped into the following families, according to their unique instruction sets: ·80x86: the "x" represents the family. Mention is therefore made to 386, 486, 586, 686, etc.

- ARM
- IA-64
- MIPS
- Motorola 6800
- PowerPC
- SPARC

This explains why a programme produced for a certain type of processor can only work directly on a system with another type of processor if there is instruction translation, called emulation. The term "emulator" is used to refer to the programme performing this translation.

INSTRUCTION SET

An instruction set is the sum of basic operations that a processor can accomplish. A processors instruction set is a determining factor in its architecture, even though the same architecture can lead to different implementations by different manufacturers. The processor works efficiently thanks to a limited number of instructions, hardwired to the electronic circuits. Most operations can be performed using basic functions. Some architecture does, however, include advanced processor functions.

CISC ARCHITECTURE

CISC (*Complex Instruction Set Computer*) architecture means hardwiring the processor with complex instructions that are difficult to create using basic instructions. CISC is especially popular in 80x86 type processors. This type of architecture has an elevated cost because of advanced functions printed on the silicone. Instructions are of variable length and may sometimes require more than one clock cycle. Because CISC-based processors can only process one instruction at a time, the processing time is a function of the size of the instruction.

RISC ARCHITECTURE

Processors with RISC (*Reduced Instruction Set Computer*)

technology do not have hardwired, advanced functions. Programmes must therefore be translated into simple instructions which complicates development and/or requires a more powerful processor.

Such architecture has a reduced production cost compared to CISC processors. In addition, instructions, simple in nature, are executed in just one clock cycle, which speeds up programme execution when compared to CISC processors. Finally, these processors can handle multiple instructions simultaneously by processing them in parallel.

TECHNOLOGICAL IMPROVEMENTS

Throughout time, microprocessor manufacturers (called *founders*) have developed a certain number of improvements that optimize processor performance.

PARALLEL PROCESSING

Parallel processing consists of simultaneously executing instructions from the same programme on different processors. This involves dividing a programme into multiple processes handled in parallel in order to reduce execution time. This type of technology, however, requires synchronization and communication between the various processes, like the division of tasks in a business: work is divided into small discrete processes which are then handled by different departments. The operation of an enterprise may be greatly affected when communication between the services does not work correctly.

PIPELINING

Pipelining is technology that improves instruction execution speed by putting the steps into parallel. To understand the pipelines mechanism, it is first necessary to understand the execution phases of an instruction. Execution phases of an instruction for a processor with a 5-step "classic" pipeline are as follows:

- *Fetch*: Retrieves the instruction from the cache;
- *Decode:* Decodes the instruction and looks for operands (register or immediate values);

- *Execute:* Performs the instruction (for example, if it is an add instruction, addition is performed, if it is a SUB instruction, subtraction is performed, etc.);
- *Memory:* Accesses the memory, and writes data or retrieves data from it;
- *Write back (retire):* Records the calculated value in a register.

Instructions are organized into lines in the memory and are loaded one after the other. Thanks to the pipeline, instruction processing requires no more than the five preceding steps. Because the order of the steps is invariable (Fetch, Decode, Execute, Memory, Write Back), it is possible to create specialized circuits in the processor for each one.

The goal of the pipeline is to perform each step in parallel with the preceding and following steps, meaning reading an instruction (Fetch) while the previous step is being read (Decode), while the step before that is being executed (Execute), while the step before that is being written to the memory (Memory), and while the first step in the series is being recorded in a register (Write back)

LI	DI	EX	MEM	ER				
	LI	DI	EX	MEM	ER			
		LI	DI	EX	MEM	ER		
			LI	DI	EX	MEM	ER	
				LI	DI	EX	MEM	ER

In general, 1 to 2 clock cycles (rarely more) for each pipeline step or a maximum of 10 clock cycles per instruction should be planned for. For two instructions, a maximum of 12 clock cycles are necessary (10+2=12 instead of 10*2=20) because the preceding instruction was already in the pipeline. Both instructions are therefore being simultaneously processed, but with a delay of 1 or 2 clock cycles. For 3 instructions, 14 clock cycles are required, etc.

The principle of a pipeline may be compared to a car assembly line. The car moves from one workstation to another by following the assembly line and is completely finished by the time it leaves the factory. To completely understand the principle, the assembly line must be looked at as a whole, and not vehicle by vehicle. Three hours are required to produce each vehicle, but one is produced every minute! It must be noted that there are many different types of pipelines, varying from 2 to 40 steps, but the principle remains the same.

SUPERSCALING

Superscaling consists of placing multiple processing units in parallel in order to process multiple instructions per cycle.

HYPERTHREADING

HyperThreading (written *HT*) technology consists of placing two logic processors with a physical processor. Thus, the system recognizes two physical processors and behaves like a multitasking system by sending two simultaneous threads, referred to as SMT (*Simultaneous Multi Threading*). This "deception" allows processor resources to be better employed by guaranteeing the bulk shipment of data to the processor.

INTRODUCTION TO PDA'S

A PDA (*Personal Digital Assistant,* also called a *pocket organizer*) is a pocket computer composed of a processor, RAM (Random Access Memory), a touch sensitive screen, and network functions bundled in an extremely small compact case.

PDA USE

A PDA is a pocket computer originally designed as an organizer. A personal assistant generally supplies the following standard applications:

- An agenda to organize time, with visual or mechanical reminders. Meetings or planned events can be contextualized in order to meet professional and personal requirements thanks to an adaptable classification system (*office, private,* etc.).
- A task manager that serves as a reminder for tasks to be done. The priority, deadlines or reminders can be assigned to each task.

- An address book (*contact manager*) that provides instant contact information (phone number, mailing address, email, etc.).
- email software that allows messages to be received and sent.

Personal assistants offer light versions of office automation tools such as text editors, spreadsheets, a calculator, and viewers for a wide variety of file formats (PDF files, images, etc).

In addition to these basic functions, more and more PDAs offer advanced multimedia tools for playing videos (in different formats, including DivX format), music (notably in mp3 format) and Flash animation.

PDAs are also used with increasing frequency for geo-referencing, mapping and road navigation by plugging them into a geo-reference device (GPS, *Global Positioning System*). In effect, it is possible to obtain a compatible, low cost and high performance GPS that helps with road navigation a using a map that continually displays the users location, speed and a visual representation of the road (eventually in 3D) with instructions both on-screen and from a synthesized voice.

OPERATING SYSTEM

PDAâ€ have operating systems adapted to their screen resolution and whose features correspond to the characteristics of the device.

Many types of operating systems exist for PDAs, usually different for each type of PDA and each manufacturer, the same as there are Mac and PC computers. The two main operating systems are:

- PalmOS, marketed by *Palm*.
- Windows Mobile or Pocket PC (formerly *Windows CE*), marketed by *Microsoft*.

These two systems have almost the same characteristics and the same functions, but with different methods of holding them and with incompatibilities between systems.

Note that there are Linux operating systems that were specifically developed for both types of machines.

TECHNICAL CHARACTERISTICS

When purchasing a PDA, it is important to pay attention to the following characteristics:

- *Weight and size:* PDAs are designed to be carried everywhere and must therefore fit into hands and pockets. Its size and weight must be as small as possible, bearing in mind ergonomic requirements and screen size.
- *Autonomy:* A PDAs autonomy is a function of its batterys characteristics.
- *Ni-Cad (Nickel / Cadmium):* a type rechargeable battery now obsolete due to its *memory effect,* meaning a progressive reduction of the maximum charge when it is recharged before being completely "empty".
- *Ni-Mh (Nickel / Metal Hybrid):* A type of rechargeable battery with higher performance than nickel-cadmium batteries.
- *Li-Ion (Lithium / Ion):* A type of rechargeable battery that is found in most computers. Li-Ion batteries give excellent performance for a moderate cost. As well, Li-Ion batteries do not suffer from memory effects, which means that they can be recharged before becoming completely empty.
- *Li-Polymer (Lithium / Polymer):* A type of rechargeable battery with performance similar to that of Li-Ion batteries, but made much lighter by replacing the electrolyte fluid and the micro-porous separator of Li-Ion batteries with a much lighter solid polymer. However, the recharging time is longer and their life expectancy is shorter.

PROGRAMMABLE LOGIC DEVICES (PLD)

Programmable logic devices (PLD) are designed with configurable logic and flip-flops linked together with programmable interconnect. PLDs provide specific functions, including device-to-device interfacing, data communication, signal processing, data display, timing and control operations, and almost every other function a system must perform.

Memory cells control and define the function that the logic performs and how the various logic functions are interconnected. Logic devices can be classified into two broad categories - fixed and programmable. As the name suggests, the circuits in a fixed logic device are permanent, they perform one function or set of functions - once manufactured, they cannot be changed. On the other hand, programmable logic devices (PLDs) are standard, off-the-shelf parts that offer customers a wide range of logic capacity, features, speed, and voltage characteristics - and these devices can be changed at any time to perform any number of functions.

With fixed logic devices, the time required to go from design, to prototypes, to a final manufacturing run can take from several months to more than a year, depending on the complexity of the device. And, if the device does not work properly, or if the requirements change, a new design must be developed. With programmable logic devices, designers use inexpensive software tools to quickly develop, simulate, and test their designs.

Then, a design can be quickly programmed into a device, and immediately tested in a live circuit. The PLD that is used for this prototyping is the exact same PLD that will be used in the final production of a piece of end equipment, such as a network router, a DSL modem, a DVD player, or an automotive navigation system. There are no NRE costs and the final design is completed much faster than that of a custom, fixed logic device. Another key benefit of using PLDs is that during the design phase customers can change the circuitry as often as they want until the design operates to their satisfaction. That's because PLDs are based on re-writable memory technology - to change the design, the device is simply reprogrammed. Once the design is final, customers can go into immediate production by simply programming as many PLDs as they need with the final software design file.

CPLDs and FPGAs

The two major types of programmable logic devices are field programmable gate arrays (FPGAs) and complex programmable logic devices (CPLDs). Of the two, FPGAs offer the highest amount of logic density, the most features, and the highest performance. The largest FPGA now shipping, part of the Xilinx Virtex™ line of devices, provides eight million "system gates" (the relative density of logic).

These advanced devices also offer features such as built-in hardwired processors (such as the IBM Power PC), substantial amounts of memory, clock management systems, and support for many of the latest, very fast device-to-device signaling technologies. FPGAs are used in a wide variety of applications ranging from data processing and storage, to instrumentation, telecommunications, and digital signal processing.

CPLDs, by contrast, offer much smaller amounts of logic - up to about 10,000 gates. But CPLDs offer very predictable timing characteristics and are therefore ideal for critical control applications. CPLDs such as the Xilinx CoolRunner™ series also require extremely low amounts of power and are very inexpensive, making them ideal for cost-sensitive, battery-operated, portable applications such as mobile phones and digital handheld assistants.

THE PLD MARKET

Today the worldwide market for programmable logic devices is about $3.5 billion, according the market researcher Gartner/Dataquest. The market for fixed logic devices is about $12 billion. However, in recent years, sales of PLDs have outpaced those of fixed logic devices built with older gate array technology.

And, high performance FPGAs are now beginning to take market share from fixed logic devices made with the more advanced standard cell technology. According to the Semiconductor Industry Association, programmable logic is now one of the fastest growing segments of the semiconductor business, and for the last few years, sales for PLDs have increased at a greater pace than sales for the overall semiconductor industry. Says EDN Magazine, a leading electronics design trade publication: "Programmable-logic devices are the fastest growing segment of the logic-device family for two fundamental reasons. Their ever-increasing logic gate count per device 'gathers up' functions that might otherwise spread over a number of discrete-logic and memory chips, improving end-system size, power consumption, performance, reliability, and cost. Equally important is the fact that in a matter of seconds or minutes you can configure and, in many cases, reconfigure these devices at your workstation or in the system-assembly line.

THE PLD ADVANTAGE

Fixed logic devices and PLDs both have their advantages. Fixed logic devices, for example, are often more appropriate for large volume applications because they can be mass-produced more economically. For certain applications where the very highest performance is required, fixed logic devices may also be the best choice.

However, programmable logic devices offer a number of important advantages over fixed logic devices, including:

- PLDs offer customers much more flexibility during the design cycle because design iterations are simply a matter of changing the programming file, and the results of design changes can be seen immediately in working parts.
- PLDs do not require long lead times for prototypes or production parts the PLDs are already on a distributor's shelf and ready for shipment.
- PLDs do not require customers to pay for large NRE costs and purchase expensive mask sets PLD suppliers incur those costs when they design their programmable devices and are able to amortize those costs over the multi-year lifespan of a given line of PLDs.
- PLDs allow customers to order just the number of parts they need, when they need them, allowing them to control inventory. Customers who use fixed logic devices often end up with excess inventory which must be scrapped, or if demand for their product

surges, they may be caught short of parts and face production delays.

- PLDs can be reprogrammed even after a piece of equipment is shipped to a customer. In fact, thanks to programmable logic devices, a number of equipment manufacturers now tout the ability to add new features or upgrade products that already are in the field. To do this, they simply upload a new programming file to the PLD, via the Internet, creating new hardware logic in the system.

Over the last few years programmable logic suppliers have made such phenomenal technical advances that PLDs are now seen as the logic solution of choice from many designers.

One reasons for this is that PLD suppliers such as Xilinx are "fabless" companies; instead of owning chip manufacturing foundries, Xilinx out sources that job to partners like IBM Microelectronics and UMC, whose chief occupation is making chips.

This strategy allows Xilinx to focus on designing new product architectures, software tools, and intellectual property cores while having access to the most advanced semiconductor process technologies. Advanced process technologies help PLDs in a number of key areas: faster performance, integration of more features, reduced power consumption, and lower cost.

Today Xilinx is producing programmable logic devices on a state-of-the-art 0.13-micron low-k copper process - one of the best in the industry. Just a few years ago, for example, the largest FPGA was measured in tens of thousands of system gates and operated at 40 MHz. Older FPGAs also were relatively expensive, costing often more than $150 for the most advanced parts at the time.

Today, however, FPGAs with advanced features offer millions of gates of logic capacity, operate at 300 MHz, can cost less than $10, and offer a new level of integrated functions such as processors and memory. Just as significant, PLDs now have a growing library of intellectual property (IP) or cores -

these are predefined and tested software modules that customer can use to create system functions instantly inside the PLD. Cores include everything from complex digital signal processing algorithms and memory controllers to bus interfaces and full-blown software-based microprocessors. Such cores save customers a lot of time and expense —it would take customers months to create these functions, further delaying a product introduction.

Chapter 3

Basic of Processor

CPU ORGANIZATION

CPU STRUCTURE AND FUNCTIONS

Processor Organization

To understand the organization of the CPU, let us consider the requirements placed on the CPU, the things that it must do:

- *Fetch instruction:* The CPU reads an instruction from memory.
- *Interpret instruction:* The instruction is decoded to determine what action is required.
- *Fetch data:* The execution of an instruction may require reading data from memory or an I/O module.
- *Process data:* The execution of an instruction may require performing some arithmetic or logical operation on data.
- *Write data:* The results of an execution may require writing data to memory or an I/O module.

To do these things, it should be clear that the CPU needs to store some data temporarily. It must remember the location of the last instruction so that it can know where to get the next instruction.

It needs to store instructions and data temporar ily while an instruction is being executed. In other words, the CPU needs a small internal memory.

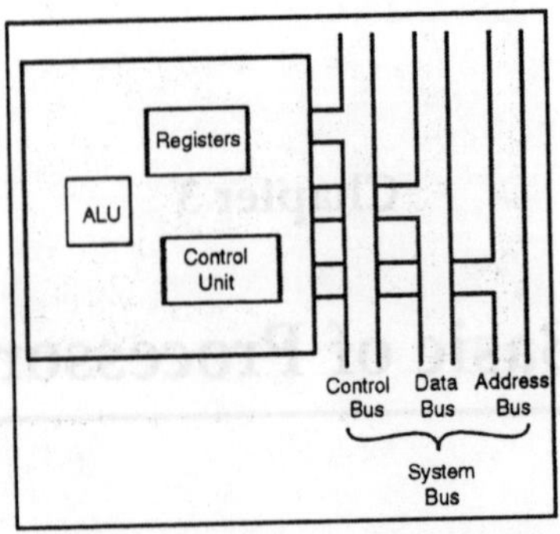

Fig. The CPU with the System Bus

Figure is a simplified view of a CPU, indicating its connection to the rest of the system via the system bus. We see that the major components of the CPU are an arithmetic and logic unit (ALU) and a control unit (CU). The ALU does the actual computation or processing of data. The con trol unit controls the movement of data and instructions into and out of the CPU and controls the operation of the ALU. In addition, a minimal internal memory, consisting of a set of storage locations, called registers. Figure is a slightly more detailed view of the CPU. The data transfer and logic control paths are indicated, including an element labeled internal CPU-bus. This element is needed to transfer data between the various registers and the ALU because the ALU in fact operates only on data in the internal CPU memory.

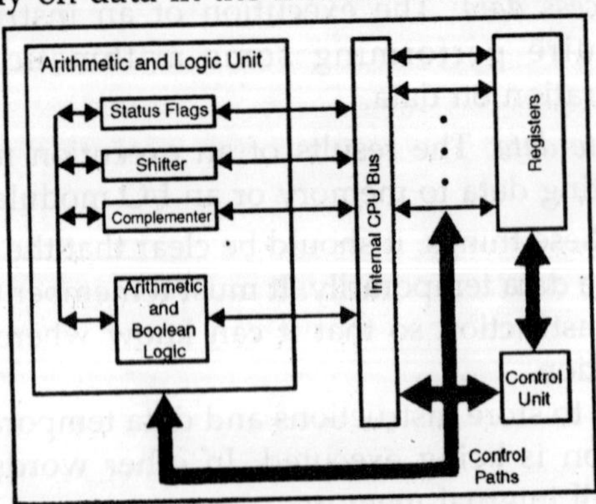

Fig. CPU Internal Structure

CONTROL UNIT

The control unit maintains order within the computer system and directs the flow of traffic (operations) and data. The flow of control is indicated by the dotted arrows on figure. The control unit selects one programme statement at a time from the programme storage area, interprets the statement, and sends the appropriate electronic impulses to the arithmetic-logic unit and storage section to cause them to carry out the instruction.

The control unit does not perform the actual processing operations on the data. Specifically, the control unit manages the operations of the CPU, be it a single-chip microprocessor or a fill-size mainframe. Like a traffic director, it decides when to start and stop(control and timing), what to do (programme instructions),where to keep information (memory), and with what devices to communicate (I/O). It controls the flow of all data entering and leaving the computer. It accomplishes this by communicating or interfacing with the arithmetic-logic unit, memory, and I/O areas. It provides the computer with the ability to function under programme control. Depending on the design of the computer, the CPU can also have the capability to function under manual control through man/ machine interfacing.

The control unit consists of several basic logically defined areas. These logically defined areas work closely with each other. Timing in a computer regulates the flow of signals that control the operation of the computer. The instruction and control portion makes up the decision-making and memory-type functions. Addressing is the process of locating the operand(specific information) for a given operation. Aninterrupt is a break in the normal flow of operation of a computer (e.g., CTRL + ALT + DEL).

Control memory is a random-access memory (RAM)consisting of addressable storage registers. Cachememory is a small, high-speed RAM buffer located between the CPU and main memory; it can increase the speed of the PC. Read-only memory (ROM) are chips with a set of software instructions supplied by the manufacturer built into them that enables the computer to perform its I/O operations. The control unit is also capable of shutting down the computer when the power supply detects abnormal conditions.

ARITHMETIC-LOGIC UNIT

The arithmetic-logic unit (ALU) performs all arithmetic operations (addition, subtraction, multiplication, and division) and logic operations. An arithmetic and logic unit (ALU) is contained within a central processor unit (CPU). The ALU is a dedicated collection of high speed circuits that performs the arithmetic and logical operations of a computer. The ALU can be physically located adjacent to, or underneath, the processor register. The ALU can be formed in the shape of a square grid.

The arithmetic and logic unit works in concert with a control unit, internal memory, and registers. All together, these functions comprise the CPU. Where the ALU performs mathematical computation, logic decisions and processing of data taken from the registers, the control unit itself will read programme instructions, farm out tasks of processing to the ALU, and ensure that the proper sequence is followed according to programme instructions.

Logic operations test various conditions encountered during processing and allow for different actions to betaken based on the results. The data required to perform the arithmetic and logical functions are inputs from the designated CPU registers and operands. The ALU relies on basic items to perform its operations. These include number systems, data routing circuits (adders/substrates), timing, instructions, operands, and registers.

Error conditions of arithmetic overflow and arithmetic underflow may occur in which the expected portions of numeric words may exceed the space provided for word length or may not be within a range to be represented and processed. Such errors may not affect precision of mathematical computations, but it is possible nevertheless. Such error conditions may be exploitable by criminal hackers (crackers) wishing to remotely install viruses, spyware, or other types of malicious software on a computer.

Because the ALU is where calculations and comparisons occur, this function can be vulnerable to error conditions if error-handling routines are not provided for the CPU as part of the overall computer operating system. Such routines and programmes are normally provided as critical and security updates to operating system software and utility software by the original software publisher. The goal is to head off exploitation by crackers of personal and business computers.

The ALU is now contained on the same chip as other necessary computing and processing components thanks to advances in miniaturization. Input/output chips (I/O), integrated circuits (ICs), random access memory (RAM), and even read only memory (ROM) now aid a microprocessor in the same physical component to smoothly perform computing functions.

While the ALU is more known for its ability to provide mathematical and logical processing, a lesser-known subset of these capabilities is found in its processing of text and character strings. An example of this capability is the event when word searches are performed through text: a word fragment is used as the search criteria and the possible matches are then compared and computed by the ALU. A "hit counter" computes the number of successful searches and other memory areas are brought into play as the successful searches are tabulated and presented to the computer operator.

REGISTER ORGANIZATION

Within the CPU, there is a set of registers that function as a level of memory above main memory and cache in the hierarchy. Every present-day CPU design includes registers for a variety of purposes, from storing the address of the currently-executed instruction to more general-purpose data storage and manipulation. CPU registers run at the same speed as the rest of the CPU; otherwise, they would be a serious bottleneck to overall system performance. The reason for this is that nearly all operations performed by the CPU involve the registers in one way or another.

The number of CPU registers (and their uses) are strictly dependent on the architectural design of the CPU itself. There is no way to change the number of CPU registers, short of migrating to a CPU with a different architecture. For these reasons, the number of CPU registers can be considered a constant, as they are changeable only with great pain and expense.

The registers in the CPU perform two roles:

- *User-visible registers:* These enable the machine- or assembly-language pro grammer to minimize main memory references by optimizing use of registers.
- *Control and status registers:* These are used by the control unit to control the operation of the CPU and by privileged, operating system programmes to control the execution of programmes.

There is not a clean separation of registers into these two categories. For example, on some machines the programme counter is user visible (e.g., Pentium), but on many it is not (e.g., PowerPC). For purposes of the following discussion, how ever, we will use these categories.

PROGRAMME COUNTER

The programme counter, PC, is a special-purpose register that is used by the processor to hold the address of the next instruction to be executed. The PLA automatically updates the PC to point to the next instruction during the op-code decode cycle. By coordinating with other hardware, in addition to the PLA, the PC is automatically incremented as each instruction is executed. The PC can also have an address dictated to it via the 'BRANCH' instruction.

The functional level block diagram of the PC designed for this microprocessor. The PC possesses the following attributes: outputs an 8-bit address, resets to zero, can be loaded with any 1 of the possible 256 addresses and produces an overflow flag if the counter exceeds 256. When the device is reset, via an external pin, the '/RESET TO ZERO' pin is pulled low by the PLA resulting in the PC being set to 00h. The PC is incremented by the PLA by pulling the '/

INCREMENT' pin low for 1 clock cycle. If the PC is incremented past its 256 word address reach the 'OVER FLOW FLAG' pin will be driven high. The PC can be forced to a specified value with the use of the 'BRANCH' command. When the PLA decodes a 'BRANCH', the PC will latch in the contents of the next 2 addresses. The processor then shifts the concatenated 8-bit address into the PC.

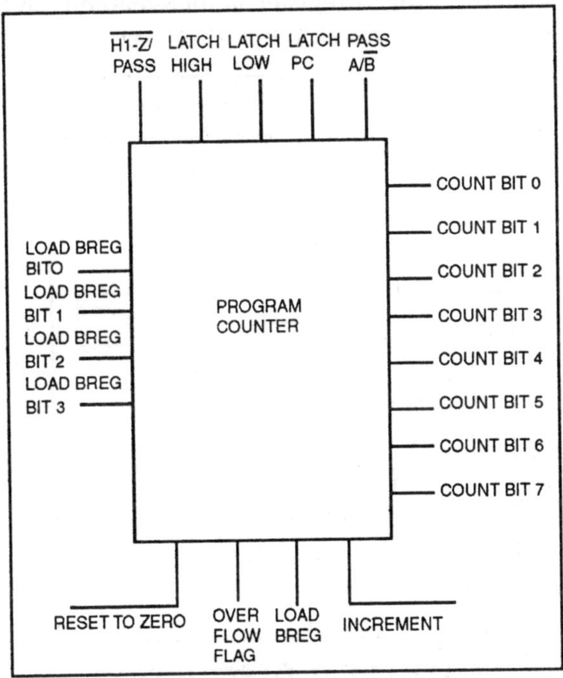

As shown in figure, the PC has several components that aid in the task of providing the address of the next instruction. During a reset, the PLA resets the incrementer to 00h and then latches the output of the incrementer into the PC. The value contained in the PC is then driven out through the multiplexer by the PLA selecting the PC data path.

For each time the PLA implements an increment PC, the incrementer is advanced by 1 and then shifted into the PC register. The value contained within the PC is then selected to pass through the multiplexer whose output is directly tied to the address pins. When the PLA decodes a 'BRANCH' op code, the contents of the next 2 addresses are shifted into the B register via the data bus controller. Once the branch address is shifted into the B register the value is then loaded into the incrementer. The PLA then proceeds to pass the contents of the B register through the multiplexer to the address pins. On the next increment PC, the value that was shifted into the incrementer from the B register is incremented, shifted into the PC and passed through the multiplexer.

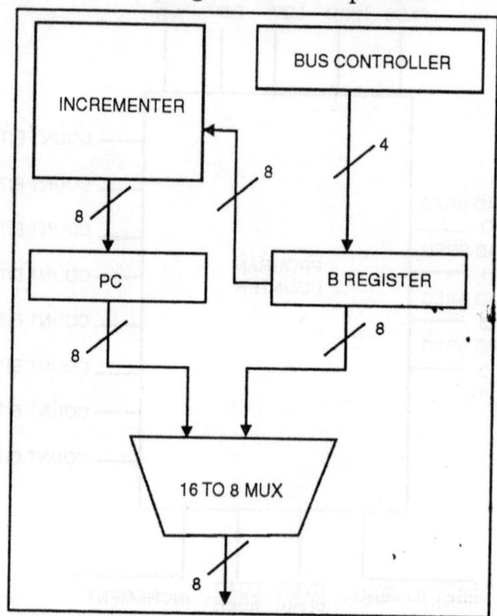

GATE LEVEL DESCRIPTION

INCREMENTER

The 8-bit incrementer is base on the circuit displayed. The incrementer circuit has the ability to be reset to 0 and to be incremented by 1. The 8-bit incrementer is constructed by routing the carry signal around to the input of the AND gate of the next incrementer circuit.

The LSB of the incrementer has the input of the AND gate tied to Vdd. The 'COUNT' signal of the MSB is used as the 'OVER FLOW FLAG', signifying that the increment has exceeded its 8-bit limit.

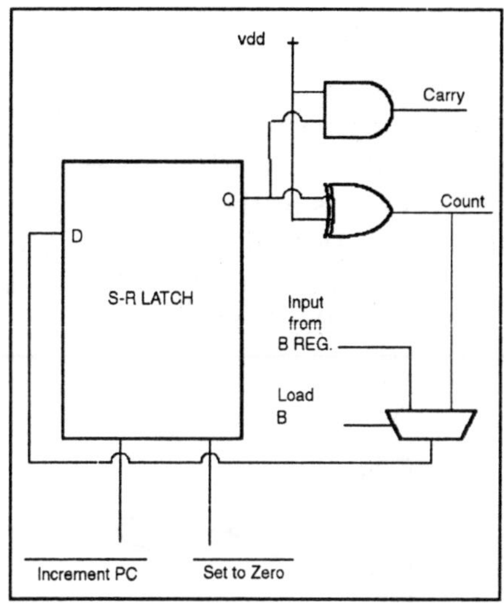

S-R LATCH

The incrementer circuit uses an S-R latch to provide the ability to reset the incrementer to 00h and to latch the current address. The gate level schematic of the S-R latch used in the incrementer design. The 'CLK' and '-CLK' signals are tied to '/INCREMENT PC' and 'INCREMENT PC' respectively. In addition, the '-RESET' is mapped to '/SET TO ZERO' in the 8-bit increment design. In the silicon implementation of the 8-bit incrementer, the 'CLK' and '-CLK' signals were heavily buffered to ensure that rising and falling edges of these signal contained very little skew. In addition, the '-SET' signal was tied to Vdd since it had no application in this design.

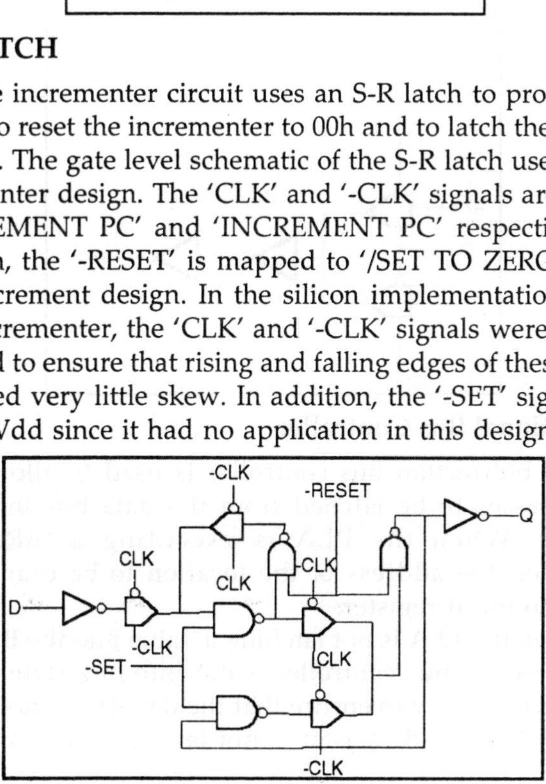

MULTIPLEXER

The multiplexer used in the PC design is used to pass either the PC register or the B register. The 16-to-8 multiplexer was constructed by concatenating 8 2-to-1 multiplexer. The 2-to-1 multiplexer is buffered by implementing 2 inverters at the output of the multiplexer. The final design of the 16-to-8 multiplexer is designed such that only 1 control signal is supplied by the PLA to either pass the PC register or the B register.

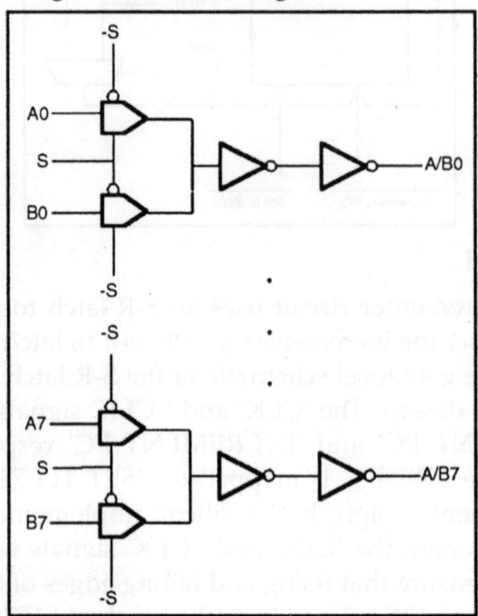

Bidirectional Bus Controller

The bidirection bus controller is used to allow the 4-bit addresses to be latched from the data bus into the B register. When the PLA is executing a 'BRANCH' instruction the address of the location to be branch to is latch into the B register.

When the PLA is not latching a value into the B register the bidirection bus controller is put into hi-z state. The hi-z state is necessary to ensure that the data bus is not heavily loaded when the B register is not latching data in.

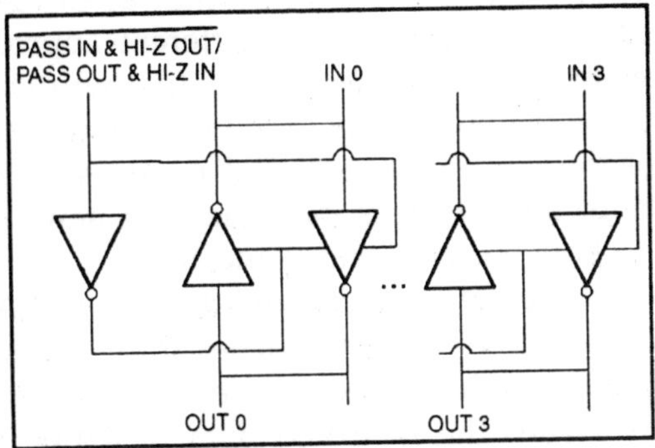

Cache Memory

The purpose of cache memory is to act as a buffer between the very limited, very high-speed CPU registers and the relatively slower and much larger main system memory – usually referred to as RAM. Cache memory has an operating speed similar to the CPU itself so, when the CPU accesses data in cache, the CPU is not kept waiting for the data. Cache memory is configured such that, whenever data is to be read from RAM, the system hardware first checks to determine if the desired data is in cache.

If the data is in cache, it is quickly retrieved, and used by the CPU. However, if the data is not in cache, the data is read from RAM and, while being transferred to the CPU, is also placed in cache (in case it is needed again later). From the perspective of the CPU, all this is done transparently, so that the only difference between accessing data in cache and accessing data in RAM is the amount of time it takes for the data to be returned.

In terms of storage capacity, cache is much smaller than RAM. Therefore, not every byte in RAM can have its own unique location in cache. As such, it is necessary to split cache up into sections that can be used to cache different areas of RAM, and to have a mechanism that allows each area of cache to cache different areas of RAM at different times. Even with the difference in size between cache and RAM, given the sequential and localized nature of storage access, a small amount of cache can effectively speed access to a large amount of RAM. When writing data from the CPU, things get a bit more complicated. There are two different approaches that can be used. In both cases, the data is first written to cache. However, since the purpose of cache is to function as a very fast copy of the contents of selected portions of RAM, any time a piece of data changes its value, that new value must be written to both cache memory and RAM.

Otherwise, the data in cache and the data in RAM would no longer match. The two approaches differ in how this is done. One approach, known as *write-through* caching, immediately writes the modified data to RAM. *Write-back* caching, however, delays the writing of modified data back to RAM. The reason for doing this is to reduce the number of times a frequently-modified piece of data must be written back to RAM.

Write-through cache is a bit simpler to implement; for this reason it is most common. Write-back cache is a bit trickier to implement; in addition to storing the actual data, it is necessary to maintain some sort of mechanism capable of flagging the cached data as clean (the data in cache is the same as the data in RAM), or dirty (the data in cache has been modified, meaning that the data in RAM is no longer current). It is also necessary to implement a way of periodically flushing dirty cache entries back to RAM.

Cache Levels

Cache subsystems in present-day computer designs may be multi-level; that is, there might be more than one set of cache between the CPU and main memory. The cache levels are often numbered, with lower numbers being closer to the CPU. Many systems have two cache levels:

- L1 cache is often located directly on the CPU chip itself and runs at the same speed as the CPU
- L2 cache is often part of the CPU module, runs at CPU speeds (or nearly so), and is usually a bit larger and slower than L1 cache

Some systems (normally high-performance servers) also have L3 cache, which is usually part of the system motherboard. As might be expected, L3 cache would be larger (and most likely slower) than L2 cache. In either case, the goal of all cache subsystems — whether single- or multi-level — is to reduce the average access time to the RAM.

MEMORY ADDRESS REGISTER (MAR)

MAR is short for memory address register. This register has its output hooked up to the address bus. This register is going to be the only way for the CPU to communicate with the bus. However, to prevent the memory address register from continously dumping its output to the address bus, we'll place a 32-bit tri-state buffer between the output of the MAR and the address bus. This allows other devices (say, I/O devices) to use the address bus, if necessary.

The MAR can hold two different kinds of addresses. Either it stores the address of an instruction, or it stores the address of data. Of course, as far as memory is concerned, an address is an address. It doesn't care what is stored at that address. However, from your perspective, as a person learning how a CPU works, it's useful to know that MAR can hold either an instruction address or a data address. Where does the MAR load its addresses? For now, we're just going to say that it comes from some other part of the CPU, which we'll discuss at a later point.

MEMORY DATA REGISTER (MDR)

MDR is short for memory data register. As you might guess, the MDR is the analog of the MAR, except it is used with the data bus, instead of the address bus. Unlike the MAR, where we either place the address on the address bus or we don't (by deactivating the tri-state buffer between the MAR and the address bus), the MDR has more operations than just placing the data on the data bus or not placing it.

In particular, data can go both ways. For a load operation, we expect to read data from the data bus into the MDR. For a store operation, we expect to place the data from the MDR onto the data bus. This means that the MDR can (parallel) load its data from one of two places: the data bus (for a load operation) and somewhere else in the CPU (for a store operation). We want to provide two choices for where the MDR should get its data. What kind of circuit should we use that allows us to select from one of two different inputs? A 2-1 MUX! Specifically, a 32-bit 2-1 MUX.

Similarly, the data from the MDR can either go to the data bus (for a store operation) or to some other part of the the CPU (for a load operation). Although it looks like we may need a DeMUX, we won't. We'll just split the data up, and both places will get the data.

This is how the diagram of the CPU looks so far.

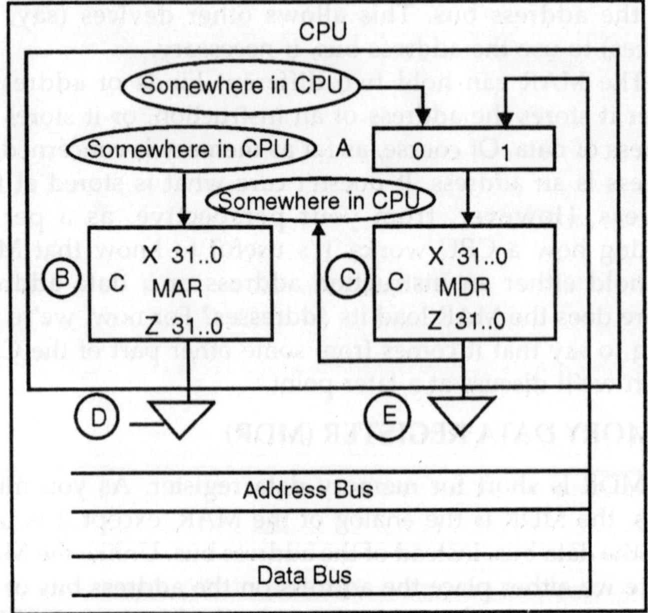

So far, the CPU contains two registers. MAR is on the left. MDR is on the right. The input to the MAR comes from some other place in the CPU, which we'll discuss later on.

The output of the MAR is hooked to the address bus using a 32-bit tri-state buffer. The inputs to the MDR comes from one of two places. Either it comes from some other place in the CPU (for store operations) or it comes from the data bus (for load operations). A MUX is used to pick which input the MDR should load from. The output of the MDR is hooked to the data bus using a 32-bit tri-state buffer. It is *also* directed to some other place in the CPU, which presumably uses the data in the MDR after it has been loaded from the data bus.

The diagram may seem confusing, but you should look it over until you feel comfortable with what's going on. I've left of the drawing of memory, which would be hooked up to the address and data bus, as shown from a previous set of notes. However, you should assume that memory is still there.

Control Signals

We have two registers, one MUX, and two tri-state buffers. Each of these devices has control inputs that tell it what to do. Each of them have a letter written beside it.

Let's list them out:

- A This is the control to the 32-bit 2-1 MUX to the MDR. Either the MDR can get its input from the data bus or from some other part of the CPU to be specified later on.
- B This is the control to the MAR. You can either load or hold.
- C This is the control to the MDR. You can either load or hold.
- D This is the control to the tri-state buffer from the MAR to the address bus. The control can either be on (allowing the bits to flow through) or off (allowing nothing to flow through).
- E This is the control to the tri-state buffer from the MDR to the data bus. The control can either be on (allowing the bits to flow through) or off (allowing nothing to flow through).

The control signals are going to become very important soon because they will allow use to control when the CPU does what. In particular, we're eventually going to talk about the design of a control unit, which will orchestrate the events in a CPU.

We're going to classify control signals into two types:

- Operations on registers (i.e., parallel load and hold)

- Operations on combinational logic devices (e.g.,. MUXes, tri-state buffers)

The biggest difference between these two kinds of signals is that one is based on a clock (i.e., sequential devices such as registers) and the other one is not (i.e., combinational logic devices). Even though the second one is not based on a clock, the entire CPU runs using a clock, and so, indirectly, the clock is important when it comes to dealing with combinational logic devices.

Hidden Registers

The MAR and MDR are considered "hidden registers". These are registers that are not used directly by the assembly language programmer. They are used to implement the instructions, however. Think of them like local variables to a function. For example, you may have been assigned to write a function that takes two parameters and returns some value. To compute the return value, you may need to declare some local variables. Whoever uses the function does not have to be aware of the local variables, and that they are used to help with the function. Similarly, users do not need to be aware of the MAR and the MDR. Over time, we may decide it's not necessary to have the MAR or the MDR. Because they are hidden, it shouldn't affect the running of the assembly language programmes, since they don't use these registers.

User-visible Registers

A user-visible register is one that may be referenced by means of the machine lan guage that the CPU executes. We can characterize these in the following categories:

- General purpose
- Data
- Address
- Condition codes

General-purpose registers: can be assigned to a variety of functions by the pro grammer. Sometimes their use within the instruction set is orthogonal to the opera tion. That is, any general—purpose register can contain the operand for any opcode. This provides true general-purpose register use. Often, however, there are restric tions. For example, there may be dedicated registers for floating-point and stack operations. In some cases, general-purpose registers can be used for addressing functions (e.g.. register indirect, displacement). In other cases, there is a partial or clean sep aration between data registers and address registers.

Data registers may be used only to hold data and cannot be employed in the calculation of an operand address. Address registers may themselves be somewhat general purpose, or they may be devoted to a particular addressing mode.

Examples include the following:

- *Segment Pointers:* In a machine with segmented addressing, a segment register holds the address of the base of the segment. There may be multiple registers: for example, one for the operating system and one for the current process.
- *Index Registers:* These are used for indexed addressing and may be auto-indexed.
- *Stack Pointer:* If there is user-visible stack addressing, then typically the stack is in memory and there is a dedicated register that points to the top of the slack. This allows implicit addressing; that is, push, pop, and other slack in structions need not contain an explicit stack operand.

Condition codes register (also referred to as flags): Condition codes are bits set by the CPU hardware as the result of operations. For example, an arithmetic operation may pro duce a positive, negative, zero, or overflow result. In addition to the result itself being stored in a register or memory, a condition code is also set. The code may sub sequently be tested as part of a conditional branch operation.

Control and Status Registers

There are a variety of CPU registers that are employed to control the operation of the CPU. Most of these, on most machines, are not visible to the user. Some of them may be visible to machine instructions executed in a control or operating system mode. Of course, different machines will have different register organizations and use different terminology. We list here a reasonably complete list of register types, with a brief description.

Four registers are essential to instruction execution:

- *Programme counter (PC):* Contains the address of an instruction to be fetched.
- *Instruction register (IR):* Contains the instruction most recently fetched.
- *Memory address registers (MAR):* Contains the address of a location in memory.
- *Memory buffer register (MBR):* Contains a word of data lo be written to mem ory or the word most recently read.

Typically, the CPU updates the PC after each instruction fetch so that the PC always points to the next instruction to be executed. A branch or skip instruction will also modify the contents of the PC. The fetched instruction is loaded into an IR, where the opcode and operand specifiers are analyzed. Data are exchanged with memory using the MAR and MBR. In a bus-organized system, the MAR connects directly to the address bus, and the MBR connects directly to the data bus. User-visible registers, in turn, exchange data with the MBR. The four registers just mentioned are used for the movement of data between the CPU and memory.

Within the CPU, data must be presented to the ALU for pro cessing. The ALU may have direct access to the MBR and user-visible registers. Alternatively, there may be additional buffering registers at the boundary to the ALU: these registers serve as input and output registers for the ALL and exchange data with the MBR and user-visible registers.

All CPU designs include a register or set of registers, often known as the programme status word (PSW), that contain status information. The PSW typically con tains condition codes plus other stains information.

Fields or flags include the following:

- *Sign:* Contains the sign bit of the result of the last arithmetic operation.

- *Zero:* Set when the result is 0.
- *Carry:* Set if an operation resulted in a carry (addition) into or borrow (sub-traction) out of a high-order hit. Used for multiword arithmetic operations.
- *Equal:* Set if a logical compare result is equality.
- *Overflow:* Used to indicate arithmetic overflow
- *Interrupt enable/disable:* Used to enable or disable interrupts.
- *Supervisor:* Indicates whether the CPU is executing in supervisor or user mode. Certain privileged instructions can be executed only in supervisor mode, and certain areas of memory can be accessed only in supervisor mode.

A number of other registers related to status and control might be found in a particular CPU design. In addition to the PSW, there may be a pointer to a block of memory containing additional status information (e.g., process control blocks).

Example Register Organizations:

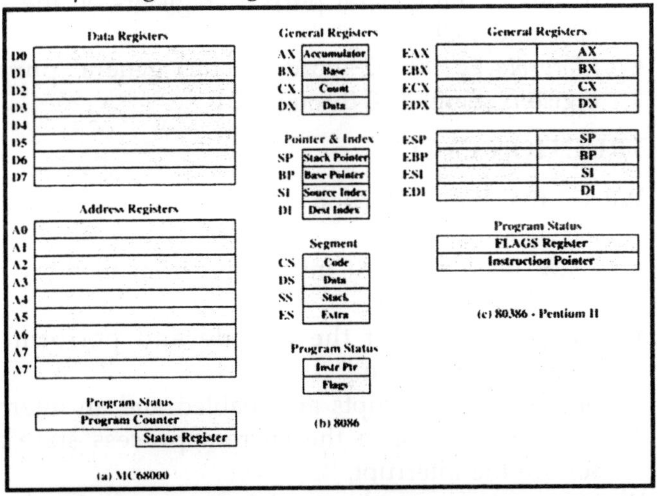

Fig. Example of Microprocessor Registers Organizations

GENERAL PURPOSE REGISTER (IR)

General purpose registers can be used as either data or **address** registers.

- *DEC VAX:* 16 word (32 bit) general purpose registers; named R0 through R15
- *IBM 360/370:* 16 full word (32 bit) general purpose registers; named 0, 1, 2, 3, 4, 5, 6, 7, 8, 9, A (or 10), B (or 11), C (or 12), D (or 13), E (or 14), and F (or 15)
- *Intel 8086/80286:* 8 word (16 bit) general purpose registers; named AX, BX, CX, DX, BP, SP, SI, and DI (high order bytes of the AX, BX, CX, and DX registers have the names AH, BH, CH, and DH and low order bytes of the AX, BX, CX, and DX registers have the names AL, BL, CL, and DL)
- *Intel 80386:* 8 doubleword (32 bit) general purpose registers; named EAX, EBX, ECX, EDX, EBP, ESP, ESI, and EDI (low order words use the same names as the general purpose registers on the Intel 8086 and 80286 and low order and high order bytes of the low order words of four of the registers use the same names as the general purpose registers on the Intel 8086 and 80286)
- *Motorola 88100:* 32 word (32 bit) general purpose registers; named r0 through r31

INSTRUCTION CYCLE

We see that the instruction cycle includes the following sub-cycles:

- *Fetch:* Read the next instruction from memory into the CPU.
- *Execute:* Interpret the opcode and perform the indicated operation.
- *Interrupt:* If interrupts are enabled and an interrupt has occurred, save the current process state and service the interrupt.

We are now in a position to elaborate somewhat on the instruction cycle. First, we must introduce one additional sub-cycle, known as the indirect cycle.

Indirect Cycle

We have seen that the execution of an instruction may

involve one or more operands in memory, each of which requires a memory access. Further, if indirect addressing is used, then additional memory accesses are required. We can think of the fetching of indirect addresses as one more instruction sub-cycle.

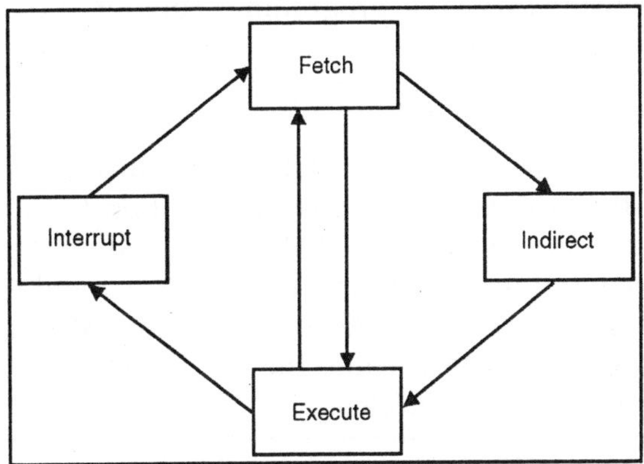

Fig. Instruction Cycle with Indirect

Another way to view this process is shown in Figure This illustrates the nature of the instruction cycle. Once an instruction is fetched, its operand specifiers must be identified. Each input Operand in memory is then fetched, and this process may require indirect addressing.

Register-based operand need not he fetched. Once the opcode is exe cuted, a similar process may be needed to store the result in main memory.

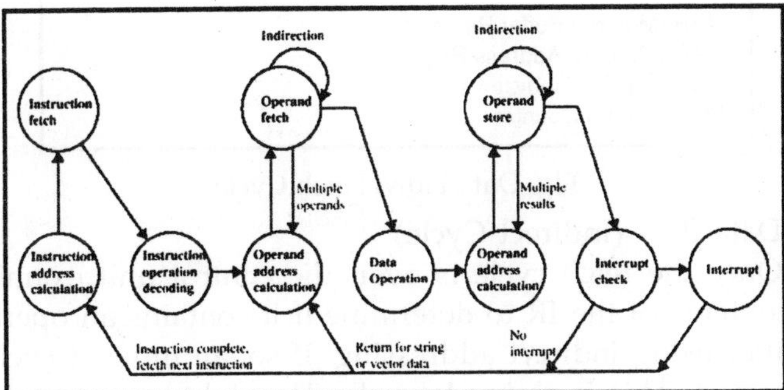

Fig. Instruction Cycle State Diagram

Data Flow

The exact sequence of events during an instruction cycle depends on the design of the CPU. We can, however, indicate in general terms what must happen. Let us assume that a CPU that employs a memory address register (MAR), a memory buffer register (MBR), a programme counter (PC), and an instruction register (IR).

Data Flow (Fetch Cycle)

Figure shows the flow of data during this cycle. The PC contains the address of the next instruc tion to be fetched. This address is moved to the MAR and placed on the address bus. The control unit requests a memory read, and the result is placed on the data bus and copied into the MBR and then moved to the IR. Meanwhile, the PC is incremented by 1 preparatory for the next fetch.

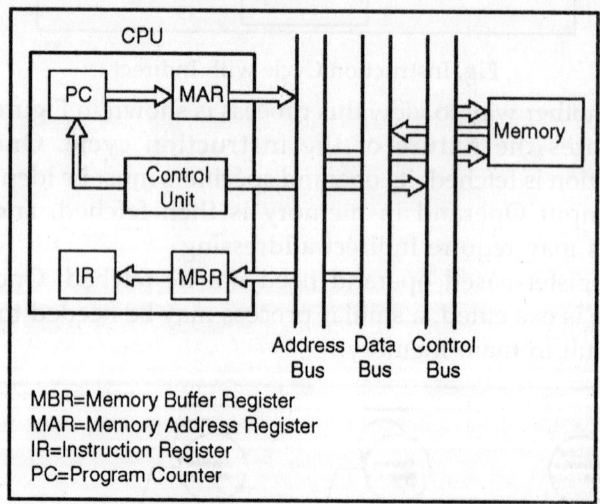

Fig. Data Flow, Fetch Cycle

Data flow (Indirect Cycle)

Once the fetch cycle is over, the control unit examines the contents of the IR to determine if it contains an operand specifier using indirect addressing. If so, an indirect cycle is performed. This is a simple cycle. The right most N bits of the MBR, which contain the address reference, are transferred to the MAR. Then the control unit requests a memory read, to get the desired address of the operand into the MBR.

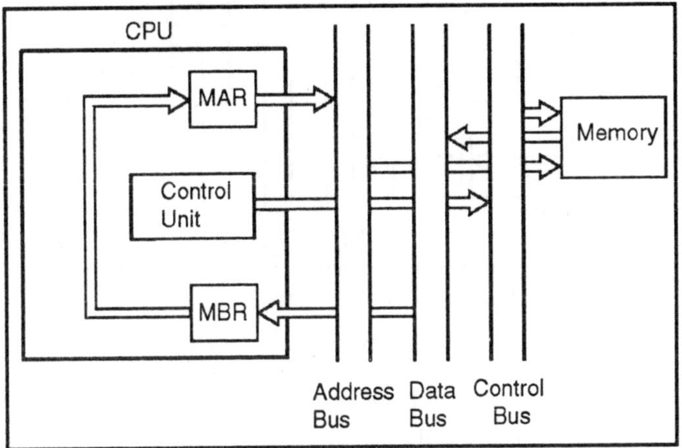

Fig. Data Flow, Indirect Cycle

Data Flow (Execute Cycle)

The fetch and indirect cycles are simple and predictable. The execute cycle takes many forms, the form depends on which of the various machine instructions is in the IR.

This cycle may involve transferring data among registers, read or write from memory or I/O, and/or the invocation of the ALU.

Data Flow (Interrupt Cycle)

Like the fetch and indirect cycles, the interrupt cycle is simple and predictable. The current contents of the PC must be saved so that the CPU can resume normal activity after the interrupt. Thus, the contents of the PC arc trans ferred to the MBR to be written into memory.

The special memory location reserved for this purpose is loaded into the MAR from the control unit. It might, for example, be a stack pointer. The PC is loaded with the address of the interrupt routine. As a result, the next instruction cycle will begin by fetching the appropriate instruction.

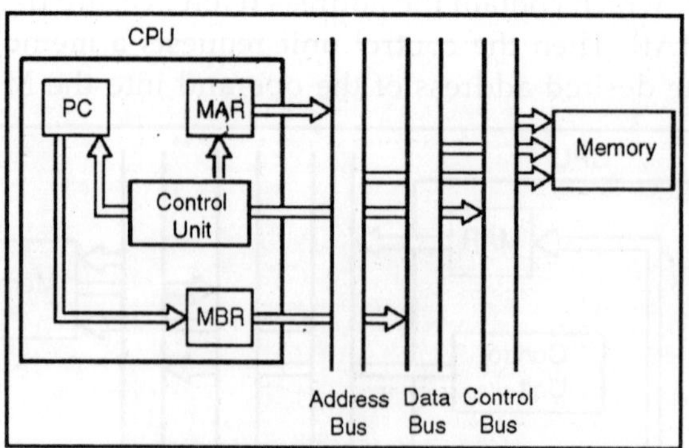

Fig. Data Flow, Interrupt Cycle

MAIN MEMORY – RAM

RAM makes up the bulk of electronic storage on present-day computers. It is used as storage for both data and programmes while those data and programmes are in use. The speed of RAM in most systems today lies between the speed of cache memory and that of hard drives, and is much closer to the former than the latter. The basic operation of RAM is actually quite straightforward. At the lowest level, there are the RAM chips — integrated circuits that do the actual "remembering."

These chips have four types of connections to the outside world:

- Power connections.
- Data connections (to enable the transfer of data into or out of the chip)
- Read/Write connections (to control whether data is to be stored into or retrieved from the chip)
- Address connections (to determine where in the chip the data should be read/written)

Here are the steps required to store data in RAM:

- The data to be stored is presented to the data connections.
- The address at which the data is to be stored is presented to the address connections.
- The read/write connection is set to write mode.

Retrieving data is just as straightforward:

- The address of the desired data is presented to the address connections.

- The read/write connection is set to read mode.
- The desired data is read from the data connections.

While these steps seem simple, they take place at very high speeds, with the time spent on each step measured in nanoseconds. Nearly all RAM chips created today are sold as *modules.* Each module consists of a number of individual RAM chips attached to a small circuit board. The mechanical and electrical layout of the module adheres to various industry standards, making it possible to purchase memory from a variety of vendors.

HARD DRIVES

All the technologies discussed so far are *volatile* in nature. In other words, data contained in volatile storage is lost when the power is turned off. Hard drives, on the other hand, are *non-volatile* — the data they contain remains there, even after the power is removed. Because of this, hard drives occupy a special place in the storage spectrum. Their non-volatile nature makes them ideal for storing programmes and data for longer-term use. Another unique aspect to hard drives is that, unlike RAM and cache memory, it is not possible to execute programmes directly when they are stored on hard drives; instead, they must first be read into RAM.

Also different from cache and RAM is the speed of data storage and retrieval; hard drives are at least an order of magnitude slower than the all-electronic technologies used for cache and RAM. The difference in speed is due mainly to their electromechanical nature. There are four distinct phases taking place during each data transfer to or from a hard drive. The following list illustrates these phases, along with the time it would take a typical high-performance drive, on average, to complete each:

- Access arm movement (5.5 milliseconds)
- Disk rotation (.1 milliseconds)
- Heads reading/writing data (.00014 milliseconds)
- Data transfer to/from the drive's electronics (.003 Milliseconds) Of these, only the last phase is not dependent on any mechanical operation.

FIXED POINT NUMBERS

Most computer languages nowadays only offer two kinds of numbers, *floating-point* and *integer fixed-point*. On present-day computers, all numbers are encoded using *binary digits* (called "bits") which are either 1 or 0.[G.1] In C, C++, and Java, floating-point variables are declared as float (32 bits) or double (64 bits), while integer fixed-point variables are declared as short int(typically 16 bits and never less), long int (typically 32 bits and never less), or simply int (typically the same as a long int, but sometimes between short and long). For an 8-bit integer, one can use the char data type (8 bits).

Since C was designed to accommodate a wide range of hardware, including old mini-computers, some latitude was historically allowed in the choice of these bit-lengths. The sizeof operator is officially the "right way" for a C programme to determine the number of bytes in various data types at run-time, *e.g.*, sizeof(long). (The word int can be omitted after short or long.) Nowadays, however, shorts are always 16 bits (at least on all the major platforms), ints are 32 bits, and longs are typically 32 bits on 32-bit computers and 64 bits on 64-bit computers (although some C/C++ compilers use long long int to declare 64-bit ints). Table gives the lengths currently used by GNU C/C++ compilers (usually called "gcc" or "cc") on 64-bit.

Table. Byte Sizes of GNU C/C++ Data Types for 64-bit Machines.

Type	Bytes	Notes
char	1	
short	2	
int	4	
long	8	(4 bytes on 32-bit machines)
long long	8	(may become 16 bytes)
type *	8	(any pointer)
float	4	
double	8	
long double	8	(may become 10 bytes)
size_t	8	(type of sizeof())
T* - T*	8	(pointer arithmetic)

A careful reader should now realise the bit pattern of 53 and 26.5 is exactly the same. The *only* difference, is the position of binary point.

In the case of 53_{10}, there is "no" binary point. Alternatively, we can say the binary point is located at the far right, at position 0. (Think in decimal, 53 and 53.0 represents the same number.)

2^5	2^4	2^3	2^2	2^1	2^0	Binary Point	2^{-1}	2^{-2}	2^{-3}
1	1	0	1	0	1		0	0	0

In the case of 26.5_{10}, binary point is located one position to the *left* of 53_{10}:

2^5	2^4	2^3	2^2	2^1	2^0	Binary Point	2^{-1}	2^{-2}	2^{-3}
0	1	1	0	1	0		1	0	0

Now, we see in class, we discuss shifting an integer to the right by 1 bit position is equivalent to dividing the number by 2. In the case of integer, since we don't have a fractional part, we simply cannot represent digit to the right of a binary point, making this shifting process an *integer division*. However, it is simply a limitation of integer representations of binary number.

In general, mathematically, given a fixed binary point position, shifting the bit pattern of a number to the right by 1 bit *always* divide the number by 2. Similarly, shifting a number to the left by 1 bit multiplies the number by 2.

The shifting process above is the key to understand fixed point number representation. To represent a real number in computers (or any hardware in general), we can define a fixed point number type simply by implicitly *fixing* the binary point to be at some position of a numeral. We will then simply adhere to this implicit convention when we represent numbers.

To define a fixed point type conceptually, all we need are two parameters:

- Width of the number representation, and
- Binary point position within the number

We will use the notation fixed<w,b> for the rest of this article, where w denotes the number of bits used as a whole (the Width of a number), and b denotes the position of binary point counting from the least significant bit (counting from 0).

For example, fixed<8,3> denotes a 8-bit fixed point number, of which 3 right most bits are fractional. Therefore, the bit pattern:

0 0 0 1 0 1 1 0 Represents a real number:

00010.110_2

$= 1 * 2^1 + 1 * 2^{-1} + 1 * 2^{-1}$

$= 2 + 0.5 + 0.25$

$= 2.75$

Note that on a computer, a bit patter can represents anything. Therefore the same bit pattern, if we "cast" it to another type, such as a fixed<8,5> type, will represents the number:

000.10110_2

$= 1 * 2^{-1} + 1 * 2^{-3} + 1 * 2^{-4}$

$= 0.5 + 0.125 + 0.0625$

$= 0.6875$

If we treat this bit patter as integer, it represents the number:

10110_2

$= 1 * 2^4 + 1 * 2^2 + 1 * 2^1$

$= 16 + 4 + 2$

$= 22$

FLOATING-POINT NUMBERS

Floating-point numbers consist of an "exponent," "significand", and "sign bit". For a negative number, we may set the sign bit of the floating-point word and negate the number to be encoded, leaving only nonnegative numbers to be considered.

Zero is represented by all zeros, so now we need only consider positive numbers. The basic idea of floating point *encoding* of a binary number is to *normalize* the number by *shifting* the bits either left or right until the shifted result lies between 1/2 and 1.

(A left-shift by one place in a binary word corresponds to multiplying by 2, while a right-shift one place corresponds to dividing by 2.) The number of bit-positions shifted to normalize the number can be recorded as a signed integer. The negative of this integer (*i.e.*, the shift required to recover the original number) is defined as the *exponent* of the floating-point encoding.

The normalized number between 1/2 and 1 is called the *significand,* so called because it holds all the "significant bits" of the number.

Floating point notation is exactly analogous to "scientific notation" for decimal numbers, *e.g.*, 1.2345×10^{-9} the number of significant digits, 5 in this example, is determined by counting digits in the "significand" 1.2345 while the "order of magnitude" is determined by the power of 10 (–9 in this case).

In floating-point numbers, the significand is stored in fractional two's-complement binary format, and the exponent is stored as a binary integer. Since the significand lies in the interval (1/2,1),[G.6]its most significant bit is always a 1, so it is not actually stored in the computer word, giving one more significant bit of precision.

Let's now restate the above a little more precisely. Let $x>0$ denote a number to be encoded in floating-point, and let $\overline{x} = x \cdot 2^{-E}$ denote the normalized value obtained by shifting x either E bits to the right (if $E>0$), or $|E|$ bits to the left (if $E<0$).

Then we have $1/2 \le \overline{x} < 1$ and $x = \overline{x} \cdot 2^{E}$ The *significand* M of the floating-point representation for x is defined as the binary encoding of [G.7] It is often the case that requires more bits than are available for exact encoding. Therefore, the significand is typically *rounded* (or truncated) to the value closest to $\overline{x}$ Given N_M bits for the significand, the encoding of $\overline{x}$ can be computed by multiplying it by 2^{N_M} (left-shifting it N_M bits), *rounding* to the nearest integer (or *truncating*toward minus infinity—as implemented by the floor() function), and encoding the N_M-bit result as a binary (signed) integer.

As a final practical note, exponents in floating-point formats may have a *bias.* That is, instead of storing E as a binary integer, you may find a binary encoding of E–B where

B is the bias. A real number (that is, a number that can contain a fractional part).

The following are floating-point numbers:

- 3.0
- –111.5
- ½
- 3E-5

The last example is a computer shorthand for scientific notation. It means 3*10-5 (or 10 to the negative 5th power multiplied by 3). In essence, computers are integer machines and are capable of representing real numbers only by using complex codes.

The term *floating point* is derived from the fact that there is no fixed number of digits before and after the decimal point; that is, the decimal point can float.

There are also representations in which the number of digits before and after the decimal point is set, called *fixed-point* representations. In general, floating-point representations are slower and less accurate than fixed-point representations, but they can handle a larger range of numbers.

Note that most floating-point numbers a computer can represent are just approximations. One of the challenges in programming with floating-point values is ensuring that the approximations lead to reasonable results. If the programmer is not careful, small discrepancies in the approximations can snowball to the point where the final results become meaningless.

Because mathematics with floating-point numbers requires a great deal of computing power, many microprocessors come with a chip, called a *floating point unit (FPU)*, specialized for performing floating-point arithmetic. FPUs are also called *math coprocessors* and *numeric coprocessors*.

FIXED VERSUS FLOATING POINT

Digital Signal Processing can be divided into two categories, fixed point and floating point. These refer to the format used to store and manipulate numbers within the devices. Fixed point DSPs usually represent each number with a minimum of 16 bits, although a different length can be used. For instance, Motorola manufactures a family of fixed point DSPs that use 24 bits. There are four common ways that these 2^{16} = 65536 possible bit patterns can represent a number. In unsigned integer, the stored number can take on any integer value from 0 to 65,535. Similarly, signed integer uses two's complement to make the range include negative numbers, from -32,768 to 32,767.

With unsigned fractionnotation, the 65,536 levels are spread uniformly between 0 and 1. Lastly, the signed fraction format allows negative numbers, equally spaced between –1 and 1. In comparison, floating point DSPs typically use a minimum of 32 bits to store each value.

This results in many more bit patterns than for fixed point, 2^{32} = 4,294,967,296 to be exact. A key feature of floating point notation is that the represented numbers are *not* uniformly spaced.

In the most common format (ANSI/IEEE Std. 754-1985), the largest and smallest numbers are $\pm 3.4 \times 10^{38}$ and 1.210^{-38}, respectively. The represented values are unequally spaced between these two extremes, such that the gap between any two numbers is about ten-million times smaller than the value of the numbers.

This is important because it places large gaps between large numbers, but small gaps between small numbers. All floating point DSPs can also handle fixed point numbers, a necessity to implement counters, loops, and signals coming from the ADC and going to the DAC. However, this doesn't mean that fixed point math will be carried out as quickly as the floating point operations; it depends on the internal architecture.

For instance, the SHARC DSPs are optimized for both floating point and fixed point operations, and executes them with equal efficiency. For this reason, the SHARC devices are often referred to as "32-bit DSPs," rather than just "Floating Point." Figure illustrates the primary trade-offs between fixed and floating point DSPs.

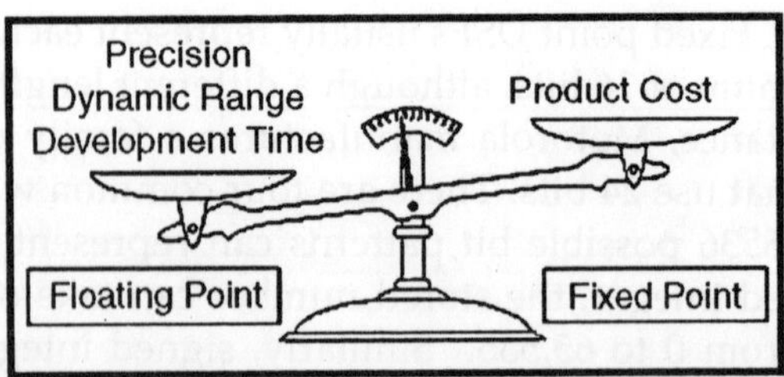

Faster than floating point in general purpose computers. However, with DSPs the speed is about the same, a result of the hardware being highly optimized for math operations. The internal architecture of a floating point DSP is more complicated than for a fixed point device.

All the registers and data buses must be 32 bits wide instead of only 16; the multiplier and ALU must be able to quickly perform floating point arithmetic, the instruction set must be larger (so that they can handle both floating and fixed point numbers), and so on.

Floating point (32 bit) has better precision and a higher dynamic range than fixed point (16 bit). In addition, floating point programmes often have a shorter development cycle, since the programmer doesn't generally need to worry about issues such as overflow, underflow, and round-off error. On the other hand, fixed point DSPs have traditionally been cheaper than floating point devices.

Nothing changes more rapidly than the price of electronics; anything you find in a book will be out-of-date before it is printed. Nevertheless, cost is a key factor in understanding how DSPs are evolving, and we need to give you a general idea.

When this book was completed in 1999, fixed point DSPs sold for between $5 and $100, while floating point devices were in the range of $10 to $300. This difference in cost can be viewed as a measure of the relative complexity between the devices. If you want to find out what the prices are *today*, you need to look *today*.

Now let's turn our attention to *performance*; what can a 32-bit floating point system do that a 16-bit fixed point can't? The answer to this question is signal-to-noise ratio. Suppose we store a number in a 32 bit floating point format. As previously mentioned, the gap between this number and its adjacent neighbour is about one ten-millionth of the value of the number.

To store the number, it must be round up or down by a maximum of one-half the gap size. In other words, each time we store a number in floating point notation, we add *noise* to the signal. The same thing happens when a number is stored as a 16-bit fixed point value, except that the added noise is much worse. This is because the gaps between adjacent numbers are much larger.

For instance, suppose we store the number 10,000 as a signed integer (running from –32,768 to 32,767). The gap between numbers is one ten-thousandth of the value of the number we are storing. If we want to store the number 1000, the gap between numbers is only one one-thousandth of the value.

Noise in signals is usually represented by its *standard deviation*. For here, the important fact is that the standard deviation of this quantization noise is about one-third of the gap size.

This means that the signal-to-noise ratio for storing a floating point number is about 30 million to one, while for a fixed point number it is only about ten-thousand to one. In other words, floating point has roughly 30,000 times less quantization noise than fixed point.

This brings up an important way that DSPs are different from traditional microprocessors. Suppose we implement an FIR filter in fixed point. To do this, we loop through each coefficient, multiply it by the appropriate sample from the input signal, and add the product to an accumulator. Here's the problem.

In traditional microprocessors, this accumulator is just another 16 bit fixed point variable. To avoid overflow, we need to scale the values being added, and will correspondingly add quantization noise on each step. In the worst case, this quantization noise will simply add, greatly lowering the signal-to-noise ratio of the system. For instance, in a 500 coefficient FIR filter, the noise on each output sample may be 500 times the noise on each input sample. The signal-to-noise ratio of *ten-thousand to one* has dropped to a ghastly *twenty to one.* Although this is an extreme case, it illustrates the main point: when many operations are carried out on each sample, it's bad, really bad. DSPs handle this problem by using an extended precision accumulator.

This is a special register that has 2-3 times as many bits as the other memory locations. For example, in a 16 bit DSP it may have 32 to 40 bits, while in the SHARC DSPs it contains 80 bits for fixed point use. This extended range virtually eliminates round-off noise hile the accumulation is in progress. The only round-off error suffered is when the accumulator is scaled and stored in the 16 bit memory. This strategy works very well, although it does limit how some algorithms must be carried out.

In comparison, floating point has such low quantization noise that these techniques are usually not necessary. In addition to having lower quantization noise, floating point systems are also easier to develop algorithms for. Most DSP techniques are based on repeated multiplications and additions. In fixed point, the possibility of an overflow or underflow needs to be considered after each operation. The programmer needs to continually understand the amplitude of the numbers, how the quantization errors are accumulating, and what scaling needs to take place. In comparison, these issues do not arise in floating point; the numbers take care of themselves (except in rare cases). To give you a better understanding of this issue, table from the SHARC user manual. This describes the ways that multiplication can be carried out for both fixed and floating point formats. First, look at how floating point numbers can be multiplied; there is only one way!

See the text for an explanation of these options is, Fn = Fx * Fy, where Fn, Fx, and Fy are any of the 16 data registers. It could not be any simpler. In comparison, look at all the possible commands for fixed point multiplication. These are the many options needed to efficiently handle the problems of round-off, scaling, and format.

Fixed Point	Floating Point
| Rn | MRF | MRB | = Rx * Ry (| S | U | | S | U | | F | I | FR |)	Fn = Fx * Fy
| Rn = MRF | Rn = MRB | MRF = MRF | MRB = MRB | + Rx * Ry (| S | U | | S | U | | F | I | FR |)	
| Rn = MRF | Rn = MRB | MRF = MRF | MRB = MRB | - Rx * Ry (| S | U | | S | U | | F | I | FR |)	
| Rn = SAT MRF | Rn = SAT MRB | MRF = SAT MRF | MRB = SAT MRB | | (SI) | (UI) | (SF) | (UF) |	
| Rn = RND MRF | Rn = RND MRB | MRF = RND MRF | MRB = RND MRB | | (SF) | (UF) |	
| MRF | MRB | = 0	
| MRxF | MRxB | = Rn	
Rn = | MRxF | MRxB |	

Fig. Fixed Versus Floating Point Instructions.

In Fig., Rn, Rx, and Ry refer to any of the 16 data registers, and MRF and MRB are 80 bit accumulators. The vertical lines indicate *options*. For instance, the top-left entry in this table means that all the following are valid commands: Rn = Rx * Ry, MRF = Rx * Ry, and MRB = Rx * Ry. In other words, the value of any two registers can be multiplied and placed into another register, or into one of the extended precision accumulators.

This table also shows that the numbers may be either signed or unsigned (S or U), and may be fractional or integer (F or I). The RND and SAT options are ways of controlling rounding and register overflow. There are other details and options in the table, but they are not important for our present discussion. The important idea is that the fixed point programmer must understand dozens of ways to carry out the very basic task of multiplication. In contrast, the floating point programmer can spend his time concentrating on the algorithm. Given these tradeoffs between fixed and floating point, how do you choose which to use?

Here are some things to consider. First, look at how many bits are used in the ADC and DAC. In many applications, 12-14 bits per sample is the crossover for using fixed versus floating point. For instance, television and other video signals typically use 8 bit ADC and DAC, and the precision of fixed point is acceptable. In comparison, professional audio applications can sample with as high as 20 or 24 bits, and almost certainly need floating point to capture the large dynamic range.

The next thing to look at is the complexity of the algorithm that will be run. If it is relatively simple, think fixed point; if it is more complicated, think floating point. For example, FIR filtering and other operations in the time domain only require a few dozen lines of code, making them suitable for fixed point.

In contrast, frequency domain algorithms, such as spectral analysis and FFT convolution, are very detailed and can be much more difficult to programme. While they can be written in fixed point, the development time will be greatly reduced if floating point is used.

Lastly, think about the money: how important is the cost of the product, and how important is the cost of the development? When fixed point is chosen, the cost of the product will be reduced, but the development cost will probably be higher due to the more difficult algorithms. In the reverse manner, floating point will generally result in a quicker and cheaper development cycle, but a more expensive final product.

Some of the major trends in DSPs. The impact that Digital Signal Processors have had on the embedded market. These are applications that use a microprocessor to directly operate and control some larger system, such as a cellular telephone, microwave oven, or automotive instrument display panel. The name "microcontroller" is often used in referring to these devices, to distinguish them from the microprocessors used in personal computers. As shown in (a), about 38% of embedded designers have already started using DSPs, and another 49% are considering the switch. The high throughput and computational power of DSPs often makes them an ideal choice for embedded designs.

As illustrated in (b), about twice as many engineers currently use fixed point as use floating point DSPs. However, this depends greatly on the application. Fixed point is more popular in competitive consumer products where the cost of the electronics must be kept very low. A good example of this is cellular telephones.

When you are in competition to sell millions of your product, a cost difference of only a few dollars can be the difference between success and failure. In comparison, floating point is more common when greater performance is needed and cost is not important.

For instance, suppose you are designing a medical imaging system, such a computed tomography scanner. Only a few hundred of the model will ever be sold, at a price of several hundred-thousand dollars each. For this application, the cost of the DSP is insignificant, but the performance is critical.

In spite of the larger number of fixed point DSPs being used, the floating point market is the fastest growing segment. As shown in , over one-half of engineers using 16-bits devices plan to migrate to floating point at some time in the near future.

Before leaving this topic, we should reemphasize that floating point and fixed point usually use 32 bits and 16 bits, respectively, *but not always*. For instance, the SHARC family can represent numbers in 32-bit fixed point, a mode that is common in digital audio applications.

This makes the 2^{32} quantization levels spaced uniformly over a relatively small range, say, between -1 and 1. In comparison, floating point notation places the 2^{32} quantization levels logarithmically over a huge range, typically $\pm 3.4 \times 10^{38}$. This gives 32-bit fixed point better *precision*, that is, the quantization error on any one sample will be lower. However,

32-bit floating point has a higher *dynamic range,* meaning there is a greater difference between the largest number and the smallest number that can be represented.

INSTRUCTIONS SETS

ADC	HL,ss	Add with carry register pair ss to HL.
ADC	A,s	Add with carry operand s to accumulator.
ADD	A,n	Add value n to accumulator.
ADD	A,r	Add register r to accumulator.
ADD	A,(HL)	Add location (HL) to accumulator.
ADD	A,(IX+d)	Add location (IX+d) to accumulator.
ADD	A,(IY+d)	Add location (IY+d) to accumulator.
ADD	HL,ss	Add register pair ss to HL.
ADD	IX,pp	Add register pair pp to IX.
ADD	IY,rr	Add register pair rr to IY.
AND	s	Logical AND of operand s to accumulator.
BIT	b,(HL)	Test bit b of location (HL).
BIT	b,(IX+d)	Test bit b of location (IX+d).
BIT	b,(IY+d)	Test bit b of location (IY+d).
BIT	b,r	Test bit b of register r.
CALL	cc,nn	Call subroutine at location nn if condition CC is true.
CCF		Complement carry flag.
CP	s	Compare operand s with accumulator.
CPD		Comapre location (HL) and acc., decrement HL and BC,
CPDR		Perform a CPD and repeat until BC=0.
CPI		Compare location (HL) and acc., incr HL, decr BC.
CPIR		Perform a CPI and repeat until BC=0.
CPL		Complement accumulator (1's complement).
DAA		Decimal adjust accumulator.
DEC	m	Decrement operand m.

DEC	IX	Decrement IX.
DEC	IY	Decrement IY.
DEC	ss	Decrement register pair ss.
DI		Disable interrupts.
DJNZ	e	Decrement B and jump relative if B=0.
EI		Enable interrupts.
EX	(SP),HL	Exchange the location (SP) and HL.
EX	(SP),IX	Exchange the location (SP) and IX.
EX	(SP),IY	Exchange the location (SP) and IY.
EX	AF,AF'	Exchange the contents of AF and AF'.
EX	DE,HL	Exchange the contents of DE and HL.
EXX		Exchange the contents of BC,DE,HL with BC',DE',HL'.
HALT		Halt computer and wait for interrupt.
IM	0	Set interrupt mode 0.
IM	1	Set interrupt mode 1.
IM	2	Set interrupt mode 2.
IN	A,(n)	Load the accumulator with input from device n.
IN	r,(c)	Load the register r with input from device (C).
INC	(HL)	Increment location (HL).
INC	IX	Increment IX.
INC	(IX+d)	Increment location (IX+d).
INC	IY	Increment IY.
INC	(IY+d)	Increment location (IY+d).
INC	r	Increment register r.
INC	ss	Increment register pair ss.
IND		(HL)=Input from port (C). Decrement HL and B.
INDR		Perform an IND and repeat until B=0.
INI		(HL)=Input from port (C). HL=HL+1. B=B-1.
INIR		Perform an INI and repeat until B=0.
JP	(HL)	Unconditional jump to location (HL).
JP	(IX)	Unconditional jump to location (IX).

JP	(IY)	Unconditional jump to location (IY).
JP	cc,nn	Jump to location nn if condition cc is true.
JR	C,e	Jump relative to PC+e if carry=1.
JR	e	Unconditional jump relative to PC+e.
JR	NC,e	Jump relative to PC+e if carry=0.
JR	NZ,e	Jump relative to PC+e if non zero (Z=0).
JR	Z,e	Jump relative to PC+e if zero (Z=1).
LD	A,(BC)	Load accumulator with location (BC).
LD	A,(DE)	Load accumulator with location (DE).
LD	A,I	Load accumulator with I.
LD	A,(nn)	Load accumulator with location nn.
LD	A,R	Load accumulator with R.
LD	(BC),A	Load location (BC) with accumulator.
LD	(DE),A	Load location (DE) with accumulator.
LD	(HL),A	Load location (HL) with accumulator.
LD	dd,nn	Load register pair dd with nn.
LD	dd,(nn)	Load register pair dd with location (nn).
LD	HL,(nn)	Load HL with location (nn).
LD	(HL),r	Load location (HL) with register r.
LD	I,A	Load I with accumulator.
LD	IX,nn	Load IX with value nn.
LD	IX,(nn)	Load IX with location (nn).
LD	(IX+d),n	Load location (IX+d) with n.
LD	(IX+d),r	Load location (IX+d) with register r.
LD	IY,nn	Load IY with value nn.
LD	IY,(nn)	Load IY with location (nn).
LD	(IY+d),n	Load location (IY+d) with value n.
LD	(IY+d),r	Load location (IY+d) with register r.
LD	(nn),A	Load location (nn) with accumulator.
LD	(nn),dd	Load location (nn) with register pair dd.
LD	(nn),HL	Load location (nn) with HL.
LD	(nn),IX	Load location (nn) with IX.
LD	(nn),IY	Load location (nn) with IY.

LD	R,A	Load R with accumulator.
LD	r,(HL)	Load register r with location (HL).
LD	r,(IX+d)	Load register r with location (IX+d).
LD	r,(IY+d)	Load register r with location (IY+d).
LD	r,n	Load register r with value n.
LD	r,r'	Load register r with register r'.
LD	SP,HL	Load SP with HL.
LD	SP,IX	Load SP with IX.
LD	SP,IY	Load SP with IY.
LDD		Load location (DE) with location (HL), decrement DE,HL,BC.
LDDR		Perform an LDD and repeat until BC=0.
LDI		Load location (DE) with location (HL), incr DE,HL; decr BC.
LDIR		Perform an LDI and repeat until BC=0.
NEG		Negate accumulator (2's complement).
NOP		No operation.
OR	s	Logical OR of operand s and accumulator.
OTDR		Perform an OUTD and repeat until B=0.
OTIR		Perform an OTI and repeat until B=0.
OUT	(C),r	Load output port (C) with register r.
OUT	(n),A	Load output port (n) with accumulator.
OUTD		Load output port (C) with (HL), decrement HL and B.
OUTI		Load output port (C) with (HL), incr HL, decr B.
POP	IX	Load IX with top of stack.
POP	IY	Load IY with top of stack.
POP	qq	Load register pair qq with top of stack.
PUSH	IX	Load IX onto stack.
PUSH	IY	Load IY onto stack.
PUSH	qq	Load register pair qq onto stack.
RES	b,m	Reset bit b of operand m.
RET		Return from subroutine.

RET	cc	Return from subroutine if condition cc is true.
RETI		Return from interrupt.
RETN		Return from non-maskable interrupt.
RL	m	Rotate left through operand m.
RLA		Rotate left accumulator through carry.
RLC	(HL)	Rotate location (HL) left circular.
RLC	(IX+d)	Rotate location (IX+d) left circular.
RLC	(IY+d)	Rotate location (IY+d) left circular.
RLC	r	Rotate register r left circular.
RLCA		Rotate left circular accumulator.
RLD		Rotate digit left and right between accumulator and (HL).
RR	m	Rotate right through carry operand m.
RRA		Rotate right accumulator through carry.
RRC	m	Rotate operand m right circular.
RRCA		Rotate right circular accumulator.
RRD		Rotate digit right and left between accumulator and (HL).
RST	p	Restart to location p.
SBC	A,s	Subtract operand s from accumulator with carry.
SBC	HL,ss	Subtract register pair ss from HL with carry.
SCF		Set carry flag (C=1).
SET	b,(HL)	Set bit b of location (HL).
SET	b,(IX+d)	Set bit b of location (IX+d).
SET	b,(IY+d)	Set bit b of location (IY+d).
SET	b,R	Set bit b of register r.
SLA	m	Shift operand m left arithmetic.
SRA	m	Shift operand m right arithmetic.
SRL	m	Shift operand m right logical.
SUB	s	Subtract operand s from accumulator.
XOR	s	Exclusive OR operand s and accumulator

Chapter 4

Data Path Design

FIXED POINT ARITHMETIC

INTRODUCTION

Fixed-point numbers, which have a specified number of digits to the right of the decimal point, are common in many kinds of applications, but they seem to have been omitted from most computer programming libraries.

This package implements fixed-point numbers as instances of a class called fixed. It consists of the library file FIXED.LIB which must be linked to every application that uses it, and the header file FIXED.H, which must be included in every source file that contains any calls on it. The library itself is made by compiling a number of source files and combining the resulting object files into a library. A makefile to do this Borland C++ is included with the source code.

Included with the source code is a test programme to perform various operations on fixed-point command-line arguments and display the results.

The precision of a fixed-point number is the number of digits to the right of the decimal point, and it normally stays the same when computations are performed on the number. The maximum value MAX_FIXED_PRECISION is defined in the header file FIXED.H as 15, but you can change this value and recompile the package. Catastrophic failure will occur if the precision is larger than 255, so don't go overboard!

The package stores a fixed-point number internally as an extra-long signed integer of a type called fixed_numerator, which represents the value of the number without its decimal point, together with the precision as an unsigned character. For example, -123.4500 is stored internally as:

value = 1234500

precision = 4

Notice that trailing zeros, as in this example, have no effect on the mathematical value of a fixed-point number, but they do affect its precision.

You must supply the fixed_numerator type from some other source. The current version of Borland C++ has a 64-bit signed integer type called __int64, which the package uses. You may supply a different type.

The fixed_numerator type must implement the following operators:

+ – * / == != > ⇒ < ⇐

Both negation (unary -) and subtraction (binary -) must be supported. It must also implement assignment from a standard integer (int), and a conversion function integer() that will convert a fixed_numerator value to a standard integer (int).

The fixed_numerator type is also responsible for detecting and handling arithmetic overflow, if this is deemed necessary. Notice that overflow may occur in some kinds of operations even though the operands and results are within range. For this reason, the fixed_numerator type should have a capacity considerably larger than the range of expected operand and result values.

The package includes an editing function that needs a buffer to hold the result. The number MAX_FIXED_LENGTH is the size of a buffer just large enough to hold the largest possible number, with a prefixed minus sign, commas, a decimal point, and a terminating nul.

If fixed_numerator is 64-bit signed twos-complement arithmetic, as in the unaltered package, then the largest and smallest possible numbers are -9,223,372,036,854,775,808. and 9,223,372,036,854,775,807., respectively. Hence MAX_FIXED_LENGTH is 28.

Every fixed-point number must have a precision, which is determined when the number is constructed and is normally not changed dynamically. There are two constructors:

```
fixed(x, p);
int x; initial value without decimal point
int p; initial precision (default value is zero)
fixed(s);
const char *s;string to be scanned for initial
value
```

For example, the following two fixed-point numbers have the same initial value and precision:

```
fixed x(1234500, 4);
fixed y("123.4500");
```

The package defines two kinds of assignment operators:

```
x = n;
x = y;
fixed x, y;
int n;
```

The precision of x is unchanged by assignment. The value to be assigned is truncated (toward zero) or padded with trailing zeros. Here are some examples:

```
fixed x(0, 4);
x = 12345678; // x becomes 12345678.0000
x = fixed("-1.2345678"); // x becomes -1.2345
```

The following function edits a fixed-point value to a displayable string form:

```
s = x.edit(options);
fixed x; a fixed-point variable or
expression
const char *s; pointer to static buffer
containing result
int options; any combination of the
following:
fixed::COMMAS include commas
fixed::DECIMAL include decimal
point
even if precision is
zero fixed::ALIGN align decimal points
the default value is fixed::COMMAS
```

If the fixed::ALIGN option is included, then the result will be padded with enough leading blanks so the decimal point will appear in the same position, no matter what the value and precision of the fixed-point number.

CAUTION: The function uses the same static buffer for every call. If the result is not to be used immediately, it must be copied elsewhere before the next call on edit(). You may *not* use more than one call on edit() in the same statement:

```
printf("x=%s and y=%s", x.edit(), y.edit());
// This will NOT produce the desired result!
```

The following member function returns, as an integer, the integral part of a fixed-point number:

```
n = x.whole();
fixed x; a fixed-point variable or expression
int n; value of integral part
```

For example,

```
fixed("1234.567").whole() produces 1234
```

The package implements the usual arithmetic operations: addition, subtraction, multiplication, division and negation (unary minus) and the usual comparison operations: ==, !=, >, ⇒, < and ⇐. It is permissible to mix precisions, and to mix fixed-point and integer operands. An integer operand is treated as a fixed-point operand with precision 0.

A sum or difference has a precision equal to the higher operand precision.

Comparisons are performed by subtracting the operands and comparing the result to zero. *WARNING:* Comparison of operands of opposite sign may produce an overflow and invalid results even if the operands themselves are in range!

A product normally has a precision equal to the sum of the precisions of the operands. If this is greater than MAX_FIXED_PRECISION, the result is truncated to MAX_FIXED_PRECISION.

A quotient has the same precision as the dividend.

The precision of a fixed-point number may be changed with the [] operator. If x is a fixed-point variable or expression, then x[p] is the same value with precision p, truncated or padded with zeros.

For example:

```
fixed x("123.456");
x[1] is 123.4
x[4] is 123.4560
```

MODEL OF FIXED POINT ARITHMETIC

- In the strict mode, the predefined arithmetic operations of a fixed point type shall satisfy the accuracy requirements specified here and shall avoid or signal overflow in the situations described.

IMPLEMENTATION REQUIREMENTS

- The accuracy requirements for the predefined fixed point arithmetic operations and conversions, and the results of relations on fixed point operands, are given below.
- The operands of the fixed point adding operators, absolute value, and comparisons have the same type. These operations are required to yield exact results, unless they overflow.
- Multiplications and divisions are allowed between operands of any two fixed point types; the result has to be (implicitly or explicitly) converted to some other numeric type. For purposes of defining the accuracy rules, the multiplication or division and the conversion are treated as a single operation whose accuracy depends on three types (those of the operands and the result). For decimal fixed point types, the attribute T'Round may be used to imply explicit conversion with rounding.
- When the result type is a floating point type, the accuracy is as given in G.2.1. For some combinations of the operand and result types in the remaining cases, the result is required to belong to a small set of values called the *perfect result set*;for other combinations, it is required merely to belong to a generally larger and implementation-defined set of values called the *close result set*. When the result type

is a decimal fixed point type, the perfect result set contains a single value; thus, operations on decimal types are always fully specified.

- When one operand of a fixed-fixed multiplication or division is of type *universal_real*, that operand is not implicitly converted in the usual sense, since the context does not determine a unique target type, but the accuracy of the result of the multiplication or division (i.e., whether the result has to belong to the perfect result set or merely the close result set) depends on the value of the operand of type *universal_real* and on the types of the other operand and of the result.
- For a fixed point multiplication or division whose (exact) mathematical result is *v*, and for the conversion of a value *v* to a fixed point type, the perfect result set and close result set are defined as follows:
- If the result type is an ordinary fixed point type with a *small* of *s*,
- If *v* is an integer multiple of *s*, then the perfect result set contains only the value *v*;
- Otherwise, it contains the integer multiple of *s* just below *v* and the integer multiple of *s* just above *v*.
- The close result set is an implementation-defined set of consecutive integer multiples of *s* containing the perfect result set as a subset.
- If the result type is a decimal type with a *small* of *s*,
- If *v* is an integer multiple of *s*, then the perfect result set contains only the value *v*;
- Otherwise, if truncation applies then it contains only the integer multiple of *s* in the direction toward zero, whereas if rounding applies then it contains only the nearest integer multiple of *s*(with ties broken by rounding away from zero).
- The close result set is an implementation-defined set of consecutive integer multiples of *s* containing the perfect result set as a subset.

- If the result type is an integer type.
- if v is an integer, then the perfect result set contains only the value v.
- Otherwise, it contains the integer nearest to the value v (if v lies equally distant from two consecutive integers, the perfect result set contains the one that is further from zero).
- The close result set is an implementation-defined set of consecutive integers containing the perfect result set as a subset.
- The result of a fixed point multiplication or division shall belong either to the perfect result set or to the close result set, as described below, if overflow does not occur. In the following cases, if the result type is a fixed point type, let s be its *small*; otherwise, i.e. when the result type is an integer type, let s be 1.0.
- For a multiplication or division neither of whose operands is of type *universal_real*, let l and r be the*smalls* of the left and right operands. For a multiplication, if $(l \cdot r) / s$ is an integer or the reciprocal of an integer (the *smalls* are said to be "compatible" in this case), the result shall belong to the perfect result set; otherwise, it belongs to the close result set. For a division, if $l / (r \cdot s)$ is an integer or the reciprocal of an integer (i.e., the *smalls* are compatible), the result shall belong to the perfect result set; otherwise, it belongs to the close result set.
- For a multiplication or division having one *universal_real* operand with a value of v, note that it is always possible to factor v as an integer multiple of a "compatible" *small*, but the integer multiple may be "too big." If there exists a factorization in which that multiple is less than some implementation-defined limit, the result shall belong to the perfect result set; otherwise, it belongs to the close result set.
- A multiplication P * Q of an operand of a fixed point type F by an operand of an integer type I, or vice-versa, and a division P / Q of an operand of a fixed

point type F by an operand of an integer type I, are also allowed. In these cases, the result has a type of F; explicit conversion of the result is never required. The accuracy required in these cases is the same as that required for a multiplication F(P * Q) or a division F(P / Q) obtained by interpreting the operand of the integer type to have a fixed point type with a *small* of 1.0.

- The accuracy of the result of a conversion from an integer or fixed point type to a fixed point type, or from a fixed point type to an integer type, is the same as that of a fixed point multiplication of the source value by a fixed point operand having a *small* of 1.0 and a value of 1.0, as given by the foregoing rules. The result of a conversion from a floating point type to a fixed point type shall belong to the close result set. The result of a conversion of a *universal_real* operand to a fixed point type shall belong to the perfect result set.
- The possibility of overflow in the result of a predefined arithmetic operation or conversion yielding a result of a fixed point type T is analogous to that for floating point types, except for being related to the base range instead of the safe range. If all of the permitted results belong to the base range of T, then the implementation shall deliver one of the permitted results; otherwise,

FIXED POINT ARITHMETIC/ ADDITION AND SUBTRACTION

ADDITION AND SUBTRACTION

The addition of fixed-point numbers requires that the binary points of the addends be aligned. The addition is then performed using binary arithmetic so that no number other than 0 or 1 is used.

For example, consider the addition of 010010.1 (18.5) with 0110.110 (6.75):

```
 010010.1    (18.5)
+0110.110    (6.75)
011001.010   (25.25)
```

Fixed-point subtraction is equivalent to adding while using the two's complement value for any negative values. In subtraction, the addends must be sign extended to match each other's length. For example, consider subtracting 0110.110 (6.75) from 010010.1 (18.5):

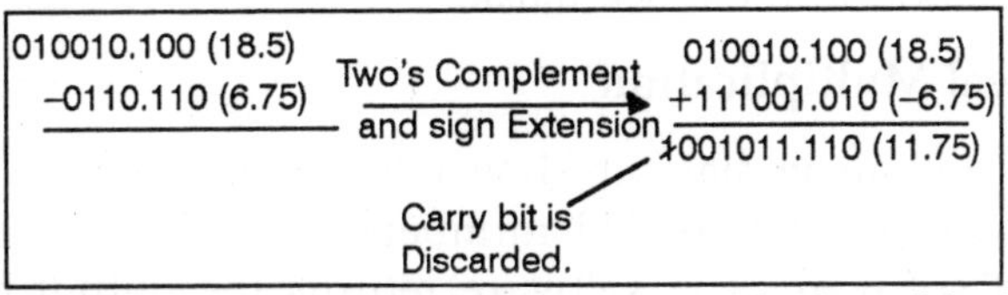

```
010010.100 (18.5)                              010010.100 (18.5)
 -0110.110 (6.75)    Two's Complement         +111001.010 (-6.75)
                   and sign Extension        1001011.110 (11.75)

                   Carry bit is
                   Discarded.
```

Most fixed-point Signal Processing Blockset blocks that perform addition cast the adder inputs to an accumulator data type before performing the addition. Therefore, no further shifting is necessary during the addition to line up the binary points.

MULTIPLICATION

The multiplication of two's complement fixed-point numbers is directly analogous to regular decimal multiplication, with the exception that the intermediate results must be sign extended so that their left sides align before you add them together.

For example, consider the multiplication of 10.11 (-1.25) with 011 (3):

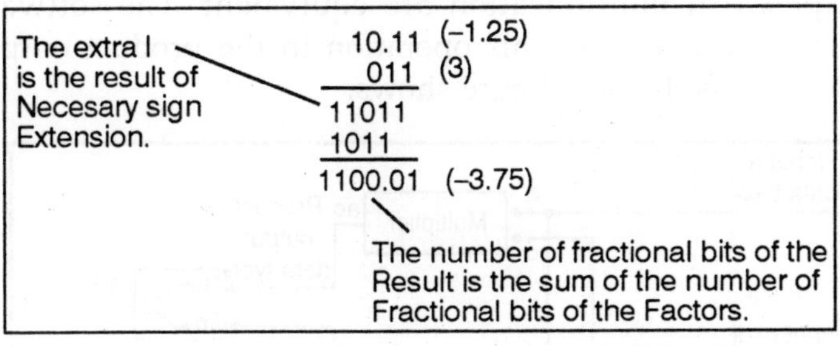

```
The extra l             10.11  (-1.25)
is the result of          011  (3)
Necesary sign          11011
Extension.             1011
                       1100.01  (-3.75)

                          The number of fractional bits of the
                          Result is the sum of the number of
                          Fractional bits of the Factors.
```

The number of fractional bits of the result's is the sum of the number of fractional bits of the factors.

Multiplication Data Types

The following diagrams show the data types used for fixed-point multiplication in Signal Processing Blockset software. The diagrams illustrate the differences between the data types used for real-real, complex-real, and complex-complex multiplication.

In most cases, you can set the data types used during multiplication in the block mask.

Real-Real Multiplication

The following diagram shows the data types used in the multiplication of two real numbers in Signal Processing Blockset software. The software returns the output of this operation in the product output data type, as the next figure shows.

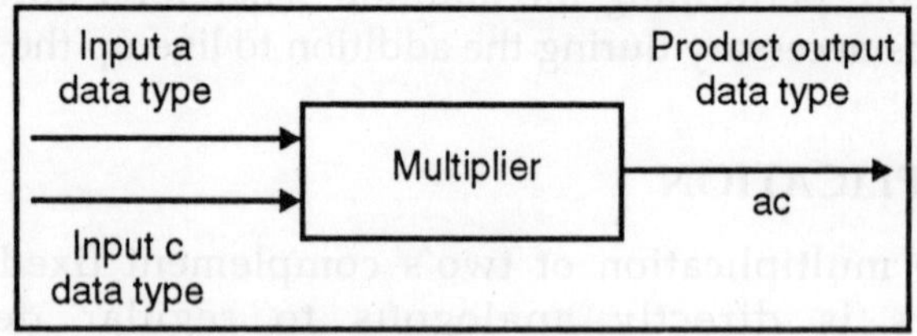

Real-Complex Multiplication

The following diagram shows the data types used in the multiplication of a real and a complex fixed-point number in Signal Processing Blockset software. Real-complex and complex-real multiplication are equivalent. The software returns the output of this operation in the product output data type, as the next figure shows.

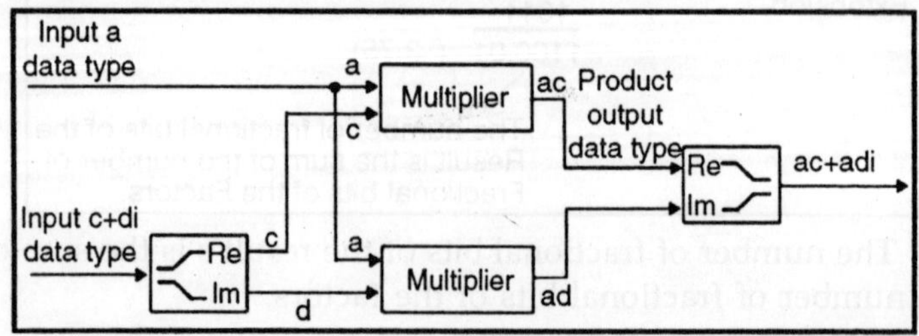

Complex-Complex Multiplication. The following diagram shows the multiplication of two complex fixed-point numbers in Signal Processing Blockset software. Note that the software returns the output of this operation in the accumulator output data type, as the next figure shows.

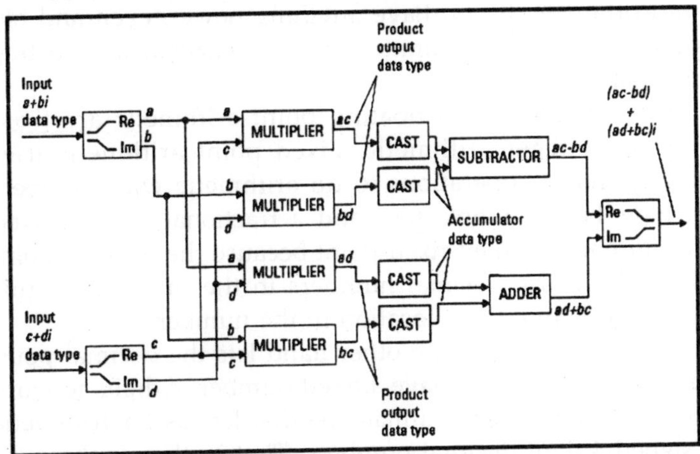

Signal Processing Blockset blocks cast to the accumulator data type before performing addition or subtraction operations. In the preceding diagram, this is equivalent to the C code

```
acc=ac;
acc-=bd;
```

for the subtractor, and

```
acc=ad;
acc+=bc;
```

for the adder, where *acc* is the accumulator.

DESCRIPTION

It seems natural to use floating point arithmetic in graphics programmes. Floating point arithmetic is easy to use and it comes closer to working the way we expect arithmetic to work than any other kind of arithmetic we can use in programmes. Interactive graphics demands speed and floating point is not usually the fastest kind of arithmetic available on personal computers. Because graphics programmes do so much arithmetic we want to do the arithmetic as fast as possible. On modern machines we want to use floating point arithmetic. If you have anything faster than a Pentium, or any of the RISC processors with floating point hardware, you might not get much by avoiding floating point arithmetic. If you have anything newer, even and old Pentium II, your programmes will run faster using floating point math.

The alternatives to floating point arithmetic are fixed point and integer arithmetic. Fixed point arithmetic uses ordinary integer operations to do arithmetic with numbers that have both a whole part and a fractional part. A fixed point number is called fixed point because the decimal point (I'm going to use decimal numbers in the first part of this discussion) is in a fixed location in the number.

(Floating point on the other hand lets the decimal point float around.) You also have a fixed number of digits to work with. Let's say we have a machine that lets us do arithmetic on signed 4 digit decimal numbers. That is, the numbers we can work with have a range from -9999 to 9999.

Let's assume we have an addition instruction that will add two of these numbers and give us a 4 digit result and a carry. We also have a subtraction instruction that subtracts two 4 digit numbers and gives us a 4 digit result and a borrow. Our example machine also has multiply and divide instructions. Multiplication and division are not like addition and subtraction. The multiplier takes two 4 digit numbers and gives us an 8 digit result. The divider divides an 8 digit number by a 4 digit number and gives us a 4 digit quotient and a 4 digit remainder.

Multiply and divide might seem a little odd, but take a look at the 386 multiply and divide instructions. The multiply takes two 32 bit numbers and gives a 64 bit result and the divider divides a 64 bit number by a 32 bit number and gives a 32 bit quotient and a 32 bit remainder. The number of digits you get when you multiply 2 numbers is the sum of the number of digits in the two numbers. This means that multiplication naturally gives you numbers twice as long as the ones you started with. Once you have the double long numbers you get from multiplying you need a divide operation that can scale them back down to 4 digits.

Having a double length intermediate value makes it possible to evaluate expressions like:

x = (a * b) / c

without getting the wrong answer. For example.

x = 1000 * 10 / 2

x = 10000 / 2

x = 5000

If products weren't allowed to be longer than normal numbers then we would have:

x = 1000 * 10 / 2

x = 0000 / 2

x = 0

because 10,000 is a five digit number and we're only allowed 4 digit numbers the 1 at the top would get lost and we would get the wrong answer. Ok, that gives us a nice definition of decimal integers. But what about fractions?

Just pretend that there is a decimal point in the middle of our numbers. This means that instead of writing "1" as 0001 we write one as 01.00. "01.00" is still a 4 digit decimal number. Inside our machine it is represented at "0100." The computer doesn't know or care about our imaginary decimal point. We call this way of looking at numbers a "2.2" fixed point format because it has 2 digits on each side of the decimal point. We could also pretend that the decimal point is all the way to left giving us a 0.4 format or, if we want to, we could use a 3.1 format with one digit of fraction and 3 digits of integer. Of course, an ordinary 4 digit integer is in 4.0 fixed point format.

If we want to add 4 + 3 in 2.2 format we set it up like this:

$$\begin{array}{r} 04.00 \\ \underline{+03.00} \\ 07.00 \end{array}$$

Notice that a normal add operation that adds 2 integers also adds 2 fixed point numbers. It doesn't matter what format they are in, it just adds.

The same is true for subtraction:

05.00
–07.00
–02.00

Integer subtraction works on fixed point numbers just like it does on integers. Remember that we are the ones deciding where the decimal point is, the hardware neither knows nor cares.

Fixed point multiplication and division are not quite as easy as addition and subtraction.

When I learned to multiply decimal fractions I was taught to do the multiplication ignoring the decimal points and then, at the end, put the decimal point in the product so that the number of digits of fraction in the product is the sum of the number of digits of fraction in the multiplier and the multiplicand. For example:

12.345 * 67.89 = 838.10205

12345 * 6789 = 83810205

The digits in the product depend on the digits in the multiplier and the multiplicand. They do not depend on where the decimal points are in the multiplier or the multiplicand.

Here are some rules to remember when multiplying fixed point numbers:

- The maximum number of digits you can have in the product is the sum of the number of digits in the multiplier and the multiplicand.
- The number of digits of fraction in the product is the sum of the number of digits of fraction in the multiplier and the number of digits of fraction in the multiplicand.
- An integer is a fixed point number with 0 digits of fraction.

This means that when you multiply a fixed point number in an M.N format by an integer the result is a number in M.N format. For example let's multiply integer 7 by 3 in 2.2 fixed point format.

0007 * 03.00 = 21.00

When you multiply 2 fixed point numbers in M.N format you get a result that has 2N digits of fraction. For example:

07.00 * 03.00 = 21.0000

To get back to an M.N format number you throw away the low order N digits of the fraction. That is, you shift the number left by N digits. Truncating the low order digits is a source of error in fixed point arithmetic. You can round the fraction instead of truncating it, but that takes longer.

These rules also imply that you can multiply numbers in different fixed points formats and get a meaningful result. For example, you might have a table of sines in 2.30 binary fixed point format (in a binary format the numbers are the number of bits, not the number of digits) that you want to multiply by numbers in an 18.14 format. The result will be numbers in a 20.44 fixed point format. You can get back to 18.14 format by throwing away the bottom 30 bits of the fraction and the top two extra bits of the integer part of the number.

When I first learned to do long division I was taught to write the answer as a quotient and a remainder. Later I learned how to continue the division to produce a decimal fraction by adding zeros to the right end of the dividend. A few years ago I realised that adding zeros is the same as shifting the dividend left. In fixed point arithmetic you shift the number left before you divide instead of adding one zero at a time as you do in long division.

Think about dividing 1 by 3. We know that the decimal fraction for 1/3 is 0.333... the threes just keep going on and on and on. But, if we divide the integer value 1 by the integer value 3 on a computer we get 0. Zero is not a very good approximation of 1/3. So, let's try adding a zero at the end of the 1. The result of dividing the integer 10 by 3 is 3. And the result of dividing 100 by 3 is 33. For every 0 we tack on to the 1 we get another 3 in the result.

In the 2.2 fixed point we've been using for our examples 1 is 01.00 which is really the integer 100 or 1 with 2 zeros tacked on the end. Dividing 01.00 by 3 is the same as dividing 0100 by 3 and we get the same 33 as a result. But, since we started with 01.00 we interpret the result as 00.33. This shows that when a fixed point number is divided by an integer the result is a fixed point number.

To divide a fixed point by a fixed point you have to tack on even more zeros to the end of the number you are dividing. This means that if we want 2 digits of fraction in the result we have to shift the dividend to the left by 2 digits before the division takes place.

0100 / 0300 = 0000
01000 / 0300 = 0003
010000 / 0300 = 0033

When we want to use fixed point arithmetic in a programme we have to decide what format to use and how to implement it within the programming language we are using.

The first thing you have to do is pick a fixed point format. On 32 bit computers it is tempting to use a 16.16 format. That is, 16 bits of fraction and 16 bits of integer. My experience with that format is that it is very easy to mess up the sign of the number during multiplies when the result of a multiply uses all the available bits. I like to leave a spare bit at the top of the format to guard against overflow. I tend to use a 17.15 format or 18.14 format to avoid these overflow problems.

You can use as many different fixed point formats as you need. If you are working with numbers that you know are always in the range 0 to 1 then an unsigned 1.31 format might be exactly what you want. If you are doing colour computation then you might use a 0.8 format and pack each number in a byte. Using the right format can prevent a lot of problems.

Your choice of fixed point formats is restricted by your choice of programming language. If you pick a 32 bit fixed point format like 16.16 then you need to be able to multiply two 32 bit numbers, get a 64 bit result, and then shift the result right to get it back into the original fixed point format. Most PC C compilers don't provide the 64 bit integer type that you need for the intermediate values you generate when you multiply 32 bit numbers.

This means that if you want to stick to "pure" high level language programming you need to restrict yourself to 16 bit fixed point formats so that the product of 2 numbers will fit in a 32 bit "long" variable. You can do 3D graphics programming using 16 bit fixed point formats in pure C. I've done it, it works, and it's a royal pain. It is especially painful when you know that with just a few lines of assembly language you can write the 32 bit fixed point multiply and divide routines you want.

My personal opinion is that you should use small amounts of assembly language in macros or in inline procedures to implement the fixed point operations and do the rest in the high level language of your choice.

When choosing a fixed point format look carefully at how many digits of fraction you need to do the job. If you only need a couple of digits of fraction then you can live with fixed point numbers with 7 bits of fraction. Two decimal digits of fraction gives you 100 steps between 0 and 1 or any two adjacent integer numbers. Seven bits of fraction gives you 128 steps between integers. If you need 3 decimal digits of fraction then 10 bits of fraction will do the job and so on.

Using more bits of fraction makes your fixed point number more precise at the expense of the range of numbers you can use. If you take 16 bits out of 32 total bits then you have limited the range of numbers you can represent to the range -32768 to 32767 for two's compliment integers or 0 to 65535 for unsigned integers.

The files fixed.cpp and fixed.h contain type definitions and in line assembly language arithmetic routines for an 18.14 fixed point format written in Watcom C including a couple of fixed point square root functions and table based sine and cosine functions.

The multiply and divide functions use assembly language to get at the hardware arithmetic capabilities that are hidden by high level programming languages. One of the fixed point square root routines uses a standard Newton iteration to extract the root. It just happens to use fixed point arithmetic to do it. The routine is surprisingly (at least to me) accurate and fast enough to be useful, but only slightly faster than a software floating point square root and not nearly as accurate as the square root provided in the Watcom math library.

The other fixed point square root routine uses the integer square root procedure that is also in fixed.cpp. This routine uses the fact that fixed point numbers are really integers. The integer square root of a fixed point number divided by the square root of 2 to the F power where F is the number of bits of fraction in the fixed point number is the square root of the original fixed point number. If you have an even number of bits of fraction you can convert the integer square root to the fixed point square root with a shift. Otherwise you have to do one divide to recover the square root.

Since the integer square root routine is simple and fast the second fixed point routine is faster than the first one. But, it is not as accurate, especially when taking the roots of large numbers.

The file demo.cpp contains code that tests the fixed point and integer square root routines and does a timing test on each of them. There is also a timing test of the C library sqrt() function. It is interesting to compare the speed and accuracy of the double precision floating point square root and the 32 bit fixed point square roots.

On my home machine, a 386/40 with no floating point coprocessor the fast fixed point square root is about 2.5 times faster than the library floating point square root.

The sine and cosine functions are implemented as arrays of 256 fixed point sine values and 256 fixed point cosine values. The trick is to use 256 "degrees" instead of 360. This lets you use a simple masking operation to make sure that you don't over run the array boundaries.

256 degrees seems to be plenty for interactive graphics applications. If it isn't good enough for your application it is easy to generate tables with 512, 1024, 2048, or more entries. If you can live with slower functions but need better accuracy then linear interpolation between adjacent table entries is a good compromise. It you need better accuracy than that you're probably not going to be happy using fixed point

arithmetic. Code for generating the sine and cosine tables is also in demo.cpp. It's worth looking at that code if you are planning to generate tables of other functions. It is very easy to build tables that have cumulative errors built into them. Errors caused by bad tables are awfully hard to find. Also remember that the tables are only as good as the source of the values in the tables.

Fixed.cpp and fixed.h also contain a couple of routines that are handy for doing integer arithmetic. I've already mentioned the integer square root routine. This routine is based on one I picked up off the net sometime ago. I tested a number of integer square root routines and this one worked, it's simple, and it's fast. After a little study I even convinced myself that I understand how it works. It seems to be an implementation of the pencil and paper root extraction algorithm you may have learned in grade school. It takes advantage of the fact that all even powers of 2 are the squares of even powers of 2.

The other routine is mulDiv(a, b, c) this function multiplies A times B and then divides by C. The nice thing about the routine is that it multiplies 32 bit numbers and keeps around the 64 bit intermediate result. This means that you can do the common (A*B)/C operation over the entire range of 32 bit numbers and get the correct answer.

TIPS AND TRICKS

The real beauty of fixed point math is in the formats, because you design them for your needs. You are not limited to only 3 formats like in floats – you can have signed and unsigned fixed point numbers, different fractional number of bits across numbers, etc. Of course all of these depend on the implementation you wish.

You might be thinking that integers can't really have a high dynamic range. Well it depends: if you know the number's range, say it's between x^74 and x^77, then you can simply use this information without needing exponents (use shifting). On the other hand, if this "range" varies here, consider floating point.

Note that if you know the range of your variables, and they have different "ranges", it's possible to use integers to represent the same thing (think of the integer being the mantissa, since the exponent is known at this code implementation, you don't need to store it). For example, given our variable being between x^74 and x^77, you only need 77-74=3 extra bits to account for this range, without any exponent at all.

You can then use shifts and other operators to make it work for other "known" ranges. This is, obviously, "special-purpose", unlike the more "general-purpose" of the floats.

Also remember that fractional parts are useless in addition and subtraction (i. e., same operations as normal integers). The only part of the fractional parts that's important in multiplication/division are the numbers between 0 and 1 (e. g., 0.5, 0.2).

When you design a fractional format, think of multiplication by 1, which must result in the same number. Then think of "dividing" the number when you multiply with numbers "under" 1.

MULTIPLYING INTEGER BY RECIPROCAL

Let's assume you want to divide x by 5, and don't want to use divide since you know it's a constant, why not multiply by 0.2? In truth, you are using integers so it might not be possible, but fixed point comes to mind. This is actually a trick, represent the number 0.2 as a fixed point type of (for example) 32 bits, all of them belonging to the fractional part!

We have 32 bits representing our fractional part, so let's start: 1<<32 equals 4294967296. Now multiply this in a calculator or something with 0.2, and the result will be the fraction we'll use:

858993459.2

Oops, we got a fractional part in our result, which means that we cannot represent 0.2 with 32 bits correctly, though. No matter, we don't care about such a small precision loss right now. Now if we multiply our x which is an integer (32.0 fixed point format:), with our "0.2" in 0.32 fixed point format:

r = (x * 858993459) >> 32

and we just divided x by 5, or multiplied it by 0.2, whatever...

ROTATION MATRIX

Here's a typical scenario where I prefer fixed points. Suppose you have a rotation matrix, and you want to multiply it with a vector. Ok, a rotation matrix has values between -1 and 1, so why waste bits with the integer part or some exponent? We can simply use all the bits we have or want to the fractional part – all except one, since we need a sign.

You can use two's complement or whatever other numbering system, though I recommend you use your processor's native negation format. Remember, the "point" in fixed point is imaginary – they are integers too like any other integer. However, I believe that you will need a "signed" right-shift if you use two's complement. In x86 asm, that is the sar instruction.

The vector can have whatever values you want – note, you don't need a fractional part since you usually don't multiply or divide vectors between them, because it's impossible (mathematically speaking; of course nothing stops you to make weird operations:). So, you don't need to have the same format for both of the values – the matrix can have 0.32 format and the vector 32.0. It depends on your specific needs. You may say that "normals" are definetely invalid if we use this vector format, but truth be told, fixed point is "specific-purpose"! You don't need to use the same format for all vectors. A standard vector can have a 32.0 format and a "normal" to a surface a 0.32 format (since it is between 0 and 1). Don't be limited to use the same formats over and over again. Specific formats are the most powerful thing of fixed point over floating point.

A common representation that people use in RGB colours besides the 24-bit one is with floating point scalars. In this case you have Red, Green and Blue stored in 32-bit float each, up to a total of 96 bits per pixel. The numbers themselves are between 0 and 1.

If you understood fixed point then you would most probably see how many bytes are wasted here, per colour! In my opinion, this floating point stuff is really silly. Even if you want better precision than 24-bit RGB, use 48-bit RGB or 72-bit RGB. The 72-bit one has the same precision as the floating point one, yet it is smaller (this is because floats waste 1 byte per colour with the exponent and sign, because they are useless in this situation).

Some guys keep telling me how are you going to do blending like multiply mode if the numbers RGB are between 0 and 255?. That's silly. Floating point is not magical, it's only the exponent that does the job. If we were to emulate this in float (that is without using the hardware FPU), then it would have been very obvious that it's a silly thing to do here. Float doesn't suck, it simply is inappropiate for this purpose. With a little math we can get this to work with "integers". Enough babble... let's get to the example.

In multiply blending mode, two colours are multiplied together. Since they are between 0 and 1, we expect a darker result unless one of them is 1. How are we going to do this if we have our numbers between 0 and 255? Very simple if we use our imagination and consider them fixed point numbers!

We can assume that each component is of the format 0.8, meaning 0 bits for integer and 8 bits for fractional (0...255). To keep the original format in the result (since we want the result to be between 0...255 too) we use the shift right, and that's it. Look how simple this is, only an extra shift after the multiplication!

r = (colour1 * colour2) >> 8

However, with this you are unable to represent the white value (255,255,255) in the multiplication since this operation requires it to be 256, not 255. We can quickly fix this with an extra increment:

r = (colour1 * (colour2+1)) >> 8

Of course you would need to do this for each component if you want to do it right. I only presented the pseudo-code example. I hope this enlightens you a bit. And unlike float, you can do a lot of other blending modes because the format is much simpler (without exponents, etc.) and you can also use the logical operators to make things even trickier. And it can be even trickier in assembly.

FLOATING POINT ARITHMETIC

INTRODUCTION

Some of the greatest achievements of the 20th century would not have been possible without the floating point capabilities of digital computers. Nevertheless, this subject is not well understood by most programmers and is a regular source of confusion.

IEEE 754 Binary Floating Point Representation

First we will describe how floating point numbers are represented. Java uses a subset of the IEEE 754 binary floating point standard to represent floating point numbers and define the results of arithmetic operations. Virtually all modern computers conform to this standard.

A float is represented using 32 bits, and each possible combination of bits represents one real number. This means that at most 2^{32} possible real numbers can be exactly represented, even though there are infinitely many real numbers (even between 0 and 1). The IEEE standard uses an internal representation similar to scientific notation, but in binary instead of base 10.

This covers a range from ±1.40129846432481707e-45 to ±3.40282346638528860e+38. with 6 or 7 significant decimal digits, including including plus infinity, minus infinity, and NaN (not a number). The number contains a sign bit *s* (interpreted as plus or minus), 8 bits for the exponent *e*, and 23 bits for the mantissa *M*. The decimal number is represented according to the following formula.

$$(-1)^s \times m \times 2^{(e-127)}$$

Sign bit s (bit 31). The most significant bit represents the sign of the number (1 for negative, 0 for positive).

Exponent field e (bits 30 – 23). The next 8 bits represent the exponent. By convention the exponent is*biased* by 127. This means that to represent the binary exponent 5, we encode 127 + 5 = 132 in binary (10000100). To represent the binary exponent –5 we encode 127 – 5 = 122 in binary (01111010). This convention is alternative to two's complement notation for representing negative integers.

Mantissa m (bits 22 – 0). The remaining 23 bits represent the mantissa, *normalized* to be between 0.5 and 1. This normalization is always possible by adjusting the binary exponent accordingly. Binary fractions work like decimal fractions: 0.1101 represents 1/2 + 1/4 + 1/16 = 13/16 = 0.825. Not every decimal number can be represented as a binary fraction. For example 1/10 = 1/16 + 1/32 + 1/256 + 1/512 + 1/4096 + 1/8192 +... In this case, the number 0.1 is approximated by the closest 23 bit binary fraction 0.000110011001100110011... One further optimization is employed. Since the mantissa always begins with a 1, there is no need to explicitly store this *hidden bit*.

As an example the decimal number 0.085 is stored as 00111101101011100001010001111011.

```
0.085:
bits:  31  30-23  22-0
binary:  0  01111011  01011100001010001111011
```

decimal: 0 123 3019899

This exactly represents the number $2^{e-127} (1 + m / 2^{23})$ = $2^{-4}(1 + 3019899/8388608)$ = 11408507/134217728 = 0.085000000894069671630859375.

A double is similar to a float except that its internal representation uses 64 bits, an 11 bit exponent with a bias of 1023, and a 52 bit mantissa. This covers a range from ±4.94065645841246544e-324 to ±1.79769313486231570e+308 with 14 or 15 significant digits of accuracy.

PRECISION VS. ACCURACY

Precision = tightness of specification. Accuracy = correctness. Do not confuse precision with accuracy. 3.133333333 is an estimate of the mathematical constant ð which is specified with 10 decimal digits of precision, but it only has two decimal digits of accuracy.

As John von Neumann once said "There's no sense in being precise when you don't even know what you're talking about." Java typically prints out floating point numbers with 16 or 17 decimal digits of precision, but do not blindly believe that this means there that many digits of accuracy! Calculators typically display 10 digits, but compute with 13 digits of precision. Kahan: the mirror for the Hubble space telescope was ground with great precision, but to the wrong specification.

Hence, it was initially a great failure since it couldn't produce high resolution images as expected. However, it's precision enabled an astronaut to install a corrective lens to counter-balance the error. Currency calculations are often defined in terms of a give precision, e.g., Euro exchange rates must be quoted to 6 digits.

ROUNDOFF ERROR

Programming with floating point numbers can be a bewildering and perilous process for the uninitiated. Arithmetic with integers is exact, unless the answer is outside the range of integers that can be represented (overflow). In contrast, floating point arithmetic is not exact since some real numbers require an infinite number of digits to be represented, e.g., the mathematical constants e and ð and 1/3. However, most novice Java programmers are surprised to learn that 1/10 is not exactly representable either in the standard binary floating point. These roundoff errors can propagate through the calculation in non-intuitive ways.

- *Rounding of decimal fractions*

```
double x1 = 0.3;
double x2 = 0.1 + 0.1 + 0.1;
StdOut.println(x1 == x2);
double z1 = 0.5;
double z2 = 0.1 + 0.1 + 0.1 + 0.1 + 0.1;
StdOut.println(z1 == z2);
```

- *Newton's method:* A more realistic example is the following code fragment whose intent is to compute the square root of c by iterating Newton's method.

Mathematically, the sequence of iterates converges to "c from above, so that t^2 - c > 0. However, a floating point number only has finitely many bits of accuracy, so eventually, we may expect t^2 to equal c exactly, up to machine precision.

```
double EPSILON = 0.0;
double t = c;
while (t*t - c > EPSILON)
  t = (c/t + t) / 2.0;
```

Indeed, for some values of c, the method works.

```
% java Sqrt 2 % java Sqrt 4 % java Sqrt 10
1.414213562373095 2.0 3.162277660168379
```

This might give us some confidence that our code fragment is correct. But a surprising thing happens when we try to compute the square root of 20. Our programme gets stuck in an infinite loop! This type of error is called *roundoff error*. *Machine accuracy* is smallest number ε such that (1.0 + ε != ε). In Java, it is XYZ with double and XYZ with float. Changing the error tolerance ε to a small positive value helps, but does not fix the problem

We must be satisfied with approximating the square root. A reliable way to do the computation is to choose some error tolerance ε, say 1E-15, and try to find a value t such that |t - c/t| < ε t. We use*relative error* instead of *absolute error*; otherwise the programme may go into an infinite loop.

```
double epsilon = 1e-15;
double t = c;
while (Math.abs(t*t - c) > c*epsilon)
t = (c/t + t) / 2.0;
```

- *Harmonic sum:* Possibly motivate by trying to estimate Euler's constant ã = limit as n approaches infinity of $ã_n = H_n$ - ln n. The limit exists and is approximately 0.5772156649. Surprisingly, it is not even known whether γ is irrational.

Programme HarmonicSum.java computes 1/1 + 1/2 +... + 1/N using single precision and double precision. With single precision, when N = 10,000, the sum is accurate to 5 decimal digits, when N = 1,000,000 it is accurate to only 3 decimal digits, when N = 10,000,000 it is accurate to only 2 decimal digits. In fact, once N reaches 10 million, the sum never increases. Although the Harmonic sum diverges to infinity, in floating point it converges to a finite number! This dispels the popular misconception that if you are solving a problem that requires only 4 or 5 decimal digits of ?precision, then you are safe using a type that stores 7. Many numerical computations (e.g., integration or solutions to differential equations) involve summing up alot of small terms. The errors can accumulate. This accumulation of roundoff error can lead to serious problems.

Better formula: $y \approx Y_n - 1/(2n) + 1/(12n^2)$ Accurate to 12 decimal places for n = 1 million. Every time you perform an arithmetic operation, you introduce an additional error of at least ε. Kernighan and Plauger: "Floating point numbers are like piles of sand; every time you move one you lose a little sand and pick up a little dirt."

If the errors occur at random, we might expect a cumulative error of sqrt(N) ε_m. However, if we are not vigilant in designing our numerical algorithms, these errors can propagate in very unfavorable and non-intuitive ways, leading to cumulative errors of N ε_m or worse.

FINANCIAL COMPUTING

We illustrate some examples of roundoff error that can ruin a financial calculation. Financial calculations involving dollars and cents involve base 10 arithmetic. The following examples demonstrate some of the perils of using a binary floating point system like IEEE 754.

Sales tax: Programme Financial.java illustrates the danger. Calculate the 9% sales tax of a 50 cent phone call. (or 5% sales tax on a $0.70 phone call). Using IEEE 754, 1.09 * 50 = xxx. This results gets rounded down to 0.xx even though the exact answer is 0.xx, which the telephone company (by law) is required to round down to 0.xx (using Banker's rounding). In contrast, a 14% tax on a 75 cent phone call yields xxx. might get rounded up to x.xx even though (by law) the phone company must round down the number (using Banker's rounding) to x.xx. This difference in pennies might not seem significant, and you might hope that the effects cancel each other out in the long run. However, taken over hundreds of millions of transactions, this salami slicing might result in millions of dollars. Reference: Superman III (1983), Hackers (1995), and Office Space (1999). In Office Space, three friends infect the accounting system with a computer virus that rounds down fractions of a cent and transfer it into their account.

For this reason, some programmers believe that you should always use integer types to store financial values instead of floating point types. The next example will show the perils of storing financial values using type int.

- *Compound interest:* This example introduces you to the dangers of roundoff error. Suppose you invest $1000.00 at 5% interest, compounded daily. How much money will you end up with after 1 year? If the bank computes the value correctly, you should end up with $1051.27 since the exact formula is

$$a * (1 + r/n)^n$$

which leads to 1051.2674964674473.... Suppose, instead, that the bank stores your balance as an integer (measured in pennies). At the end of each day, the bank calculates your balance and multiplies it by 1.05 and rounds the result to the nearest penny. Then, you will end up with only $1051.10, and have been cheated out of 17 cents. Suppose instead the bank rounds *down* to the nearest penny at the end of each day. Now, you will end up with only $1049.40 and you will have been cheated out of $1.87. The error of not storing the fractions of a penny accumulate and can eventually become significant, and even fraudulent. Programme CompoundInterest.java.

Instead of using integer or floating point types, you should use Java's BigDecimal library. This library has two main advantages. First, it can represent decimal numbers exactly. This prevents the sales tax issues of using binary floating point. Second, it can store numbers with an arbitrary amount of precision. This enables the programmer to control the degree to which roundoff error affects the computation.

OTHER SOURCE OF ERROR

In addition to roundoff error inherent when using floating point arithmetic, there are some other types of approximation errors that commonly arise in scientific applications.

- *Measurement error:* The data values used in the computation are not accurate. This arises from both practical (inaccurate or imprecise measuring instruments) and theoretical (Heisenberg uncertainty principle) considerations. We are primarily interested in models and solution methods whose answer is not highly sensitive to the initial data.
- *Discretization error:* Another source of inaccuracy results from discretizing continuous system, e.g., approximating a transcendental function by truncating its Taylor expansion, approximating an integral using a finite sum of rectangles, finite difference method for finding approximate solutions to differential equations, or estimating a continuous function over a lattice. Discretization error would still be present even if using exact arithmetic. It is often unavoidable, but we can reduce truncation error by using more refined discretization. Of course, this comes at the price of using more resources, whether it be memory or time. Discretization error often more important than roundoff error in practical applications.
- *Statistical error:* Not enough random samples.

CATASTROPHIC CANCELLATION

Devastating loss of precision when small numbers are computed from large numbers by addition or subtraction. For example if x and y agree in all but the last few digits, then if we compute z = x - y, then z may only have a few digits of accuracy. If we subsequently use z in a calculation, then the result may only have a few digits of accuracy.

- *Plotting a function:* Try plotting f(x) = (1 - cos x) / (x^2) from x = -4 * 10^-8 to 4 * 10^-8. In this region the mathematical function f(x) is approximately constant, with the value 0.5. However, in IEEE floating point, it is most definitely not! Programme Catastrophic.java does this, with some very surprising results.

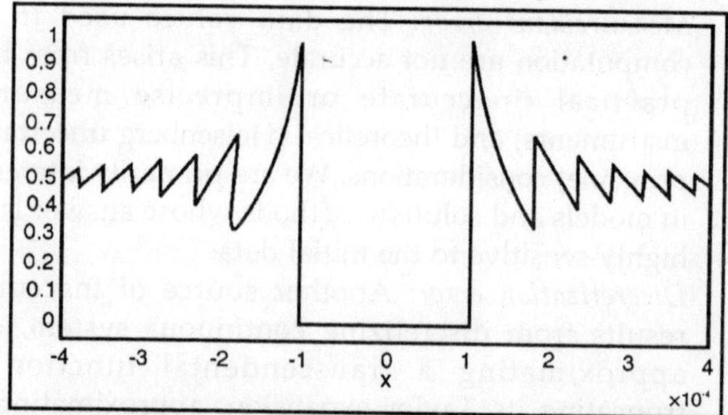

- *Exponential function:* Now we consider a more subtle and pernicious consequence of catastrophic cancellation. Programme Exponential.java computes ex using the Taylor series

  ex = 1 + x + x2/2! + x3/3! + x4/4! +...

This series converges uniformly and absolutely for all values of x. Nevertheless, for many negative values of x (e.g., -25), the programme obtains no correct digits, no matter how many terms in the series are summed. For example when x = -25, the series converges in floating point to -7.129780403672078E-7 (a negative number!), but the true answer is 1.3887943864964021E-11. To see why, observe that term 24 in the sum is 2524/24! and term 25 is -2525/25!. In principle, they should exactly cancel each other out. In practice, they cancel each other out catastrophically. The size of these terms (5.7 * 109) is 20 orders of magnitude greater than the true answer, and any error in the cancellation is magnified in the calculated answer. Fortunately, in this case, the problem is easily rectified

NUMERICAL ANALYSIS

Lloyd Trefethen "Numerical analysis is the study of algorithms for the problems of continuous mathematics."

- *Stability:* A mathematical problem is well-conditioned if its solution changes by only a small amount when the input parameters changes by a small amount. An algorithm is numerically stable if the output of the algorithm changes by only a small amount when the input data changes by a small amount. Numerical stability captures how errors are propagated by the algorithm. Numerical analysis is the art and science of finding numerically stable algorithms to solve well-conditioned problems. Accuracy depends on the conditioning of problem and the stability of the algorithm. Inaccuracy can result from applying a stable algorithm to an ill-conditioned problem or an unstable algorithm to a well-conditioned problem.
  - *Exponential function:* For a simple example, computing f(x) = exp(x) is a well conditioned problem since f(x + ?) =.... One algorithm for computing exp(x) is via its Taylor series. Suppose we estimate f(x) = exp(x) using the first four terms of its Taylor approximation: g(x) = 1 + x + x2/2 + x3/3!. Then f(1) = 2.718282, g(1) = 2.666667. However, it is unstable since if x < 0..... A stable algorithm is to use the Taylor series if x is nonnegative, but if x is negative, compute e-x using a Taylor series and take the reciprocal.
  - *(1 - cos x) / (x^2) function:* Give a stable way to evaluate this function.
- *Conditioning:* We saw an example of a non-stable algorithm for computing exp(x). We also saw a stable algorithm for computing it. Sometimes, we are not always so lucky. We say that a problem is ill-conditioned if there is no stable algorithm for solving it.

Addition, multiplication, exponentiation, and division of positive numbers are all well-conditioned problems. So is computing the roots of a quadratic equation. Subtraction is ill-conditioned. So is finding the roots of a general polynomial. The conditioning of the problem of solving Ax = b depends on the matrix A. Population dynamics: The Verhulst equation is a simplified model of population dynamics.

$$x_n = (R + 1)x_{n-1} - R\,(x_{n-1})^2$$

Programme Verhulst.java reads in a command line parameter R and iterates the Verhulst equation for 100 iterations, starting with $x_0 = 0.5$. It orders the computation in four different, but mathematically equivalent, ways. All lead to significantly different results when R = 3, none of which is remotely correct

	(R+1)x-R(xx)	(R+1)x-(Rx)x	((R+1)-(Rx))x	x + R(x-xx)	correct
0:	0.5000000000	0.5000000000	0.5000000000	0.5000000000	0.5000000000
10:	0.3846309658	0.3846309658	0.3846309658	0.3846309658	0.3846309658
20:	0.4188950250	0.4188950250	0.4188950250	0.4188950250	0.4188950250
30:	0.0463994725	0.0463994756	0.0463994787	0.0463994775	0.0463994768
40:	0.3201767255	0.3201840912	0.3201915468	0.3201885159	0.3201870617
50:	0.0675670955	0.0637469566	0.0599878799	0.0615028942	0.0622361944
60:	0.0011449576	0.2711150754	1.0005313342	1.2945078734	0.0049027225
70:	1.2967745569	1.3284619999	1.3296922488	0.1410079704	0.5530823827
80:	0.5530384607	0.8171627721	0.0219521770	0.0184394043	0.1196398067
90:	0.0948523432	0.1541841695	0.0483069438	1.2513933889	0.3109290854
100:	0.0000671271	0.1194574394	1.2564956763	1.0428230334	0.7428865400

When R > 2.57, this system exhibits chaotic behaviour. The system itself is ill-conditioned, so there is no way to restructure the computation to iterate the system using floating point arithmetic. Although we cannot expect our floating point algorithms to correctly handle ill-conditioned problem, we can ask that they report back an error rangle associated with the solution so that at least we are alerted to potential problems. For example, when solving linear systems of equations, we can compute something called a *condition number*: this quantity can be used to bound the error of the resulting solution.

Ill-conditioning is not just a theoretical possibility. Astrophysicists have determined that our Solar System is chaotic. The trajectory of Pluto's orbit is chaotic, as in the motion of the Jovian planets, Halley's comet, and asteroidal zone trajectories. Upon a close encounter with Venus, Mercury could be ejected from the Solar System in less than 3.5 billion year!

- *Calculating special functions:* When learning calculus, we derive convergent Taylor series formulas for calculating exponential and trigometric functions. (e.g., exp(x), log(x), sin(x), cos(x), arctan(x), etc.). However, we must take great care when applying such formulas on digital computers. Not all special functions are built in to Java's Math library, so there are times when you must create your own. Give example, e.g., error function.

Numerical analysts have derived accurate, precise, and efficient algorithms for computing classic functions (e.g., hyperbolic trigometric functions, gamma function, beta function, error function, Bessel functions, Jacobian elliptic functions, spherical harmonics) that arise in scientific applications. We strongly recommend using these proven recipes instead of devising your own ad hoc routines.

REAL-WORLD NUMERICAL CATASTROPHES

The examples we've discussed above are rather simplistic. However, these issues arise in real applications. When done incorrectly, disaster can quickly strike.

- *Ariane 5 rocket:* Ariane 5 rocket exploded 40 seconds after being launched by European Space Agency. Maiden voyage after a decade and 7 billion dollars of research and development. Sensor reported acceleration that so was large that it caused an overflow in the part of the programme responsible for recalibrating inertial guidance. 64-bit floating point number was converted to a 16-bit signed integer, but the number was larger than 32,767 and the conversion failed. Unanticipated overflow was caught by a general systems diagnostic and dumped debugging data into an area of memory used for guiding the rocket's motors. Control was switched to a backup computer, but this had the same data. This resulted in a drastic attempt to correct the nonexistent problem, which separated the motors from their mountings, leading to the end of Ariane 5.

- *Patriot missile accident:* On February 25, 1991 an American Patriot missile failed to track and destroy an Iraqi Scud missile. Instead it hit an Army barracks, killing 26 people. The cause was later determined to be an inaccurate calculate caused by measuring time in tenth of a second. Couldn't represent 1/10 exactly since used 24 bit floating point. Software to fix problem arrived in Dhahran on February 26. Here is moreinformation.
- *Intel FDIV Bug* Error in Pentium hardwire floating point divide circuit. Discovered by Intel in July 1994, rediscovered and publicized by math professor in September 1994.
- *Sinking of Sleipner oil rig:* Sleipner A $700 million platform for producing oil and gas sprang a leak and sank in North Sea in August, 1991. Error in inaccurate finite element approximation underestimate shear stress by 47%.
- *Vancouver stock exchange:* Vancouver stock exchange index was undervalued by over 50% after 22 months of accumulated roundoff error. The obvious algorithm is to add up all the stock prices after Instead a "clever" analyst decided it would be more efficient to recompute the index by adding the net change of a stock after each trade. This computation was done using four decimal places and truncating (not rounding) the result to three.

DESCRIPTION

Arithmetic operations on floating point numbers consist of addition, subtraction, multiplication and division the operations are done with algorithms similar to those used on sign magnitude integers (because of the similarity of representation) — example, only add numbers of the same sign. If the numbers are of opposite sign, must do subtraction.

ADDITION

Example on decimal value given in scientific notation:
3.25 x 10 ** 3
<u>+ 2.63 x 10 ** -1</u>
First step: align decimal points
Second step: add
3.25 x 10 ** 3
+ <u>0.000263 x 10 ** 3</u>
3.250263 x 10 ** 3
(presumes use of infinite precision, without regard for accuracy)
Third step: Normalize the result (already normalized!)
example on fl pt. value given in binary:
.25 = 0 01111101 00000000000000000000000
100 = 0 10000101 10010000000000000000000
To add these fl. pt. representations,
Step 1: align radix points

Shifting the mantissa LEFT by 1 bit decreases the exponent by 1. Shifting the mantissa right by 1 bit increases the exponent by 1. We want to shift the mantissa right, because the bits that fall off the end should come from the least significant end of the mantissa

Choose to shift the.25, since we want to increase it's exponent.
Shift by 10000101
<u>-01111101</u>
00001000 (8) places.
0 01111101 00000000000000000000000 (original value)
0 01111110 10000000000000000000000 (shifted 1

place) (note that hidden bit is shifted into
msb of mantissa)
0 01111111 01000000000000000000000 (shifted 2 places)
0 10000000 00100000000000000000000 (shifted 3 places)
0 10000001 00010000000000000000000 (shifted 4 places)
0 10000010 00001000000000000000000 (shifted 5 places)
0 10000011 00000100000000000000000 (shifted 6 places)
0 10000100 00000010000000000000000 (shifted 7 places)
0 10000101 00000001000000000000000 (shifted 8 places)
Step 2: add (don't forget the hidden bit for the 100)
0 10000101 1.10010000000000000000000 (100)
+ 0 10000101 0.00000001000000000000000 (.25)
0 10000101 1.10010001000000000000000
Step 3: normalize the result (get the "hidden bit" to be a 1)
It already is for this example.
Result is
0 10000101 10010001000000000000000

Subtraction

Like addition as far as alignment of radix points then the algorithm for subtraction of sign mag. numbers takes over. before subtracting, compare magnitudes (don't forget the hidden bit!) change sign bit if order of operands is changed. don't forget to normalize number afterward.

Multiplication

Example on decimal values given in scientific notation:
3.0 x 10 ** 1
+ 0.5 x 10 ** 2
algorithm: multiply mantissas
add exponents
3.0 x 10 ** 1
+ 0.5 x 10 ** 2
1.50 x 10 ** 3
Example in binary:use a mantissa that is only 4 bits so that I don't spend all day just doing the multiplication part.
0 10000100 0100

x 1 00111100 1100

mantissa multiplication: 1.0100

(don't forget hidden bit) x 1.1100

00000

00000

10100

10100

10100

1000110000

becomes 10.00110000

add exponents: always add true exponents

(otherwise the bias gets added in twice)

biased:

10000100

\+ 00111100

10000100 01111111 (switch the order of the subtraction,

\- 01111111 - 00111100 so that we can get a negative value)

00000101 01000011

true exp true exp is 5. is -67 Add true exponents 5 + (-67) is -62.

re-bias exponent: -62 + 127 is 65.

unsigned representation for 65 is 01000001.

put the result back together (and add sign bit).

1 01000001 10.00110000

normalize the result:

(moving the radix point one place to the left increases the exponent by 1.)

1 01000001 10.00110000

becomes

1 01000010 1.000110000

this is the value stored (not the hidden bit!):

1 01000010 000110000

Division

The IEEE standard is very specific about how all this is done. Unfortunately, the hardware to do all this is pretty slow.

Some comparisons of approximate times:

2's complement integer add 1 time unit

fl. pt add 4 time units

fl. pt multiply 6 time units

fl. pt. divide 13 time units

There is a faster way to do division. Its called division by reciprocal approximation. It takes about the same time as a fl. pt. multiply. Unfortunately, the results are not always the same as with true division.

Division by reciprocal approximation:

Instead of doing a / b

They do a x 1/b

Figure out a reciprocal for b, and then use the fl. pt

Multiplication Hardware

Example of a result that isn't the same as with true division.

True division: 3/3 = 1 (exactly)

Reciprocal approx: 1/3 =.33333333

3 x.33333333 =.99999999, not 1

It is not always possible to get a perfectly accurate reciprocal.

Issues in Floating Point

Note: this discussion only touches the surface of some issues that people deal with. Entire courses could probably be taught on each of the issues.

Rounding

Arithmetic operations on fl. pt. values compute results that cannot be represented in the given amount of precision. So, we must round

Results

There are many ways of rounding. They each have "correct" uses, and exist for different reasons. The goal in a computation is to have the computer round such that the end result is as "correct" as possible. There are even arguments as to what is really correct.

Methods of Rounding

Round toward 0 — also called truncation.figure out how many bits (digits) are available. Take that many bits (digits)

for the result and throw away the rest. This has the effect of making the value represented closer to 0.

Example

.7783 if 3 decimal places available,.778
if 2 decimal places available,.77
round toward + infinity –
regardless of the value, round towards +infinity.

Example

1.23 if 2 decimal places, 1.3
-2.86 if 2 decimal places, -2.8
round toward - infinity –
regardless of the value, round towards -infinity.
Example:
1.23 if 2 decimal places, 1.2
-2.86 if 2 decimal places, -2.9
in binary – rounding to 2 digits after radix point
round toward + infinity –
1.1101
|
1.11 | 10.00
– – –
1.001
|
1.00 | 1.01
– –
round toward nearest –

Odd Case: if there is anything other than 1000... to the right of the number of digits to be kept, then rounded in IEEE standard such that the least significant bit (to be kept) is a zero.

USE OF STANDARDS

- Allows all machines following the standard to exchange data and to calculate the exact same results.
- IEEE fl. pt. standard sets parameters of data representation (# bits for mantissa vs. exponent)
- Pentium architecture follows the standard

Overflow and Underflow

Just as with integer arithmetic, floating point arithmetic operations can cause overflow. Detection of overflow in fl. pt. comes by checking exponents before/during normalization. Once overflow has occurred, an infinity value can be represented and propagated through a calculation.

Underflow occurs in fl. pt. representations when a number is to small (close to 0) to be represented. (show number line!) If a fl. pt. value cannot be normalized (getting a 1 just to the left of the radix point would cause the exponent field to be all 0's) then underflow occurs.

EXPLANATION

Floating point arithmetic derives its name from something that happens when you use exponential notation. Consider the number 123:

it can be written using exponential notation as:

- $1.23 * 10^{2}$
- $12.3 * 10^{1}$
- $123 * 10^{0}$
- $123 * 10^{3}$
- $1230 * 10^{-1}$

All of these representations of the number 123 are numerically equivalent. They differ only in their "normalization": where the decimal point appears in the first number. In each case, the number before the multiplication operator ("*") represents the significant figures in the number (which distinguish it from other numbers with the same normalization and exponent); we will call this number the "significand" (also called the "mantissa" in other texts, which call the exponent the "characteristic").

Notice how the decimal point "floats" within the number as the exponent is changed. This phenomenon gives floating point numbers their name. Only two of the representations of the number 123 above are in any kind of standard form. The first representation, $1.23 * 10^{2}$, is in a form called "scientific notation", and is distinguished by the normalization of the significand:

In scientific notation, the significand is always a number greater than or equal to 1 and less than 10. Standard computer normalization for floating point numbers follows the fourth form in the list above. The significand is greater than or equal to.1, and is always less than 1. Of course, in binary computer, all numbers are stored in base 2 instead of base 10; for this reason, the normalization of a binary floating point number simply requires that there be no leading zeroes after the binary point (just as the decimal point separates the 10^{0} place from the 10^{-1} place, the binary point separates the 2^{0} place from the 2^{-1} place). We will continue to use the decimal number system for our numerical examples, but the impact of the computer's use of the binary number system will be felt as we discuss the way those numbers are stored in the computer.

FLOATING POINT FORMATS

Over the years, floating point formats in computers have not exactly been standardized. While the IEEE (Institute of Electrical and Electronics Engineers) has developed standards in this area, they have not been universally adopted. This is due in large part to the issue of "backwards compatibility": when a hardware manufacturer designs a new computer chip, they usually design it so that programmes which ran on their old chips will continue to run in the same way on the new one. Since there was no standardization in floating point formats when the first floating point processing chips (often called "coprocessors" or "FPU"s: "Floating Point Units") were designed, there was no rush among computer designers to conform to the IEEE floating point standards (although the situation has improved with time).

For this reason, we will discuss both the IEEE standards as well as the floating point formats implemented in the very common Intel chips (such as the 80387, 80486 and the Pentium series). Each of these formats has a name like "single precision" or "double precision", and specifies the numbers of bits which are used to store both the exponent and the significand. We will defined the notion of "precision" in the following way: if the significand is stored in n bits, it can represent a decimal number between 0 and $2^n - 1$ (since a significand is stored as an unsigned integer). If we find the largest number "m" such that $10^m - 1$ is less than or equal to $2^n - 1$, m will be the precision. Consider the following:

$2^4 - 1 = 15$	$10^1 - 1 = 9$
$2^8 - 1 = 255$	$10^2 - 1 = 99$
$2^{12} - 1 = 4{,}095$	$10^3 - 1 = 999$
$2^{16} - 1 = 65{,}535$	$10^4 - 1 = 9{,}999$
$2^{20} - 1 = 1{,}048{,}575$	$10^6 - 1 = 999{,}999$

From the last example, it is easy to see that a 20 bit significand provides just over 6 decimal digits of precision. In the other examples, there is more precision than we have indicated. For example, a 16 bit significand is certainly sufficient to represent many decimal numbers with more than 4 digits; however, not all 5 digit decimal numbers can be represented in 16 bits, and so the precision of a 16 bit significand is said to be "> 4" (but less than 5). Some texts attempt to more accurately describe the precision using fractions, but we do not feel the need to do so.

The following table describes the IEEE standard formats as well as those used in common Intel processors:

Precision	Sign	Exponent	Signific and	Total Length	Decimal digits
	(# of bits)	(# of bits)	(# of bits)	(in bits)	of precision
IEEE / Intel single	1	8	23	32	> 6
IEEE single extended	1	>= 11	>= 32	>= 44	> 9
IEEE / Intel double	1	11	52	64	> 15
IEEE double extended	1	>= 15	>= 64	>= 80	> 19
Intel internal	1	15	64	80	> 19

Note first that all of the formats reserve one bit to store the sign of the number; this is necessary because the significand is stored as an unsigned fraction in all of these formats (often the first bit of the significand is not even stored, because it is always 1 in a properly normalized floating point number). The rows describing the IEEE extended formats specify the minimum number of bits which the exponent and significand must have in order to satisfy the standard. The Intel "internal" format is an extended precision format used inside the CPU chip, which allows consecutive floating point operations to be performed with greater precision than that which will eventually be stored.

Exponents are commonly stored in these formats as unsigned integers; however, an exponent can be negative as well as positive, and so we must have some technique for representing negative exponents using unsigned integers. This technique is called "biasing": a positive number is added to the exponent before it is stored in to the floating point number. The stored exponent is then called a "biased exponent". If the exponent contains 8 bits, the bias number 127 is added to the exponent before it is stored so that, for example, an exponent of 1 is stored as 128.

Since the unsigned exponent can represent numbers between 0 and 255, it should be theoretically possible to store exponents whose values range from -127 to +128 (-127 would stored as the biased exponent value 0, and +128 would be stored as the biased value 255). In practice, the IEEE specification reserves the values 0 and 255, which means that an 8 bit exponent can represent exponent values between -126 and +127.

If the stored (biased) exponent has the value 0, and the significand is 0 as well, the value of the floating point number is exactly 0. A floating point number with a stored exponent of 0 and a nonzero significand is of course unnormalized. If the stored exponent has the value 255 (all ones),

The floating point number has one of two special meanings:

- If the significand is 0, the number represents infinity.
- If the significand is not zero, that number represents a "NaN" ("Not a Number"): the result of a division by zero.

In general, if n bits are used to store the exponent, the bias value is $2^{n-1} - 1$, the range of exponents which can be represented are from $-2^{n-1} + 2$ to $+2^{n-1} - 1$, and a biased exponent of $2^n - 1$ indicates either infinity or a NaN (as above). The Intel double precision floating point format, which has an 11 bit exponent field, uses a bias of $2^{10} - 1 = 1{,}023$, and can represent exponents between $-2^{10} + 2 = -1{,}022$ to $+2^{10} - 1 = +1{,}023$. Note that while all of our examples use the decimal number system (for your convenience), the computer uses binary as the base for the exponents as well (although in the past, some computers used 16 as the base for the exponents). So, for example, the number 1 has a normalized binary floating point value of

$.1_2 * 2^1$ (with a 1 in the 2^{-1} place, this is equivalent to 1/2 * 2); the number 3 has the normalized binary floating point value of $.11_2 * 2^2$ (with a 1 in the 2^{-1} place and a 1 in the 2^{-2} place, this is equivalent to (1/2 + 1/4) * 4), etc. In contrast, of course, you would represent these numbers in decimal as $.1 * 10^1$ and $.3 * 10^1$, respectively.

EXAMPLES

In order to illustrate some of the details of floating point arithmetic, we will consider an imaginary floating point format in which the exponent is stored in 5 bits, the significand is stored in 10 bits, and 1 bit is used to store the sign of the number. Using exponent biasing and reserving the values 0 and 31 ($2^5 - 1$), our bias value will be 15 and our exponent will therefore be able to represent the values -14 to 15. Since the significand is stored in 10 bits, and $2^{10} - 1 = 1{,}023$, we see that our imaginary format provides us with three decimal digits of precision (since all of the numbers from 0 to 999 fit in 10 bits, but not all those from 0 to 9,999 fit). We will do all of our examples using decimal, but always keep in mind that the computer always uses binary! For our first example, consider the sum 122 + 12.

We first normalize these numbers as $.122 * 10^3$ and$.12 * 10^2$. But already there is a complication: we can't simply add two decimal numbers which are multiplied by different exponents! That is, the answers .242 * 10^3 or.242 * 10^2 are obviously incorrect! To solve this problem, the number with the smaller exponent must be denormalized before the addition can take place .12 * 10^2 becomes.012 * 10^3.

Now it is clear that we can simply add the decimal numbers, since a * 10^x + b * 10^x = (a + b) * 10^x, and we get the answer .134 * 10^3 which is of course 134. If the relative sizes of the two numbers are too different, we may have one of two errors. As an example of the first type of error, consider the sum 1220 + 14. In our hypothetical computer, these numbers are normalized as .122 * 10^4 and.14 * 10^2. But when we denormalize the smaller number before adding, the fact that we have only 3 decimal digits of precision causes a truncation error .14 * 10^2 becomes.001 * 10^4; that is, the second significant digit was lost: it was denormalized out of existence.

In fact, if we consider the sum 1220 + 1.4, we see that the second operand (1.4) is denormalized to zero .14 * 10^1 becomes.000 * 10^4! This is called an "underflow" error; it and the truncation errors are called "representation errors". You are already familiar with representation errors: some numbers have no finite representation in the decimal number system, such as 1/3 (which cannot be written down as a finite string of numbers to the right of the decimal point).

For the same reasons, many numbers have no finite representation in binary. This includes all so-called "non-terminating" numbers in decimal, as well as any fraction with a power of 5 in the denominator (which may have finite representations in decimal; ie., 1/5 =.2). And of course there is representation error any time you need more precision than the computer provides: 1273 is represented on our hypothetical computer as .127 * 10^4, because, again, we only have 3 decimal digits of precision! Representation errors can also occur during multiplication. Consider the product 125 * 21. This product is represented in normalized form as .125 * 10^3 *.21 * 10^2. Now the convenience of exponential notation for multiplication has not been lost on the computer architects (this is why they choose exponential representations in the first place!). Since x * 10^a * y * 10^b = (x * y) * 10^{a+b}, the product is computed by us as (.125 *.21) * 10^5 =.02625 * 10^5 but because of the finite precision inherent in the computer (which here has only 3 digits of precision), the result is truncated (before normalization!) to .026 * 10^5 and is then normalized to .26 * 10^4.

In general, in order to perform any floating point arithmetic operation, the computer must:

- First represent each operand as a normalized number within the limits of its precision (which may result in representation error due to truncation of less significant digits);
- Denormalize the smaller of the numbers if an addition or subtraction is being performed (which may again result in representation error due to the denormalization);
- Perform the operation (which again may result in representation error due to the finite precision of the floating point processor); and finally
- Renormalize the result

The step which actually performs the operation can result in another kind of error: overflows can occur in floating point arithmetic as well as in fixed, but they are detected in the exponent rather than the significand. If we attempt to multiply 2 * 10^7 times 7 * 10^7, the normalized product is .2 * 10^8 *.7 * 10^8 =.14 * 10^{16}; but our imaginary computer can only represent numbers with exponents up to 15!

It is therefore useful to know the range of exponents which your computer can represent. As an example, the Intel double precision format supports exponents in the range -1,022 to +1,023. Since these are exponents of 2, the range of numbers which can be represented as floating point doubles in an Intel CPU are $2^{-1,022}$ to $2^{1,023}$, which is (approximately) decimal 2.225 * 10^{-308} to 8.988 * 10^{307}. Any results with exponents outside those ranges will result in an overflow error. It is worth noting that floating point operations are much slower than their corresponding fixed point counterparts. For example, on a 1.4 GHz Pentium 4 CPU, two 32 bit fixed point numbers can be added in about 71 billionths of a second (71 nanoseconds). A fixed point multiply of two

32 bit numbers may take 4 or 5 times longer. By comparison, floating point operations may take tens or even hundreds of times longer to perform.

FLOATING POINT PIPELINES

In the MIPS pipeline that we have studied last semester, only one pipeline stage, EX, is allowed for the numerical calculations to take place. As long as the numerical calculations can be done by a simple ALU, the amount of time available during one pipeline stage should be adequate. However, more complicated arithmetic operations, such as multiply, divide and floating point operations, can require complex hardware with significantly longer delays than a simple ALU. One solution might be to extend the super pipelining idea to the EX stage and have multi-ple EX stages. Well designed integer multiply hardware has about twice the delay of the carry chain in the ALU. This could be incorporated with two EX stages.

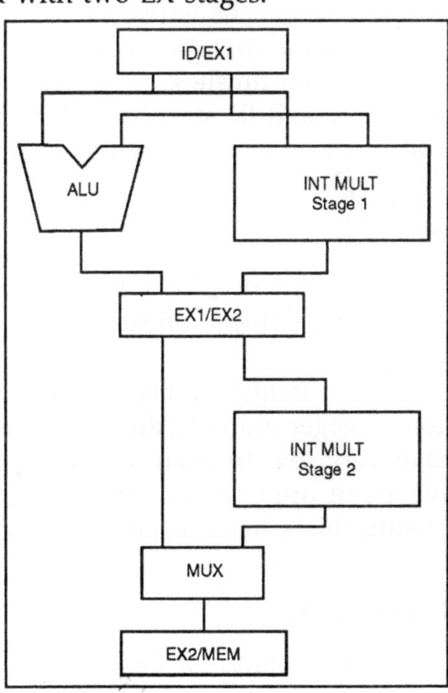

The throughput for ALU instructions is unaffected by this scheme, but the increased pipe-line latency will require additional operand forwarding and longer instruction latencies. The same technique is not practical for integer division. Multiplication can be compressed into a few pipeline stages because most of the computation can be done in parallel. Unfor-tunately, division algorithms are highly sequential and only a limited amount of work can be done in each pipeline stage which requires a large number of stages to complete the algorithm. Floating point operations also require many pipeline stages.

SINGLE PIPELINES

When all instructions run through a pipeline with the same number of stages, it is usually not practical to make the pipeline long enough to accommodate the longest multi-stage instruction since it would take too many stages. Instead, the multi-stage instructions are broken down into simpler parts. The EX stage contains all of the hardware for each step and the EX stage is repeated the appropriate number of times until the multi-stage instruction finishes.

Meanwhile, the IF and ID stages are stalled if EX takes more than one clock cycle.This scheme preserves the simplicity of the simple linear pipeline and does not increase the latency of the simple ALU instructions (only one EX cycle). The multi-stage instructions cause many stall cycles (the instructions become essentially unpipelined), but as long as the instruction frequency of the multi-stage instructions is low, stalls will be infrequent.

Typical instruction frequency data show that the multi-stage instructions (integer multiply/divide and floating point operations) have very low frequencies except in the most intense floating point applications. Division is frequently implemented using this scheme even in high performance superscalar processors.

PARALLEL PIPELINES

Different parallel pipelines for different instructions can

reduce the number of stalls caused by the multi-stage instructions. The IF and ID stages are not automatically

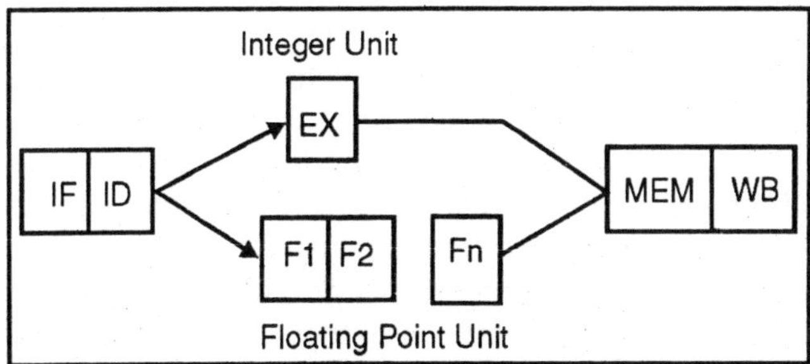

Stalled when a multi-stage instruction begins execution. The multi-stage instructions still have high instruction latencies, but the stalls are reduced since a new instruction can start executing every clock cycle. The high instruction latency means that later instructions that need the results of previous multi-stage instructions have to be stalled until the latency period is over.

Division would require the longest pipeline, but has the lowest instruction frequency of the multi-stage instructions. The low instruction frequency makes it uneconomical to devote extensive hardware to a long division pipeline. Instead, the division instruction repeatedly uses the same EX hardware over and over again.

Since the pipelines for the different instruction types are in parallel, ALU instructions can proceed before the multi-stage instructions finish. If the ALU instructions use the results of a multi-stage instruction still in its pipeline, a RAW data hazard is possible. These can be avoided by stalling or operand forwarding similar to the fixed length pipelines studied previously. The problem is that there are many more situations that can cause stalls which complicates the design.

If ALU instructions do not use results from any multi-stage instructions already in the pipeline, then the ALU instructions might finish before a previous multi-stage instruction (and multiplies might finish before previous divides, etc.). WAW and WAR data hazards only because instructions start and finish in order in a nor-mal pipeline.

The variable length pipeline on the previous page does not cause WAR hazards because instructions start and read their operands in ID in order before writes of subsequent instructions. Thus, subsequent writes will automatically be after previous reads. Another problem is that more than one instruction might get to MEM and WB at the same time. It is possible to have duplicate MEM and WB stages on the end of each pipeline, but this would require multiple ports on the memory and register file (too expensive usually).

It is true that many processors provide a separate register file for floating point operations so that an integer and floating point instruction could be in WB at the same time. How-ever, floating point operations could still cause structural hazards with other floating point operations. A single MEM and WB stage as on the previous page makes a structural haz-ard that must be avoided by stalling instructions so that only one instruction at a time enters MEM and WB.

Maintaining Precise Exceptions

Since instructions can finish out of order in floating point pipelines, it makes it much more difficult to make precise exceptions. We see that our previous method of making precise exceptions was to handle them in order as the instructions reached the WB stage. Now, instructions do not necessarily reach WB in order. We have already mentioned that precise exceptions are necessary for virtual memory systems so that page faults are handled in order. The IEEE floating point standard also requires precise exceptions. The standard defines several exceptions which allow the exception handler the opportunity to "fix" the arithmetic result causing the exception. Thus, the floating point exception handlers must be insured to run before any following instructions use the result of the floating point instruction.

The solution to the problem of precise floating point exceptions falls into the four catego-ries below:

- Give the processor two modes of operation, one with precise floating point exceptions and one without. The imprecise exception mode is faster because more floating point instructions can be in the pipeline at the same time. With precise exceptions, new floating point instructions are started only when it is determined that previous floating point instructions will not cause exceptions. This solution is used by the DEC alpha, IBM power-1 and power-2 and MIPS R8000.

- Make precise exceptions by storing the results of an instruction temporarily until all previous instructions have finished. Since the instruction results (register or memory writes) are written in order only after exceptions for each instruction are handled, the register file always has the correct values to restart the pipeline after the exception is handled. This is similar to handling all exceptions in the WB stage in the simple MIPS pipeline. This solution requires more sophisticated hardware which will be studied in more detail later. This technique is used by most superscalar processors.
- Allow imprecise exceptions and leave it up to the exception handler software to make the exceptions precise. The exception handler software must have access to sufficient information about every instruction in the pipeline. In architectures with a single inte-ger unit as the MIPS pipeline, the integer instructions finish in order and only the float-ing point instructions in the pipeline need to be considered by the exception handler. A queue of pending exceptions is needed to execute the exception handler software in order. It is also difficult to restart the pipeline after the exception handler is finished. Consider the following instruction sequence.
- Always require that previous instructions cannot cause exceptions before allowing a new instruction to start execution. This is most effective when exception detection hardware is added early in the multiple EX floating point pipeline stages. This solution is used in the MIPS R2000/3000, MIPS R4000 and the Intel Pentium.

Chapter 5

Control Design

CONTOL UNIT

The Control Unit can be thought of as the brain of the CPU itself. 0It controls based on the instructions it decodes, how other parts of the CPU and in turn, rest of the computer systems should work in order that the instruction gets executed in a correct manner.

There are two types of control units, the first type is called hardwired control unit. Hardwired control units are constructed using digital circuits and once formed cannot be changed.

The other type of control unit is microprogrammed control unit. A microprogrammed control unit itself decodes and execute instructions by means of executing micro-programs.

There are two approaches of Control Unit Design and implementation:

- Microprogrammed implementation
- Hardwired logic implementation

The figure illustrated the control unit inputs. Two techniques have been used to implemente the CU. In a hardwired implementation, the control unit is essentially considered as a logic circuit.

Its input logic signals are transformed into the set of ouput logic signals, which are the control signals. The approach of microprogrammed implementation is studied in this chapter.

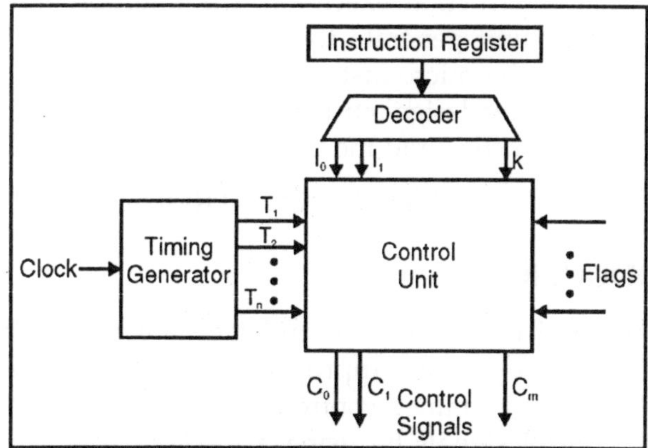

Fig. Control Unit with Decoded Inputs

The ideal of microprogrammed Control Unit is that the Control Unit design must include the logics for sequencing through micro-operations, for executing micro-operation, for executing micro-instructions, for interpreting opcodes and for making decision based on ALU flags. So the design is relatively inflexible. It is difficul to change the design if one wishes to add a new machine instruction.

The principal disadvantage of a microprogrammed control unit is that it will be slower than hardwired unit of comparable technology. Despite this, microprogramming is the dominant technique for implementing control unit in the contemporary CISC processor, due to its ease of implementation.

The control unit operates by performing consecutive control storage reads to generate the next set of control function outputs. Performing the series of control memory accesses is, in effect, executing a programme for each instruction in the machine's instruction set — hence the term microprogramming.

The two basic tasks performed by a microprogrammed control unit are as follows:

- Micro-instruction sequencing: the microprogrammed control unit get the next mico-instruction from the control memory

- Micro-instruction execution: the microprogrammed control unit generate the control signals needed to execute the micro-instruction.

The control unit design must consider both affect the format of the micro-instruction and the timing of the control unit.

HARDWIRED CONTROL

INTRODUCTION

Hardwired control is a control mechanism to generate control signals by using appropriate finite state machine (FSM). Micro programmed control is a control mechanism to generate control signals by using a memory called control storage (CS), which contains the control signals. Although micro programmed control seems to be advantageous to CISC machines, since CISC requires systematic development of sophisticated control signals, there is no intrinsic difference between these 2 control mechanism.

The pair of"microinstruction-register" and "control storage address register" can be regarded as a "state register" for the hardwired control.

Note that the control storage can be regarded as a kind of combinational logic circuit. We can assign any 0, 1 values to each output corresponding to each address, which can be regarded as the input for a combinational logic circuit. This is a truth table.

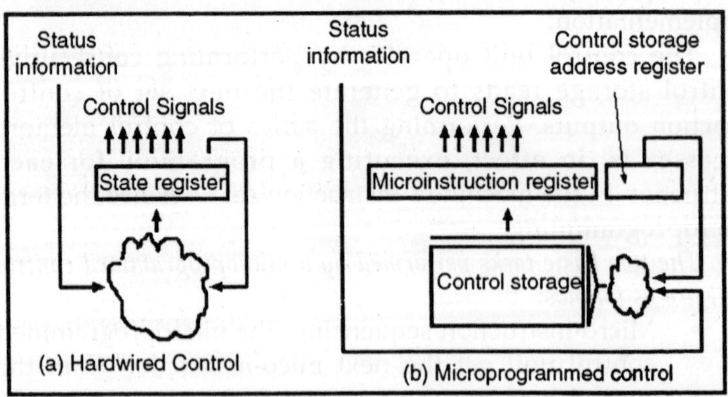

(a) Hardwired Control
(b) Microprogrammed control

CISC also can be implemented by using hardwired control:

In the above sense, the microprogrammed control is not always necessary to implement CISC machines. Hardwired control also can be used for implementing sophisticated CISC machines.

The bases of this opinion are as follows:

- The same field configuration (state assignment) can be used for both of these two types of control. This is clear because of the above identification.
- We can use any large FSM ,which has horizontal microcode like state assignment, since the delay for the hardwired control logic (FSM) does not matter at all so long as it is less than or equal to the delay for the data-path, which includes adders, shifters and so on, since the control logic circuit works in parallel with the data-path.
- The horizontal microcode like state assignment has became very easy to be implemented because of the spread of the hardware description language(HDL)s. In Verilog HDL, 'define statements enable us to get perfect net-list for the large FSM in a very short time by using appropriate logic synthesizer.

To execute instructions, a computer's processor must generate the control signals used to perform the processor's actions in the proper sequence. This sequence of actions can either be executed by another processor's software (for example in software emulation or simulation of a processor) or in hardware.

Hardware methods fall into two categories: the processor's hardware signals are generated either by hardwired control, in which the instruction bits directly generate the signals, or by microprogrammed control in which a dedicated microcontroller executes a microprogram to generate the signals.

Before microprocessors, hardwired control usually was implemented using discrete components, flip-chips, or even rotating discs or drums. This can be generally done by two methods.

Method1: The classical method of sequential circuit design. It attempts to minimize the amount of hardwire, in particular, by using only $\log_2 p$ flip flops to realise a p state circuit.

Method2: An approach that uses one flip flop per state. While expensive in terms of flip flops, this method simplifies controller unit design and debugging.

In practice, processor control units are often so complex that no one design method by itself can yield a satisfactory circuit at an acceptable cost. The most acceptable design may consist of several linked, but independently designed, sequential circuits.

Microprogramming made it possible to re-wire, as it were, a computer by simply downloading a new microprogram to it. This required dedicated hardware or an external processor. For example, some of DEC's PDP-10 processors used a PDP-11 as a front-end which uploaded a microprogram to the main processor at boot time.

Traditionally, a sewing machines' stitch patterns and a washing machine's wash programmes were implemented as hardwired, usually mechanical, controls. In modern machines, these are instead implemented as software which controls a computer which controls the machine hardware. This makes it possible, for example, to download additional stitch patterns for a small fee[citation needed] or upgrade a machine without having to buy a complete new machine. It also opens up for intellectual property rights issues.

The term hardwired is also used in a biological context to denote behaviour that is innately determined by an organism's genetically determined neurophysiology. Such hardwired behaviour would include the well-known knee-jerk reflex. Non-hardwired behaviour is dependent upon learning during the lifetime of the individual organism. As such the term is used in a way that is directly analogous to its use in computing.

DESCRIPTION

Figure is a block diagram showing the internal organization of a hard-wired control unit for our simple computer. Input to the controller consists of the 4-bit opcode of the instruction currently contained in the Instruction Register and the negative flag from the accumulator. The controller's output is a set of 16 control signals that go out to the various registers and to the memory of the computer, in addition to a HLT signal that is activated whenever the leading bit of the op-code is one. The controller is composed of the following functional units: A ring counter, an instruction decoder, and a control matrix.

The ring counter provides a sequence of six consecutive active signals that cycle continuously. Synchronized by the system clock, the ring counter first activates its T0 line, then its T1 line, and so forth. After T5 is active, the sequence begins again with T0. Figure shows how the ring counter might be organized internally.

The instruction decoder takes its four-bit input from the op-code field of the instruction register and activates one and only one of its 8 output lines. Each line corresponds to one of the instructions in the computer's instruction set. Figure shows the internal organization of this decoder.

The most important part of the hard-wired controller is the control matrix. It receives input from the ring counter and the instruction decoder and provides the proper sequence of control signals. Figure is a diagram of how the control matrix for our simple machine might be wired.

To understand how this diagram was obtained, we must look carefully at the machine's instruction set shows which control signals must be active at each ring counter pulse for each of the instructions in the computer's instruction set (and for the instruction fetch operation). The table was prepared by simply writing down the instructions in the left-hand column. (In the circuit these will be the output lines from the decoder). The various control signals are placed horizontally along the top of the table.

Entries into the table consist of the moments (ring counter pulses T0, T1, T2, T3, T4, or T5) at which each control signal must be active in order to have the instruction executed. This table is prepared very easily by reading off the information for each instruction given in Table. For example, the Fetch operation has the EP and LM control signals active at ring count 1, and ED, LI, and IPC active at ring count 2. Therefore the first row (Fetch) of Table 2 has T0 entered below EP and LM, T1 below R, and T2 below IP, ED, and LI.

Once Table has been prepared, the logic required for each control signal is easily obtained. For each an AND operation is performed between any active ring counter (Ti) signals that were entered into the signal's column and the corresponding instruction contained in the far left-hand column.

If a column has more than one entry, the output of the ANDs are ORed together to produce the final control signal. For example, the LM column has the following entries: T0 (Fetch), T3 associated with the LDA instruction, and T3 associated with the STA instruction. Therefore, the logic for this signal is:

LM = T0 + T3*LDA + T3*STA This means that control signal LM will be activated whenever any of the following conditions is satisfied: (1) ring pulse T0 (first step of an instruction fetch) is active, or (2) an LDA instruction is in the IR and the ring counter is issuing pulse 3, or (3) and STA instruction is in the IR and the ring counter is issuing pulse 3. The entries in the JN (Jump Negative) row of this table require some further explanation. The LP and EI signals are active during T3 for this instruction if and only if the accumulator's negative flag has been set. Therefore the entries that appear above these signals for the JN instruction are T3*NF, meaning that the state of the negative flag must be ANDed in for the LP and EI control signals.

Figure gives the logical equations required for each of the control signals used on our machine. These equations have been read from Table as explained above. The circuit diagram of the control matrix is constructed directly from these equations.

It should be noticed that the HLT line from the instruction decoder does not enter the control matrix, Instead this signal goes directly to circuitry (not shown) that will stop the clock and thus terminate execution.

MICRO-PROGRAMMED CONTROL UNIT

As we have seen, the controller causes instructions to be executed by issuing a specific set of control signals at each beat of the system clock. Each set of control signals issued causes one basic operation (micro-operation), such as a register transfer, to occur within the data path section of the computer. In the case of a hard-wired control unit the control matrix is responsible for sending out the required sequence of signals.

An alternative way of generating the control signals is that of micro-programmed control. In order to understand this method it is convenient to think of sets of control signals that cause specific micro-operations to occur as being "microinstructions" that could be stored in a memory.

Each bit of a microinstruction might correspond to one control signal. If the bit is set it means that the control signal will be active; if cleared the signal will be inactive. Sequences of microinstructions could be stored in an internal "control" memory. Execution of a machine language instruction could then be caused by fetching the proper sequence of microinstructions from the control memory and sending them out to the data path section of the computer. A sequence of microinstructions that implements an instruction on the external computer is known as a micro-routine. The instruction set of the computer is thus determined by the set of micro-routines, the "microprogram," stored in the controller's memory. The control unit of a microprogram-controlled computer is essentially a computer within a computer.

Figure is a block diagram of a micro-programmed control unit that may be used to implement the instruction set of the computer we described above. The heart of the controller is the control 32 X 24 ROM memory in which upt to 32 24-bit long microinstructions can be stored. Each is composed of two main fields: a 16-bit wide control signal field and an 8-bit wide next-address field.

Each bit in the control signal field corresponds to one of the control signals discussed above. The next-address field contains bits that determine the address of the next microinstruction to be fetched from the control ROM. Words selected from the control ROM feed the microinstruction register. This 24-bit wide register is analogous to the outer machine's instruction register. Specifically, the leading 16 bits (the control-signal field) of the microinstruction register are connected to the control-signal lines that go to the various components of the external machine's data path.

Addresses provided to the control ROM come from a micro-counter register, which is analogous to the external machine's programme counter. The micro-counter, in turn, receives its input from a multiplexer which selects from: (1) the output of an address ROM, (2) a current-address incrementer, or (3) the address stored in the next-address field of the current microinstruction. The logic that selects one of these three alternatives will be explained shortly.

The controller's address ROM is fed by the outer computer's instruction register. The address ROM maps the op-code of the instruction currently contained in the op-code field of the instruction register to the starting address of the corresponding microroutine in the control ROM. Address zero of the address ROM contains the control-ROM address of the fetch routine; each other addresses in the address-ROM corresponds to one of the op-codes of the computer's instruction set. Table shows the contents of the address ROM for the instruction set of our simple computer. To see how the address ROM works, let us assume that an ADD instruction has been fetched into the outer computer's instruction register. Since the op-code of the ADD instruction is 3, the number stored at location 3 of the address ROM (a 9) is the starting address in the control ROM of the microroutine that implements the ADD instruction.

Details of a microinstruction's next address field are shown in Figure. The 5-bit CRJA (Control ROM Jump Address) sub-field holds a microinstruction address. Thus, the address of the next microinstruction may be obtained from the current microinstruction. This permits branching to other sections within the microprogram. The combination of the MAP bit, the CD (condition) bit, and the negative flag from the accumulator of the external machine provide input to the logic that feeds the select lines of the multiplexer and thereby determine how the address of the next microinstruction will be obtained. If the MAP bit is one, the logic attached to the multiplexer's select lines produces a 01 which selects the address ROM. Therefore, the address of the micro-routine corresponding to the instruction in the outer machine's instruction register will be channeled to the control ROM. It should be clear that the MAP bit must be set in the last microinstruction of the "fetch" micro-routine, since it is at that moment that we want the newly-fetched instruction to be executed.

If the MAP bit is zero and the CD bit is zero, (unconditional branch), the multiplexer logic produces a 10, which selects the CRJA field of the current instruction. Therefore, the next instruction will come from the address contained in the current instruction's next-address field. With MAP=0 and CD=1 (conditional branch), the logic that feeds the multiplexer will produce either a 00 or a 10, depending on the value of the negative flag. If the flag is set, it is a 10, which selects the jump address contained in the current microinstruction. If the negative flag is cleared, the select lines to the multiplexer receive a 00, which causes the incrementer to be selected.

The next microinstruction will come from the next address in sequence. It should be noticed that with this scheme, if we are not doing branching, the CRJA field should contain the address of the next microinstruction and the CD bit should be cleared. This will cause "branch to the next microinstruction" to occur.

The one exception to this rule is the case of the last microinstruction within a micro-routine. Normally we would then want to branch back to the "fetch" micro-routine. Since this routine starts at control-ROM location 00000, that address should be contained in the CRJA field and CD should be 0.

The HLT bit is used to terminate execution. If it is set, the clock that synchronizes activities within the entire machine is stopped. Notice that the micro-counter is triggered by a rising clock edge, and the microinstruction register by a falling edge. Thus, we see that on each positive edge, the micro-counter receives the address of the microinstruction and presents it to the control ROM, which has until the next negative edge to output the addressed control word to the microinstruction register. Since all operation in the data path section are positive-edge triggered, there is adequate time for the signals specified in the control word contained in the microinstruction register to go out to all sections of the external machine. The sequence of latching the address of microinstruction i+1 into the micro-counter while microinstruction i executes (positive edge) and then presenting the control word of microinstruction i+1 to the microinstruction register (negative edge) continues until a set HLT bit stops the clock.

Table shows a microprogram which, when loaded into the control ROM, will implement the instruction set of the computer we have been describing. For each microinstruction, the control ROM address has been expressed in hexadecimal, and the contents in binary. The order of the bits in the control signal field is the same as that shown in table 2: IP, LP, EP, LM, R, W, LD, ED, LI, EI, LA, EA, A, S, EU, LB, reading from left to right. The last four columns of table 4 express the status of the CD, MAP, and HLT bits, and the Control ROM Jump Address, expressed in hexadecimal. In order to clarify how the microprogram works, a description is now given of the "fetch" and JN (jump on negative) micro-routines.

The "fetch" micro-routine occupies control ROM addresses 0, 1, and 2. The active EP and LM control-signal bits in its first microinstruction cause a register transfer from the programme counter to the memory address register to occur. The MAR will now contain the address in RAM of the next instruction.

Since CD and MAP are both zero (unconditional branch), the next microinstruction will come from the address stored in the CRJA field (01) – the next consecutive location. The microinstruction stored at that location has only the R bit active. Thus, the word stored in the memory location being accessed by the MAR (presumably the next instruction) will be gated to the Memory Data Register (MDR). The zeroes in CD and MAP again cause the microinstruction to be fetched from the address specified in the CRJA field, (02). Active control signal bits for that microinstruction are ED, LI, and IP. The first two transfer the word in the MDR to the Instruction Register, and the last increments the programme counter. The new instruction is safely in the IR, and the PC is pointing to the next instruction in sequence. We have completed an instruction fetch. Since the MAP field in the last microinstruction of this "fetch" micro-routine is equal to 1, the address of the next microinstruction is determined by the address ROM, which, in turn, depends upon the opcode of the instruction that has just been loaded into the instruction register.

When the JN instruction is executed, control is supposed to be transferred to the address specified by the least significant eight bits of the number contained in the instruction register if the negative flag is set. If the negative flag is not set, execution should continue with the next instruction in sequence. Let us see how the micro-routine stored at control-ROM locations 0F, 10, and 11 implement this conditional jump. In the first microinstruction, none of the control signal bits is set. Thus, nothing will occur in the data path section of the computer. However, the fact that the CD bit is set means that if the negative flag is set, the next microinstruction will be fetched from the control-ROM address specified in the CRJA field (11 in this case). The microinstruction stored at that location has the EI and LP control signal bits set.

Thus, the contents of the instruction register (the least significant eight bits) will be transferred to the programme counter. The zeroes stored in the CD and MAP bits cause the next microinstruction to be fetched from the address contained in the CRJA field -- a 00 in this case. This is the start of the"fetch" micro-routine. Thus we see that if the negative flag is set, the JN micro-routine places the jump address in the programme counter and transfer to the fetch routine. When that fetch is performed, control will have been transferred to the jump address. If, on the other hand, the negative flag is NOT SET when the JN micro-routine executes, then the set CD bit in its first microinstruction causes the current address stored in the micro-counter to be incremented.

Thus, the next microinstruction would be fetched from location 10. That microinstruction also has no active control signals bits, but with CD=0 and CRJA=00, the next microinstruction will be the first one in the "fetch" routine. Notice that in this case, the JN instruction simply returns us to the next fetch. Since the programme counter has not been altered, that fetch will be from the next sequential memory location, as usual.

HARDWIRED VS. MICRO-PROGRAMMED COMPUTERS

It should be mentioned that most computers today are micro-programmed. The reason is basically one of flexibility. Once the control unit of a hard-wired computer is designed and built, it is virtually impossible to alter its architecture and instruction set. In the case of a micro-programmed computer, however, we can change the computer's instruction set simply by altering the microprogram stored in its control memory.

In fact, taking our basic computer as an example, we notice that its four-bit op-code permits up to 16 instructions. Therefore, we could add seven more instructions to the instruction set by simply expanding its microprogram. To do this with the hard-wired version of our computer would require a complete redesign of the controller circuit hardware.

Another advantage to using micro-programmed control is the fact that the task of designing the computer in the first place is simplified. The process of specifying the architecture and instruction set is now one of software (micro-programming) as opposed to hardware design. Nevertheless, for certain applications hard-wired computers are still used. If speed is a consideration, hard-wiring may be required since it is faster to have the hardware issue the required control signals than to have a "programme" do it.

Summary

The intent of this article has been to present, through example, the distinction between hardwired and micro-programmed computers. In the process, it is hoped that the reader has gained insight into what really occurs inside a digital computer as a programme executes.

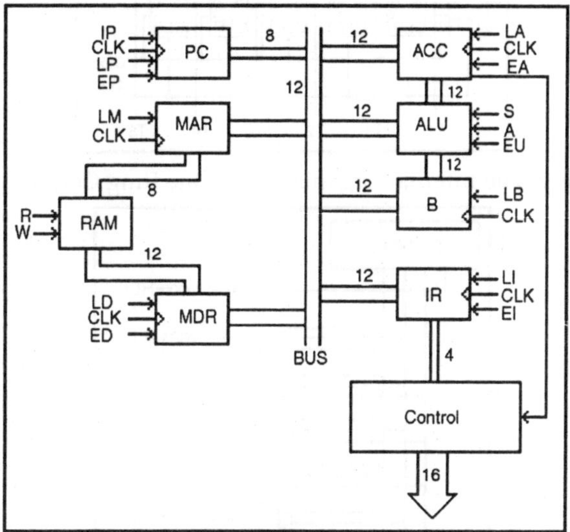

Fig. A Simple Single-Bus Basic Computer

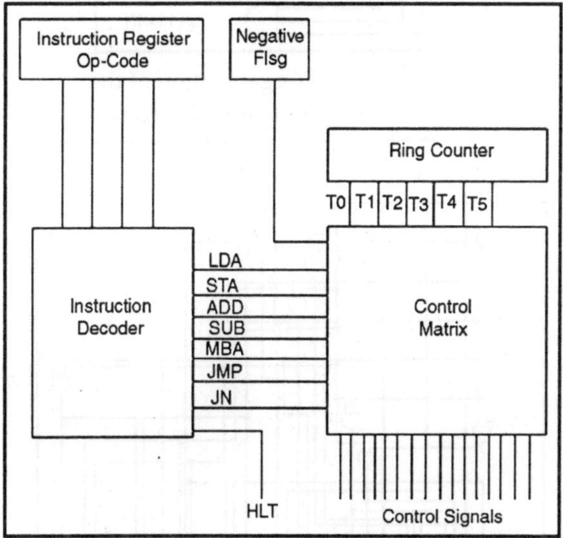

Fig. A Block Diagram of the Basic Computer's Hard-wired Control Unit

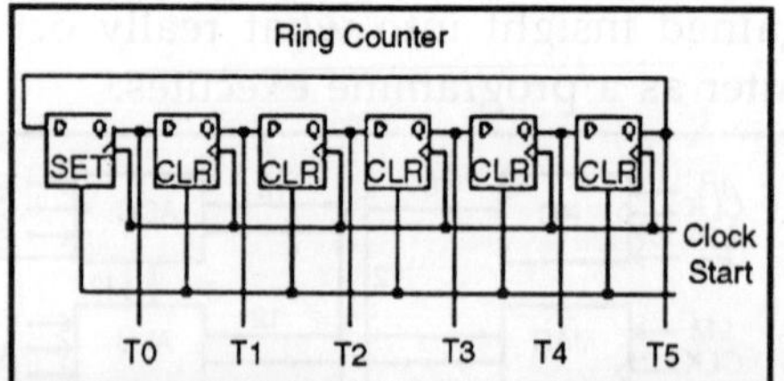

Fig. The Internal Organization of the Ring Counter

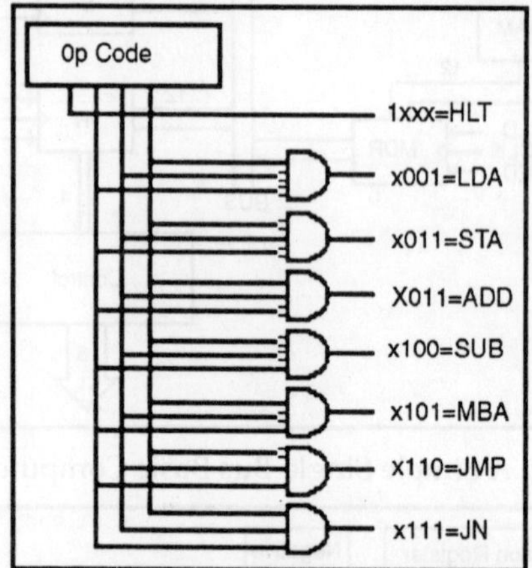

Fig. The Internal Organization of the Hard-wired Instruction Decoder

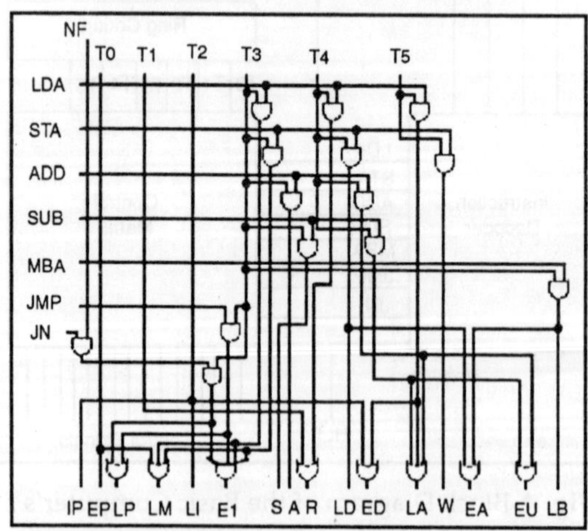

Fig. The Internal Organization of the Hard-wired Control Matrix

IP = T2
W = T5*STA
LP = T3*JMP + T3*NF*JN
LD = T4*STA
LA = T5*LDA + T4*ADD + T4*SUB
EA = T4*STA + T3*MBA
EP = T0
S = T3*SUB
A = T3*ADD
LI = T2
LM = T0 + T3*LDA + T3*STA
ED = T2 + T5*LDA
R = T1 + T4*LDA
EU = T3*ADD+T3*SUB
EI = T3*LDA + T3*STA + T3*JMP + T3*NF*JN
LB = T3*MBA

The logical equations required for each of the hardwired control signals on the basic computer.

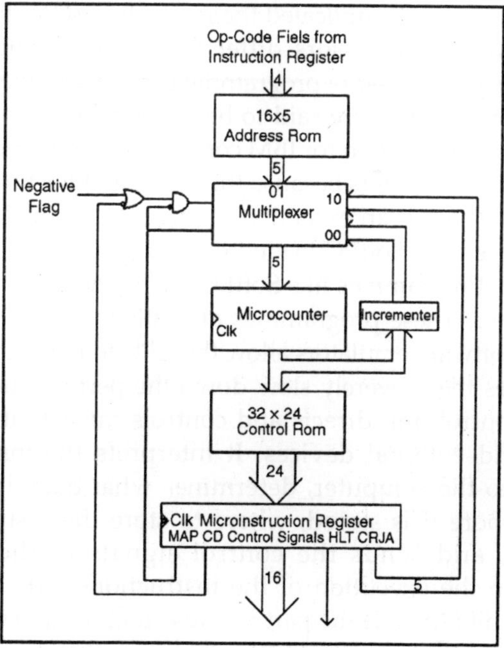

Fig. A Microprogrammed Control Unit for the Simple Computer

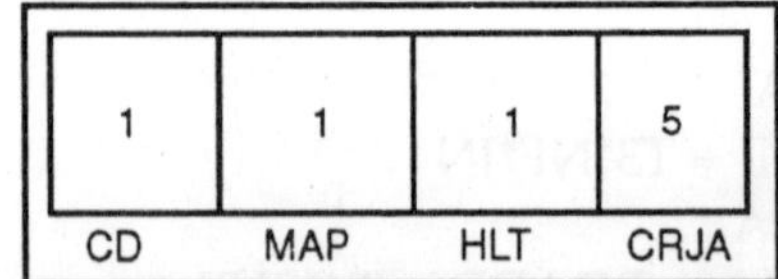

Fig. Next Address Field of the Microinstruction Register. CD is the Condition bit, MAP Causes the Address of the Next microinstruction to be obtained from the address ROM, HLT stops the clock and CRJA is the control ROM jump address field.

CPU CONTROL UNIT

CENTRAL PROCESSING UNIT

The main unit inside the computer is the CPU. This unit is responsible for all events inside the computer. It controls all internal and external devices, performs arithmetic and logic operations. The operations a microprocessor performs are called the *instruction set* of this processor. The instruction set is "hard wired" in the CPU and determines the machine language for the CPU. The more complicated the instruction set is, the slower the CPU works. Processors differ from one another by the instruction set. If the same programme can run on two different computer brands they are said to be compatible.

Programmes written for IBM compatible computers will not run on Apple computers because these two architectures are not compatible. There is an exception to this rule. Apple Macintosh with a programme SoftPC loaded can run programmes written for IBM PC. Programmes like SoftPC make one CPU "pretend" to be another. These programmes are called *software emulators.* Although software emulators allow the CPU to run incompatible programmes they severely slow down the performance.

The control unit directs and controls the activities of the internal and external devices. It interprets the instructions fetched into the computer, determines what data, if any, are needed, where it is stored, where to store the results of the operation, and sends the control signals to the devices involved in the execution of the instructions. The arithmetic and logic unit (ALU) is the part where actual computations take place. It consists of circuits which perform arithmetic operations (e.g. addition, subtraction, multiplication, division) over data received from memory and capable to compare numbers.

The CPU is composed of several units.

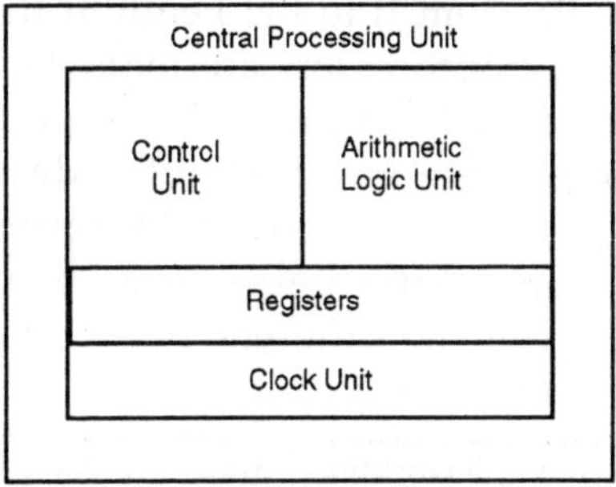

Fig. A Simplified Diagram of the CPU

While performing these operations the ALU takes data from the temporary storage area inside the CPU named registers. Registers are a group of cells used for memory addressing, data manipulation and processing. Some of the registers are general purpose and some are reserved for certain functions. It is a high-speed memory which holds only data for immediate processing and results of this processing. If these results are not needed for the next instruction, they are sent back to the main memory and registers are occupied by the new data used in the next instruction.

The microprocessor — also known as a CPU or central processing unit — is a complete computation engine that is fabricated on a single chip. The first microprocessor was the Intel 4004, introduced in 1971. The 4004 was not very powerful, all it could do was add and subtract, and it could only do that 4 bits at a time. But it was amazing that everything was on one chip. Prior to the 4004, engineers built computers either from collections of chips or from discrete components (transistors wired one at a time). The 4004 powered one of the first portable electronic calculators. The first microprocessor to make it into a home computer was the Intel 8080, a complete 8-bit computer on one chip, introduced in 1974. The first microprocessor to make a real splash in the market was the Intel 8088, introduced in 1979 and incorporated into the IBM PC (which first appeared around 1982). If you are familiar with the PC market and its history, you know that the PC market moved from the 8088 to the 80286 to the 80386 to the 80486 to the Pentium to the Pentium II to the Pentium III to the Pentium 4. All of these microprocessors are made by Intel and all of them are improvements on the basic design of the 8088. The Pentium 4 can execute any piece of code that ran on the original 8088, but it does it about 5,000 times faster!

The following table helps you to understand the differences between the different processors that Intel has introduced over the years.

Name	Date	Transistors	Microns	Clock Speed	Data width	MIPS
8080	1974	6,000	6	2 MHz	8 bits	0.64
8088	1979	29,000	3	5 MHz	16 bits, 8-bit bus	0.33
80286	1982	134,000	1.5	6 MHz	16 bits	1
80386	1985	275,000	1.5	16 MHz	32 bits	5
80486	1989	1,200,000	1	25 MHz	32 bits	20
Pentium	1993	3,100,000	0.8	60 MHz	32 bits, 64-bit bus	100
Pentium II	1997	7,500,000	0.35	233 MHz	32 bits, 64-bit bus	~300
Pentium III	1999	9,500,000	0.25	450 MHz	32 bits, 64-bit bus	~510
Pentium IV	2000	42,000,000	0.18	1.5 GHz	32 bits, 64-bit bus	~1,700

CHIP

A chip is also called an integrated circuit. Generally it is a small, thin piece of silicon onto which the transistors making up the microprocessor have been etched. A chip might be as large as an inch on a side and can contain tens of millions of transistors. Simpler processors might consist of a few thousand transistors etched onto a chip just a few millimeters square.

The date is the year that the processor was first introduced. Many processors are re-introduced at higher clock speeds for many years after the original release date. Transistors is the number of transistors on the chip. You can see that the number of transistors on a single chip has risen steadily over the years. Microns is the width, in microns, of the smallest wire on the chip. For comparison, a human hair is 100 microns thick. As the feature size on the chip goes down, the number of transistors rises.

Clock speed is the maximum rate that the chip can be clocked at. Clock speed will make more sense in the next section. Data Width is the width of the ALU. An 8-bit ALU can add/subtract/multiply/etc. two 8-bit numbers, while a 32-bit ALU can manipulate 32-bit numbers. An 8-bit ALU would have to execute four instructions to add two 32-bit numbers, while a 32-bit ALU can do it in one instruction. In many cases, the external data bus is the same width as the ALU, but not always. The 8088 had a 16-bit ALU and an 8-bit bus, while the modern Pentiums fetch data 64 bits at a time for their 32-bit ALUs.

MIPS stands for "millions of instructions per second" and is a rough measure of the performance of a CPU. Modern CPUs can do so many different things that MIPS ratings lose a lot of their meaning, but you can get a general sense of the relative power of the CPUs from this column. From this table you can see that, in general, there is a relationship between clock speed and MIPS. The maximum clock speed is a function of the manufacturing process and delays within the chip. There is also a relationship between the number of transistors and MIPS. For example, the 8088 clocked at 5 MHz but only executed at 0.33 MIPS (about one instruction per 15 clock cycles). Modern processors can often execute at a rate of two instructions per clock cycle. That improvement is directly related to the number of transistors on the chip and will make more sense in the next section.

The arithmetic logic unit (ALU) is a digital circuit that calculates an arithmetic operation (addition, subtraction, etc.) and logic operations (Exclusive Or, AND, etc.) between two numbers. The ALU is a fundamental building block of the central processing unit of a computer.

Many types of electronic circuits need to perform some type of arithmetic operation, so even the circuit inside a digital watch will have a tiny ALU that keeps adding 1 to the current time, and keeps checking if it should beep the timer, etc.

By far, the most complex electronic circuits are those that are built inside the chip of modern microprocessors like the Pentium. Therefore, these processors have inside them a powerful and very complex ALU. In fact, a modern microprocessor (or mainframe) may have multiple cores, each core with multiple execution units, each with multiple ALUs.

Many other circuits may contain ALUs inside: GPUs like the ones in NVidia and ATI graphic cards, FPUs like the old 80387 co-processor, and digital signal processor like the ones found in Sound Blaster sound cards, CD players and High-Definition TVs. All of these have several powerful and complex ALUs inside.

A control unit is the part of a CPU or other device that directs its operation. The outputs of the unit control the activity of the rest of the device. A control unit can be thought of as a finite state machine.

At one time control units for CPUs were ad-hoc logic, and they were difficult to design. Now they are often implemented as a microprogram that is stored in a control store. Words of the microprogram are selected by a microsequencer and the bits from those words directly control the different parts of the device, including the registers, arithmetic and logic units, instruction registers, buses, and off-chip input/output. In modern computers, each of these subsystems may have its own subsidiary controller, with the control unit acting as a supervisor. The control unit is the circuitry that controls the flow of information through the processor, and coordinates the activities of the other units within it. In a way, it is the "brain within the brain", as it controls what happens inside the processor, which in turn controls the rest of the PC.

The functions performed by the control unit vary greatly by the internal architecture of the CPU, since the control unit really implements this architecture. On a regular processor that executes x86 instructions natively, the control unit performs the tasks of fetching, decoding, managing execution and then storing results.

On a processor with a RISC core the control unit has significantly more work to do. It manages the translation of x86 instructions to RISC micro-instructions, manages scheduling the micro-instructions between the various execution units, and juggles the output from these units to make sure they end up where they are supposed to go. On one of these processors the control unit may be broken into other units (such as a scheduling unit to handle scheduling and a retirement unit to deal with results coming from the pipeline) due to the complexity of the job it must perform.

Chapter 6

Memory Organization

STORAGE UNIT

The memory of a computer holds (stores) programme instructions (what to do),data (information), operands (affected, manipulated, or operated upon data), and calculations (ALU results). The CPU controls the information stored in memory. Information is fetched, manipulated (under programme control) and/or written (or written back) into memory for immediate or later use. The internal memory of a computer is also referred to as main memory, global memory, main storage, or primary storage. Do not confuse it with secondary or auxiliary memory (also called mass storage) provided by various peripheral devices. In newer computers you also will encounter a number of small and independent local memories that are used for variety of purposes by embedded microprocessors.

MEMORY ORGANIZATIONAND OPERATION

The main memory of a computer is used for storingprograms, data, calculations, and operands.Memory is used in all types of computer systems includ-ing mainframes, minicomputers, and microcomputers. The amount of main memory each type of computer hasvaries according to the configuration. A wide varietyof memory types is being used. To simplify ourdiscussion, we have divided memory into two generalcategories: read/write (random access) memory andread-only memory. Within the read/write group, we discuss magnetic (core and film) memories and semiconductor (static and dynamic) memories. Read-onlymemory can be subdivided into factory programmedparts called read-only memory (ROM) and user pro-grammable devices called programmable read-onlymemory (PROM). This classification system is illus-trated in figure

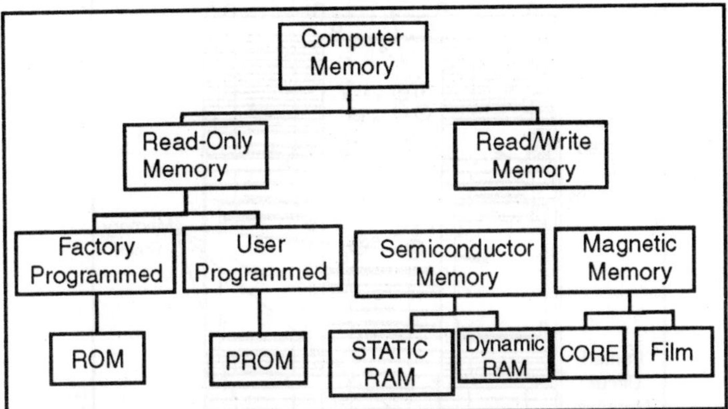

Memory organization is two-fold. First we discuss the hardware (physical) organization, then the internal architecture. The type of computer and its size do not reflect the type of memories that the computer uses. Some computers have a mixture of memory types. For example, they may use some type of magnetic memory(core or film) and also a semiconductor memory (static or dynamic).

They also have a read-only memory which is usually a part of the CPU. Memory in a computer can vary from one or more modules to one or more pcb's, depending on the computer type. The larger mainframe computers use the modular arrangement, multiple modules (four or more), to make up their memories. Whereas, minicomputers and microcomputers use chassis or assemblies, cages or racks, and motherboard or backplane arrangements. Minis and micros use multiple components on one pcb or groups of pcb's to form the memory.

MEMORY MODULES

Memory modules are made up of multiple pcb's(support circuitry) and memory components (stacks[core or film] or semiconductor pcb's with supportcircuitry) to form one memory module or unit. Figure below is an illustration of a large memory module; one offour to a single computer set.

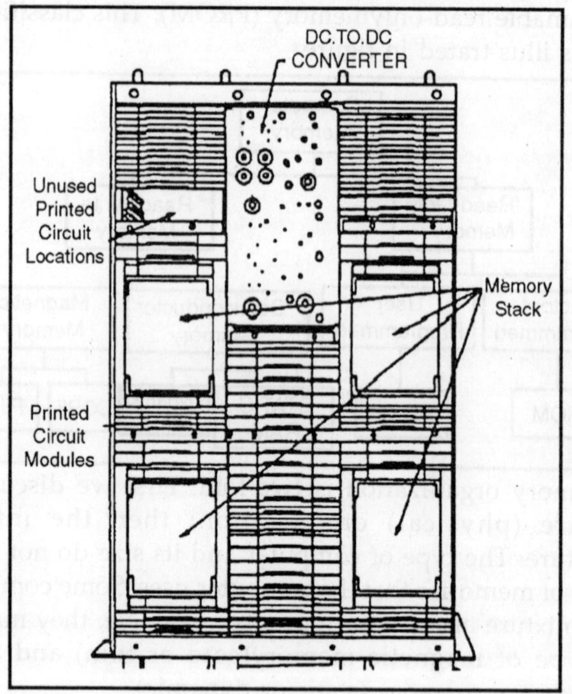

Memory modules are interchangeable with other modules of the same type and size in the same computer set. Each module provides a fixed number of memory words with a fixed number of bit positions for each word. Some memory modules are designed with the capability to receive requests from more than one central processing unit orI/O section. These multiported memory modules process memory requests on a priority basis. While the module is processing a request from one section, the remaining possible requesters are locked out, so to speak, by the module logic until the completion of the pending request. If two requests are received simultaneously, then the highest priority requestor is cycled first. Memory modules may contain magnetic or semiconductor memory types. Some computers use both but in different modules. The size of memory in terms of bits and arrangement contained on each ofthese types depends on the requirements and design of the computer. Consult your technical manual for the exact size and arrangement.

MEMORY PCB'S

Computers that use a small number of pcb's as their memories are usually of the semiconductor type. In mainframe semiconductor memory, pcb's and support circuitry are contained in a module or unit. In minicomputers and microcomputers, memory can be contained on as few as one pcb, or as many as half-a-dozen pcb's. When there is more than one pcb, they are usually arranged in a group together in the computer's frame or cabinet. Micros can also use a bank of IC chips for their memories. The IC chips are mounted on single inline memory modules (SIMMs)(fig. 6-3), single inline packages (SIPS), or single inline

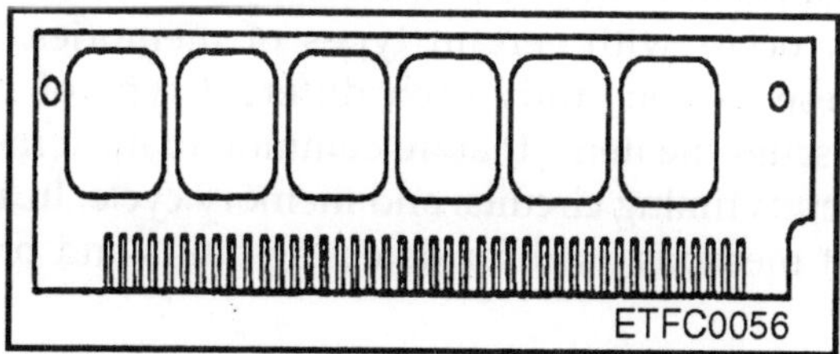

pin packages (SIPPs). Memory pcb's also operate on are quest basis, but unlike memory modules, there is nota priority sequence to go through. The request is madeby requestor, the control circuitry selects either a read or a write operation, and the timing circuitry initiates the read and/or write operations.

MEMORY ARCHITECTURE

The memory architecture, regardless of the memory type, is consistent. Memories are typically organized in square form so they have an equal number of rows(x) and columns(y). Each intersection of a row and column comprises a memory wordaddress. Each memory address contains a memoryword. The selected memory address can contain oneor more bits. But for speed and practicality, for a given computer design, the word size typically relates to the CPU and is usually the size of its registers in bits. Word sires typically range in increments of 8, 16, 32, or 64bits. Figure represents an address with an 8-bitword. The methods used for the arrangement of therows and columns vary in a given type of memory. Therows and columns are arranged in arrays, memory planes, or matrices.

MEMORY OPERATIONS

Memories operate on a request, selection, and initiate basis. A memory request or selection and a memory word location are transmitted from the requestor (CPU or I/O sections) to the memory section. The computer's internal bus system transmits the memory request or selection and location to the memory section. The memory operations, regardless ofthe computer type, share some basic commonalities. Key events must occur to access and store data in memory. Some items only occur with certain types of memories, and we discuss these as you study each different type of memory. We also discuss the items thatare common to most memories: control circuits,timing circuits, and memory cycle. In addition, we present methods used for detecting faults and protecting memory

MULTIPLE LEVEL MEMORIES

The most common and most often used computer memory is your RAM which stands for Random Access Memory. Random Access Memory is considered random access because you can access any cell of the memory at any time for any piece of information either for retrieval or storage if you know the row and column that intersect at that cell. For example: let's say we are working within an Excel spreadsheet and we want to change the value in cell A1 from 100 to 90.

In order to do this the computer has to know where on the RAM chip that cell's contents are located. Fortunately for the user, it does and the user doesn't have to. Once the change is made the computer replaces the contents in RAM, which was the value 100, with the new value of 90 and leaves it in that location until the user decides to change the value again or closes up the spreadsheet itself. Once that happens, the contents in RAM of that particular location are lost. Hopefully before doing this the user will have saved his spreadsheet to his computer's hard drive.

RAM can also be broken down into different types. First there is SRAM, which is Static Random Access Memory. This type of memory is usually used for a computer's cache memory. Then there is DRAM, which is Dynamic Random Access Memory. This type of memory has memory cells with a paired transistor and capacitor which need constant refreshing.

Then there is EDO DRAM which is Extended Data Out Dynamic Random Access Memory. This is very fast memory which doesn't wait until processing of the first bit is completed before moving on to the next bit. Then we have SDRAM, which is Synchronous Dynamic Random Access Memory. This type of memory takes advantage of the fact that in most cases the data that needs to be accessed is sequentially stored and therefore using a very fast method of accessing this memory. The rate of this memory is about 528 Mbps, which is extremely fast.

The opposite of RAM is SAM, or Sequential Access Memory. This is memory that has to be accessed in sequence, one cell at a time until the location the user is looking for is found. This memory is very good for buffer memory because items stored in the buffer are usually stored sequentially anyway as the user continues his work. SAM is slower than RAM as far as access time goes.

Another type of memory is what is known as ROM or Read Only Memory. Read Only Memory is also known as Firmware. This is an integrated circuit programmed with certain data when it is manufactured. ROM is not only used in computers but in a number of electronic devices like your Xbox or any video game console box. Without ROM just about any electronic item today that has built in functions simply wouldn't work.

Most computer memory refers to temporary types of memory. Since every action on your computer requires some form of memory, whether it is actual or virtual memory. When those actions take place, if memory was not used, everything on your system would be slow or possibly non-working at all. This is the primary function of memory in your computer. It helps the CPU access things in memory to avoid running your computer down accessing them from their original place of storage.

The average computer comes with four types of primary memory: Level one and two cache, RAM, virtual and hard disk memory. When your computer tries to access memory, it uses these different levels to access, open and utilize computer processes. The hard disk is one of the cheapest types of memory. It is a permanent storage device, but it can consume too much time to open and read data from it. So, virtual memory comes into play in conjunction with the CPU to help read the hard disk and make it a bit quicker to read the unit.

Next up comes the RAM. RAM is not fast enough to keep up with the CPU. So, there are different levels of cache to help RAM process actions quicker and keep up with the CPU. Caches utilize the data and actions that are most used by a computer. Level one cache utilizes small amounts of memory in the CPU whereas level two hides out in a chip near the CPU. It actually connects to the CPU itself and helps to keep it from over clocking when accessing its own memory.

The RAM helps sync these types of memory together, but since they do not directly connect and interact with the CPU, the cache levels help fuse everything together so that your computer runs faster when accessing data at different intervals. While there is much more to memory than just these facets, this is just a basic overview of how it all works together to keep your computer running. So, the next time you think your computer is slow, perhaps, it is time for a memory upgrade.

- Multiple levels of memory with different speeds and sizes

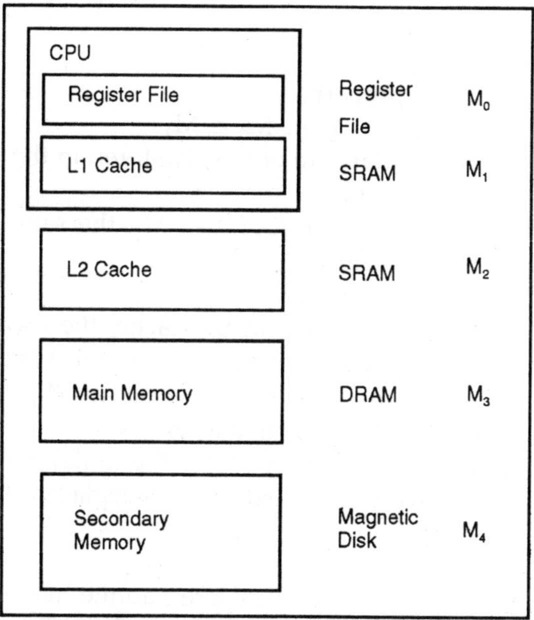

- *Access time:* $t_{Ai} < t_{Ai+1}$
- *Cost per bit:* $c_i > c_{i+1}$
- *Storage capability:* $s_i < s_{i+1}$
- The unit of data transfers between CPU and cache is called block (e.g., a 4-word block contains 32x4 bits)
- Cache consists of blocks.
- Main memory is divided into pages
  oe.g., a 4K-byte page contains 256 blocks
- *Hit:* data requested by the processor appears in the upper level, otherwise, there is a *miss.*
- When there is a hit, the data can be accessed from the upper level memory. When there is a miss, the data has to be accessed from the lower level memory.
- *Hit ratio (rate):* The ratio of hit in the *i*th level memory (h_i)
- *Miss rate:* $1 - h_i$
- *Hit time:* Time to access the *i*th level memory (t_{Ai})
- *Miss penalty:* Time to replace a block with the requested one from the lower level memory for a miss, plus the time to access the data

- Block miss
- Page miss

locality principles

- Inclusion property

$$M_1 \subset M_2 \subset M_3$$

  - All the data are originally stored in the outermost level memory
  - If the data are found in M_1, the same copy can be found in M_2, and so on.
- Coherence Property

OIf a word is modified in the cache, the copies of that word must be updated at all higher level memories

  - Write-through policy: update M_{i+1} if change occurs in M_i immediately
  - Write-back policy: delay the update in M_{i+1} until the word modified in M_i is replaced or removed from M_i
- Locality of References
  - 90-10 rule: a typical programme may spend 90% of its execution time on only 10% of the code such as a nested loop
- Temporal Locality
- Recently referenced items (instruction or data) are likely to be referenced again in the near future (e.g., loop, local variable)
- Spatial Locality
  - Tendency for a process to access items whose addresses are near one another (e.g., array elements, functions)

DESIGN FOR MEMORY HIERARCHY

- Assume that $h_0 = 0$, $h_n = 1$ ($h_3 = 1$ in our example)
- Access frequency:
  - $f_i = (1-h_1)(1-h_2)...(1-h_{i-1})h_i$
  - $sum_{i=1 \text{ to } n} (f_i) = 1$
  - $f_1 = h_1$
  - $f_1 >> f_2 >> f_3 >> ... >> f_n$
- *Goal:*

- Achieve as high a hit ratio as possible at M_1
- Effective access time of a memory hierarchy

- $T_{eff} = sum_{i=1 \text{ to } n} (f_i t_i)$
- $= h_1 t_1 + (1 - h_1) h_2 t_2 + (1 - h_1)(1 - h_2) h_3 t_3$
- *Cost:*
  - $sum_{i=1}{}^n (c_i s_i)$
- Given a cost budget, minimize T_{eff}
- *Constraints:*
  - s_i, t_i, $i=1, 2,..., n$
  - $C_{total} = sum_{i=1}{}^n (c_i s_i) < C_0$
- Linear programming
- Tradeoff among t_i, c_i, s_i, f_i, h_i

For a Memory Hierarchy of 3 Levels

	Access Time	Capacity	Cost/Kbyte	Hit ratio
Cache	$t_1 = 25ns$	$s_1 = 512K$	$c_1 = \$1.25$	0.9
Main Memory	$t_2 = ?$	$s_2 = 32M$	$c_2 = \$0.2$	0.98
Disk	$t_3 = 4ms$	$s_3 = ?$	$c_2 = \$0.0002$	

To achieve

- Total cost = \$15000
  - $c_{total} = c_1 s_1 + c_2 s_2 + c_3 s_3 <= 15000$
  - s_3 = 39.8Gbyte
- T_{eff} = 10.04us
  - $t = h_1 t_1 + (1-h_1) h_2 t_2 + (1-h_1)(1-h_2) h_3 t_3 <= 10.04$
  - t_2 = 20.6us
- If the capacity of M2 doubles: 32M → 64M
  - The capacity of M3 has to be decreased under the same cost
  - h_1 is the same
  - h_2 will be higher
  - T_{eff} will decrease

BASICS OF CACHES

- *Cache* was the name to represent the level of the memory hierarchy between the CPU and main memory
  - Also used to refer to any storage managed to take advantage of locality of access
- The concept of cache
- How do we know if a data item is in the cache? And if it is, how do we find it?
- The simplest cache structure is called *direct mapped*

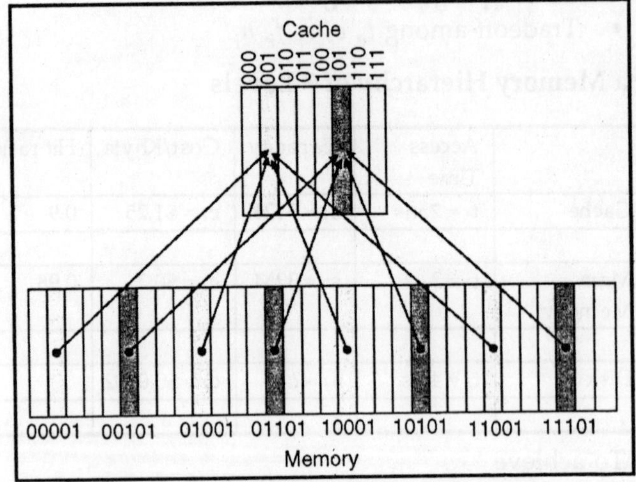

- The cache consists of
  - Data
  - *Tags:* to identify whether a word in the cache corresponds to the requested word.
  - *Valid bit:* to indicate whether an entry contains a valid address.
- The operation of cache access
- To take advantage of temporal locality: recently accessed words replace less recently referenced words
- Figure shows how a referenced address is divided into
  - A cache index (to select a block)

- A tag field (to compare with the value of the tag field of the cache)
- A valid bit

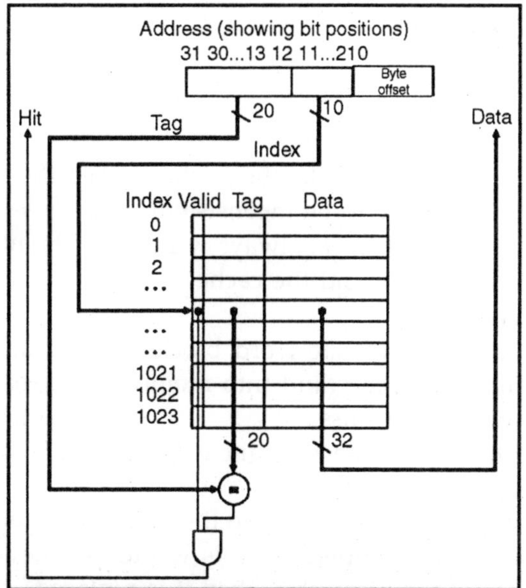

- Assume a 32-bit byte address, a direct-mapped cache of size 2^n words with one-word (4-byte) blocks will require.
  - A tag field whose size is 32 - (n+2) bits, the 2 bits are for the byte offset and n bits are for the index.
- The total number of bits in a direct-mapped cache is 2^n x (block size + tag size + valid field size)
  - The block size is one word (32 bits)
  - The address size is 32 bits
  - The number of bits is $2^n \times (32 + (32 - n - 2) + 1) = 2^n \times (63 - n)$
- For a direct-mapped cache with 64 KB of data and one-word blocks, assuming a 32-bit address
  - There are 2^{14} words
  - There are 2^{14} blocks
  - Each block has 32 bits of data with a tag of (32-14-2) bits and a valid bit

- The total cache size is 2^{14}x(32+(32-14-2)+1) = 2^{14}x49 = 784Kbits (about 98KB)
- About 1.5 times as for just the data storage

Cache Operations

- Read
  - Read miss
- Write
  - The write into the cache makes the cache and memory to be inconsistent
  - *Write-through*: always write the data into both the memory and the cache
- Write miss
- For cache of one-word blocks, just write the word into the cache (and into memory), regardless of the write hit or miss
- Reduce the performance due to the access of the memory
- *Write-back*: only to write the data to the cache
  - The modified block is written to the lower level of the hierarchy when it is replaced
  - Performance improvement
  - More complex control

Taking Advantage of Spatial Locality

- To take advantage of spatial locality, a cache block has to be larger than one word
- When a miss occurs, fetch multiple words that are adjacent and carry a high probability of being needed shortly
- Figure a cache that holds 64 KB of data, with blocks of four words (16 bytes) each.
  - An extra block index field is used to control the MUX
  - The total number of tags and valid bits is smaller (each tag and valid bit is used for four words)

A cache with 64 blocks and a block size of 16 bytes

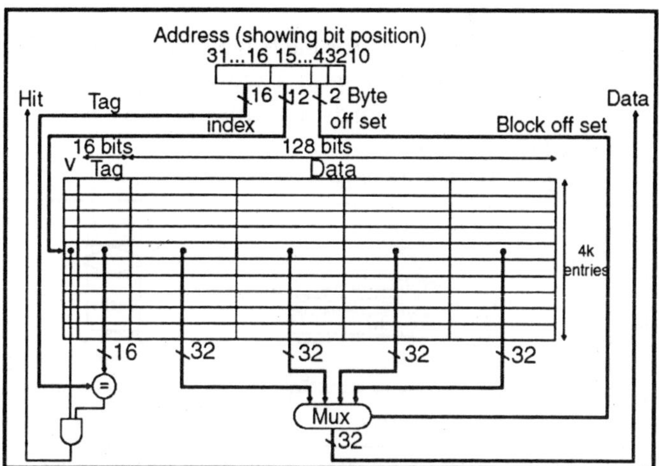

- For the cache with multi-word blocks
  - *Read miss:* brings back the entire block (the same as the cache with one-word blocks
  - *Write miss:* brings back the entire block and write the data
- Figure compares the miss rate of using one-word and 4-word blocks
- If the block size is increasing
  - The miss rate will decrease firstly due to the spatial locality
  - The miss rate will go up eventually if the block size becomes a significant fraction of the cache size
- The number of blocks will become small (when the cache size is fixed)
  - The miss penalty will increase as the blocks become larger.

MEMORY BUS ORGANIZATION

Cache misses result in the access from the main memory, which is constructed from DRAMs.

- One-word-wide memory organization
- The miss penalty (an example):
  - 1 clock cycle to send address

- 15 clock cycles for each DRAM access initiated
- 1 clock cycle to send a word of data

- For a block of 4 words, the miss penalty is

1 + 4 x (15+1) = 65

(4 x 4)/65 = 0.25 bytes/clk

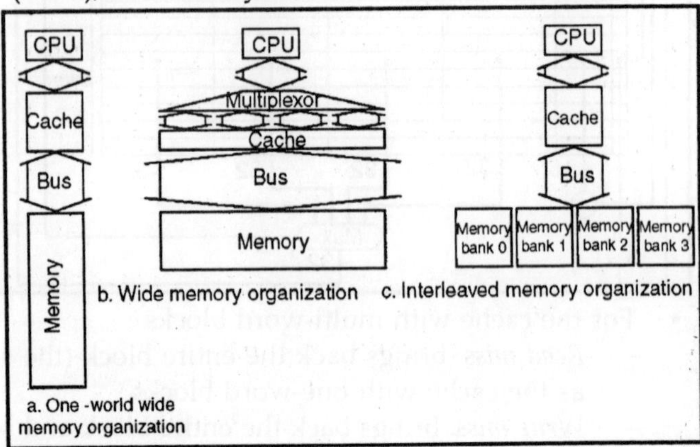

Wide Memory Organization

- Simply duplicate the bus by 2 or 4
  - 64-bit bus
  - 1 + 2 x (15 + 1) = 33
- (4x4)/33 = 0.48 bytes/clk
- 128-bit bus
- 1 + 1 x (15 + 1) = 17
- (4x4)/17 = 0.94 bytes/clk
- Access the data in parallel
- Cost/overhead
  - Wider bus
  - Increase the cache access time due to the multiplexor and its control

Interleaved Memory Organization

- Interleaving
  - Distribute the data into different banks with the same address
  - Once the address is applied, data can be read simultaneously

  - Since the bus retains the same width, data has to be transferred one by one
- Split the memory to 4 smaller ones
- Sent the address at the same time
- Access the data one by one
  - 1 + 1 x 15 + 4 x 1 = 20
  - (4 x 4)/20 = 0.8 bytes/clk
  - About three times the efficiency for the one-word-wide bus organization.

ADDRESS TRANSLATION

One of the amazing ideas we often use in developing computer software is to add "levels of indirection" to the processing. While we all know this doesn't improve their performance it often allows us to make changes without interfering with other software components that are using our resources.

Virtual Memory is a rather old idea, being first described in an academic paper in 1959. Since that time it has been rediscovered numerous times by various operating systems groups as they tried to find ways to avoid issues related to the amount of physical memory present in the system.

To do this, Windows divides up all the physical memory in the system into a series of pages (on the x86 architecture this is normally 4KB but driver writers should use the manifest constant PAGE_SIZE). It also divides up the virtual address space into a series of comparably sized pages as well. Finally, Windows and the underlying hardware platform agree upon a means to tell the hardware how to translate the address of a virtual page into a corresponding physical page.

Of course, since there is generally far less physical memory than there is virtual memory, part of this mechanism defines what the hardware should do if a virtual page is accessed but there is no translation defined to a physical page. In Windows terminology, this is defined to be a page fault.

When a page fault occurs, the hardware cannot do anything else with the instruction that caused the page fault and thus it must transfer control to an operating system routine (this is the page fault handler). The page fault handler must then decide how to handle the page fault. It can do one of two things: It can decide the virtual address is just simply not valid. In this case, Windows will report this error back by indicating an exception has occurred (typically STATUS_ACCESS_VIOLATION). It can decide the virtual address is valid. In this case, Windows will find an available physical page, place the correct data in that page, update the virtual-to-physical page translation mechanism and then tell the hardware to retry the operation. When the hardware retries the operation it will find the page translation and continue operations as if nothing had actually happened.

Once you have a virtual-to-physical page translation there's always the temptation to add features to it. So for all the Windows platforms each page can support specific types of access:

- User mode access. This access indicates if code running in user mode (that is the CPU operating mode with the least privilege, CPL 3 on the x86) can access the page. Code in kernel mode (that is the CPU operating mode with the most privilege, CPL 0 on the x86) can always access the page.
- Write access. This access indicates if code accessing the page is allowed to modify the contents of the virtual page. This applies to all running code.

If either of these two access restrictions is violated, the hardware transfers control to Windows so that Windows can hande the event properly. While Windows might throw this error back by raising a STATUS_ACCESS_VIOLATION it might also modify the page tables to resolve the problem.

The final "trick" here is that by telling the hardware to use different page tables at different times, we can substitute one set of virtual-to-physical translations for a different set of translations. Thus, when we switch from one process to a different process, we change the page tables. This means the new process has a different "virtual address space".

To summarize then, a page fault is nothing more than the computer hardware reporting to Windows that it either is not allowed to access the virtual page as requested by the running code (because of the access) or it cannot translate the virtual page to a physical page. In either case, it is Windows' responsibility to "do the right thing" and allow the system to continue running.

MEMORY ALLOCATION

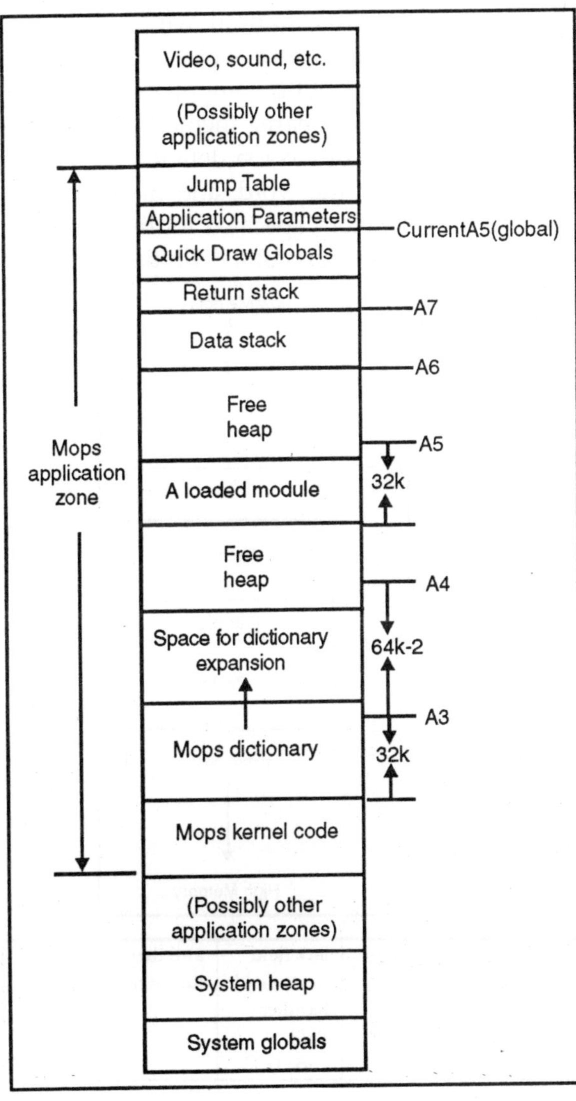

Because of the way the Macintosh manages memory, Mops has several distinct areas in which it stores data. The following diagram gives a typical picture of the Mac's memory while a Mops programme is running. If you're new to Mac programming, don't worry about what everything in the diagram means at this stage—we'll describe the main things you need to know as we go along. Near the beginning of this manual we said that a Mops programme builds a dictionary of words. Each word and its definition occupies a portion of the computer's memory. A Mops definition consists of several parts, including information like whether a word is a value or a colon definition, the numbers or other data associated with the word, and machine instructions which carry out the operations specified for that word. In Mops, the areas reserved for those parts of a definition are called fields.

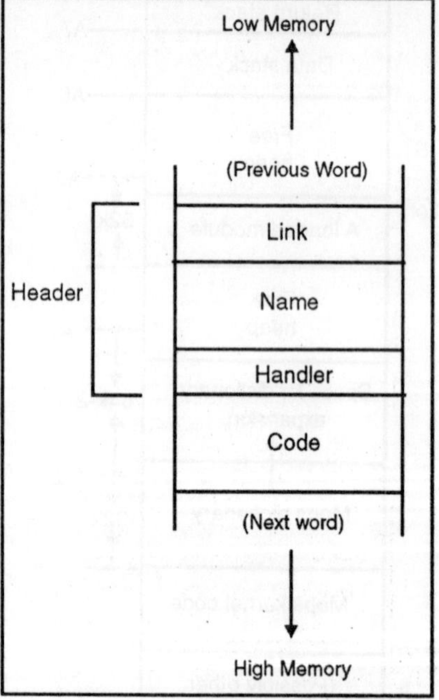

Most Mops words have four fields that you should be aware of:	link field name field handler field code field	and they look like this in memory:

The link, name and handler fields are usually grouped together as the header field. The name field holds the actual name of the word. Its length varies with the length of the name. The link field helps Mops programmes compile quickly. In the link field is the address of an earlier word in the dictionary. This facilitates the search through the dictionary each time you type a previously defined word.

The search starts at the most recently defined word (the word nearest high memory). If there is no match in the first word, the search looks to the link field for the address of the next word on which to attempt a match, and so on backward through the dictionary. The length of the name and parameter fields can change from definition to definition so there is not a fixed memory interval between words.

The content of the handler field specifies whether the word is a colon definition, a value, and so on. The handler field usually contains a negative integer, unique for each word type. When the word is compiled, the handler field is used to transfer control to the right part of the Mops compiler to compile words of this type.

For normal colon definitions, the code field contains executable code—the code that was compiled when the definition of that word was read by Mops. If you later type the word name at the keyboard, Mops looks at the handler field, sees that it is a colon definition, and transfers control to the beginning of the code field. Your compiled code is then executed. At the end of the definition, where you had put the semicolon, there is a machine language "return" (RTS) instruction. This causes control to return to the Mops interpreter.

If, instead of typing your word at the keyboard, you put it into another definition, the process is rather similar, except that instead of calling your definition directly, Mops compiles a machine language call instruction at that point, to do the calling.

For Mops word types other than colon definitions, the code field doesn't necessarily contain code. For example, for values and constants it contains the actual 4-byte value. In this case we call this field the "data field", since it contains data. But it is really the same field by a different name.

The Kernel or Nucleus

In the diagram, you'll see that above some memory areas used by the Mac system is the Mops kernel code. The kernel (also known as nucleus) is the lowest, most elemental part of the Mops dictionary-that part of Mops without any predefined classes. It is what is loaded into memory when you double-click the Mops application icon itself. Saved Mops images, such as Mops.dic, appear to the Finder as documents with Mops as their owner.

Therefore, when you open a saved Mops image, the Finder starts the Mops kernel as the application, and passes the name of the saved image file to the Mops kernel as a parameter. The Mops kernel then determines whether the file is a valid Mops image file, and, if so, loads it in an area of memory above the kernel. (This way of doing things is very efficient for development, since the image saved is the document you have been working on. You may save many variations of this document without changing the application itself). With PowerMops we're abandoning the idea of separate nucleus and dictionary files.

This came from a time when everything had to fit on a floppies, and would have added pointless complexity to the PowerMops architecture. So now, when you do a save, you get a new application generated, which has everything in it, and you just doubleclick on that to relaunch it. The memory area dedicated to the Mops kernel and other specifics of your programme is known as the application heap, or simply theheap.

THE HEAP

The heap is a region of memory that can be divided into smaller sections, called blocks. When a programme needs some memory temporarily, it can ask the Macintosh Memory Manager for a block of heap, and later give it back when it is done. This is what the Mops kernel does at startup in order to acquire memory for future expansion of the Mops dictionary. Mops requests a block of heap that will be large enough to allow for expansion of the user dictionary, but will leave enough room for both the system and Mops to use on a temporary basis (dynamic heap) as the programme executes. Many parts of Mops and the Mac Operating System rely upon dynamic heap. For instance, when your application requires a resource, such as a font, to be loaded from disk, the Font Manager places the font in the dynamic heap.

Mops modules (described below) are loaded into the dynamic heap, and any class can be told to create an object whose data exists on the dynamic heap instead of in the dictionary. Whenever you see a System Error 25, it usually means that heap has become used up or fragmented. You can remedy this situation either by leaving more dynamic heap with the Install utility or by being more careful to release the heap used by your application's modules or heap objects once they are no longer needed. The Mops dictionary can grow until it exhausts its allotted block of heap. The Mops word ROOM will return the amount in bytes of available dictionary space at any time.

STACKS

The two Mops stacks-data (parameter) and return stacks-are allocated above the application heap. Both grow downward: the return stack grows towards the base of the data stack. The Mops kernel allocates room for 1500 32-bit cells on the return stack. The data stack is limited only by the maximum address to which the heap is permitted to grow, and is allocated about 50000 in the distributed Mops system. Macintosh Toolbox routines allocate their local variables on the stack, which accounts for the relatively large size of the data stack.

Various system errors can be caused by one of the stacks growing beyond its bounds. This type of error can be difficult to detect, but you should be particularly alert for return stack problems when writing recursive routines. The return stack also gets heavy use when you use a lot of named parameters and/or local variables in your methods or Mops words, since the previous values of these quantities are saved on the return stack. The data stack is used not only by Mops, but also by the Toolbox when you invoke one of its routines. Toolbox routines allocate their local data and do parameter passing on the system stack, which is actually the same as the Mops data stack. This makes the Mops/Toolbox interface fairly easy.

RELOCATABLE AND ABSOLUTE

For speed, we normally hold all addresses in the normal Mac form (which we'll call absolute since its the actual address which is directly used by the hardware). This does mean, however, that we have to do some juggling to handle addresses that are stored in the dictionary and then saved in a dictionary image which is reloaded later. In general, these addresses won't be valid any longer, since the programme may well be located at a different place in memory.

For this kind of operation we have defined a relocatable address format, and the words @abs and reloc! to respectively fetch and store a relocatable address with conversion to/from absolute. We have also provided two classes, DicAddr and X-Addr which use the relocatable format internally. (DicAddr is for addresses of data, and X-Addr for executable word addresses.) These have access methods that incorporate the conversion. You should always use one of these mechanisms for accessing relocatable addresses. Note that relocatable conversion does not need to be done nearly as often as , so that we really do gain by standardizing on absolute addresses.

HANDLES AND POINTERS

Handles and pointers are fundamental to programming on the Mac, relying as it does on dynamic allocation and reallocation of memory for flexibility. When you allocate a block of memory in the heap, you can ask for either a Handle or a Pointer. A pointer points directly at the memory you allocated (i.e. it contains the address of that block of memory), while a handle points at what is called a Master Pointer, which is what actually points to the memory. Briefly, using a handle allows the Memory Manager to move the block of memory around, and thus allow memory to be used more efficiently. When the Memory Manager moves a block of memory, it updates the master pointer so that programmes can still know where the block of memory is, since the programme knows the address of the master pointer, and that doesn't change. However, blocks accessed via a pointer can't be moved, since the Memory Manager has no way of knowing where the pointer. In Mops, we used to encourage the use of handles rather than pointers, since the ability of handle-based blocks of memory to move around made memory allocation in a small memory space easier. But today's machines have so much memory that the extra housekeeping associated with handles is usually not worth the trouble—this is why the new Reference feature uses pointer-based blocks of memory.

Both handles and pointers are objects, with appropriate methods defined for them. If you want to do a number of operations quickly on a block of memory allocated via a handle, you may lock it in memory so the Memory Manager won't move it while you are accessing it. You may then retrieve the actual address of the block, and know that it will remain valid until you unlock the block. The methods lock: and unlock: of class Handle perform this function.

An accidental clobbering of a handle or pointer can produce a bug that can have very nasty and generally unrepeatable results, and be very hard to track down. Making them objects helps discourage doing dangerous things with them, and also allows a degree of error checking. An unallocated handle or pointer object is given a value which should always cause a trap if it is used as an address. (The actual values we use in 68k Mops are $ FFA00101 for unallocated handles, and $ FFA00103 for unallocated pointers. These two values are defined as constants with the names NilH and NilP respectively). As we have seen, you may define objects which are created in memory allocated on the heap, with a reference or a pointer or a handle pointing to them. String variables (String, String+, Bytestring) are based on Handles, and are therefore able to grow and shrink as required, since the memory they occupy is allocated dynamically.

CACHE MEMORY

Computer memory is organized into a hierarchy. At the highest level (closest to the processor) are the processor registers. Next comes one or more levels of cache. When multiple levels are used, they are denoted L1, L2, etc... Next comes main memory, which is usually made out of a dynamic random-access memory (DRAM). All of these are considered internal to the computer system. The hierarchy continues with external memory, with the next level typically being a fixed hard disk, and one or more levels below that consisting of removable media such as ZIP cartridges, optical disks, and tape. As one goes down the memory hierarchy, one finds decreasing cost/bit, increasing capacity, and slower access time. It would be nice to use only the fastest memory, but because that is the most expensive memory, we trade off access time and cost by using more of the slower memory. The trick is to organize the data and programmes in memory so that the memory words needed are usually in the fastest memory. In general, it is likely that most future accesses to main memory by the processor will be to locations recently accesses. So the cache automatically retains a copy of some of the recently used words from the DRAM. If the cache is designed properly, then most of the time the processor will request memory words that are already in the cache.

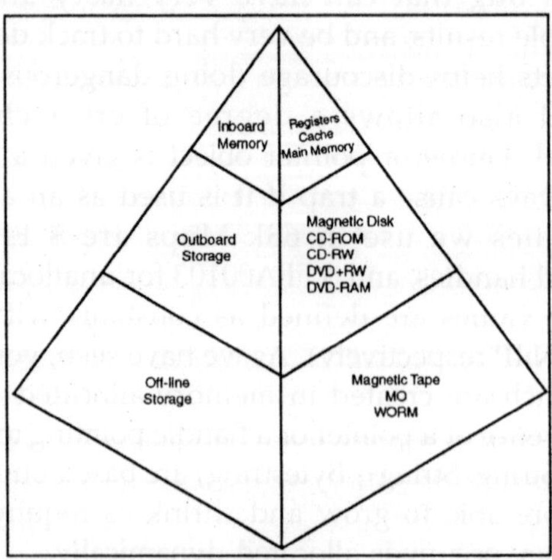

As one goes down the hierarchy: (a) decreasing cost per bit; (b) increasing capacity; (c) increasing access time; (d) decreasing frequency of access of the memory by the processor. Thus smaller, more expensive, faster memories are supplemented by larger, cheaper, slower memories. The key to the success of this organization is item (d). Locality of Reference principle.

- Memory references by the processor, for both data and instructions, cluster
- Programmes contain iterative loops and subroutines once a loop or subroutine is entered, there are repeated references to a small set of instructions
- Operations on tables and arrays involve access to a clustered set of data word Cache Operation Overview
- Processor requests the contents of some memory location
- The cache is checked for the requested data
  - If found, the requested word is delivered to the processor
  - If not found, a block of main memory is first read into the cache, then the requested word is delivered to the processor.

When a block of data is fetched into the cache to satisfy a single memory reference, it is likely that there will be future references to that same memory location or to other words in the block – locality or reference principle. Each block has a tag added to identify it.

ELEMENTS OF CACHE DESIGN

Cache Size

- Small enough so overall cost/bit is close to that of main memory
- Large enough so overall average access time is close to that of the cache alone
  - Access time = main memory access time plus cache access time
- Large caches tend to be slightly slower than small caches

Mapping Function

An algorithm is needed to map main memory blocks into cache lines. A method is needed to determine which main memory block occupies a cache line. Three techniques used: direct, associative, and set associative. Assume the following:

- Cache of 64 Kbytes
- Transfers between main memory and cache are in blocks of 4 bytes each – cache organized as 16K = 2^14 lines of 4 bytes each
- Main memory of 16 Mbytes, directly addressable by a 24-bit address (where 2^24 = 16M) – main memory consists of 4M blocks of 4 bytes each

Direct Mapping

- Each block of main memory maps to only one cache line
  - Cache line #" = "main memory block #"% "number of lines in cache"
- Main memory addresses are viewed as three fields
  - Least significant w bits identify a unique word or byte within a block
  - Most significant s bits specify one of the 2^s blocks of main memory

Tag field of s-r bits (most significant) Line field of r bits – identifies one of the m = 2^r lines of the cache

Direct Mapping Cache Organization

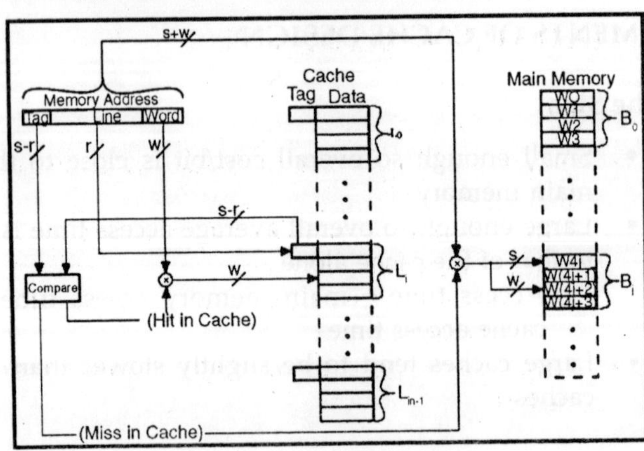

Direct Mapping Summary

- Address length = (s+w) bits
- Number of addressable units = 2^(s+w) words or bytes
- Block size = line size = 2^w words or bytes
- Number of blocks in main memory = 2^(s+w)/2^w = 2^s
- Number of lines in cache = m = 2^r
- Size of tag = (s-r) bits

Direct Mapping Pros and Cons

- Simple
- Inexpensive
- Fixed location for a given block
  - If a programme accesses two blocks that map to the same line repeatedly, then cache misses are very high.

Associative Mapping

- A main memory block can be loaded into any line of the cache
- A memory address is interpreted as a tag and a word field
- The tag field uniquely identifies a block of main memory
- Each cache line's tag is examined simultaneously to determine if a block is in cache

Associative Mapping

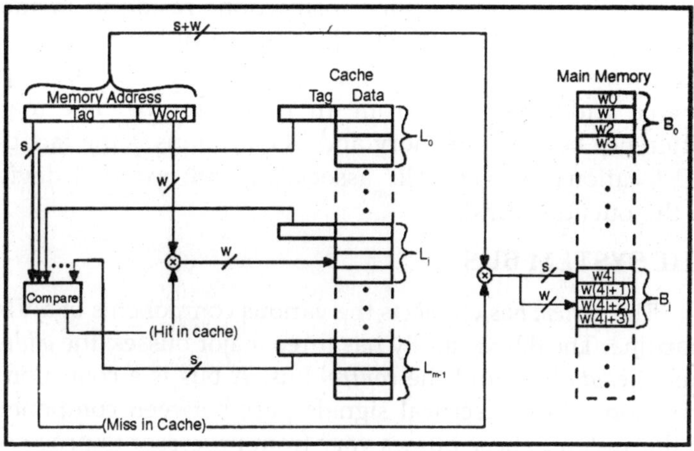

Chapter 7

System Organization

BASIC SYSTEM COMPONENTS

The basic operational design of a computer system is called its *architecture*. John Von Neumann, a pioneer in computer design, is given credit for the architecture of most computers in use today. For example, the 80x86 family uses the *Von Neumann architecture* (VNA). A typical Von Neumann system has three major components: the *central processing unit* (or *CPU*), *memory*, and *input/output* (or *I/O*). The way a system designer combines these components impacts system performance.

In VNA machines, like the 80x86 family, the CPU is where all the action takes place. All computations occur inside the CPU. Data and machine instructions reside in memory until required by the CPU. To the CPU, most I/O devices look like memory because the CPU can store data to an output device and read data from an input device. The major difference between memory and I/O locations is the fact that I/O locations are generally associated with external devices in the outside world.

THE SYSTEM BUS

The *system bus* connects the various components of a VNA machine. The 80x86 family has three major busses: the *address* bus, the*data* bus, and the *control* bus. A bus is a collection of wires on which electrical signals pass between components in the system. These busses vary from processor to processor. However, each bus carries comparable information on all processors; e.g., the data bus may have a different implementation on the 80386 than on the 8088, but both carry data between the processor, I/O, and memory.

A typical 80x86 system component uses *standard TTL logic levels*[1]. This means each wire on a bus uses a standard voltage level to represent zero and one[2]. We will always specify zero and one rather than the electrical levels because these levels vary on different processors (especially laptops).

The Data Bus

The 80x86 processors use the *data bus* to shuffle data between the various components in a computer system. The size of this bus varies widely in the 80x86 family. Indeed, this bus defines the "size" of the processor.

Every modern x86 CPU from the Pentium on up employs a 64-bit wide data bus. Some of the earlier processors used 8-bit, 16-bit, or 32-bit data busses, but such machines are sufficiently obsolete that we do not need to consider them here.

You'll often hear a processor called an *eight, 16, 32, or 64 bit processor*. While there is a mild controversy concerning the size of a processor, most people now agree that the minimum of either the number of data lines on the processor or the size of the largest general purpose integer register determines the processor size. The modern x86 CPUs all have 64-bit busses, but only provide 32-bit general purpose integer registers, so most people classify these devices as 32-bit processors.

Although the 80x86 family members with eight, 16, 32, and 64 bit data busses *can* process data up to the width of the bus, they can also access smaller memory units of eight, 16, or 32 bits. Therefore, anything you can do with a small data bus can be done with a larger data bus as well; the larger data bus, however, may access memory faster and can access larger chunks of data in one memory operation.

Address Bus

The data bus on an 80x86 family processor transfers information between a particular memory location or I/O device and the CPU. The only question is, *"Which memory location or I/*

O device? " The address bus answers that question. To differentiate memory locations and I/O devices, the system designer assigns a unique memory address to each memory element and I/O device. When the software wants to access some particular memory location or I/O device, it places the corresponding address on the address bus. Circuitry associated with the memory or I/O device recognizes this address and instructs the memory or I/O device to read the data from or place data on to the data bus. In either case, all other memory locations ignore the request. Only the device whose address matches the value on the address bus responds.

With a single address line, a processor could create exactly two unique addresses: zero and one. With *n* address lines, the processor can provide 2^n unique addresses (since there are 2^n unique values in an *n*-bit binary number). Therefore, the number of bits on the address bus will determine the *maximum* number of addressable memory and I/O locations. Early x86 processors, for example, provided only 20 bit address busses. Therefore, they could only access up to 1,048,576 (or 2^{20}) memory locations. Larger address busses can access more memory.

Table: 80x86 Family Address Bus Sizes			
Processor	**Address Bus Size**	**Max Addressable Memory**	**In English!**
8088, 8086, 80186, 80188	20	1,048,576	One Megabyte
80286, 80386sx	24	16,777,216	Sixteen Megabytes
80386dx	32	4,294,976,296	Four Gigabytes
80486, Pentium	32	4,294,976,296	Four Gigabytes
Pentium Pro, II, III, IV	36	68,719,476,736	64 Gigabytes

Future 80x86 processors (e.g., the AMD "Hammer") will probably support 40, 48, and 64-bit address busses. The time is coming when most programmers will consider four gigabytes of storage to be too small, much like they consider one megabyte insufficient today.

Control Bus

The control bus is an eclectic collection of signals that control how the processor communicates with the rest of the system. Consider for a moment the data bus. The CPU sends data to memory and receives data from memory on the data bus. This prompts the question, "Is it sending or receiving?" There are two lines on the control bus, *read* and *write*, which specify the direction of data flow. Other signals include system clocks, interrupt lines, status lines, and so on. The exact make up of the control bus varies among processors in the 80x86 family. However, some control lines are common to all processors and are worth a brief mention. The *read* and *write* control lines control the direction of data on the data bus. When both contain a logic one, the CPU and memory-I/O are not communicating with one another. If the read line is low (logic zero), the CPU is reading data from memory (that is, the system is transferring data from memory to the CPU). If the write line is low, the system transfers data from the CPU to memory. The *byte enable lines* are another set of important control lines. These control lines allow 16, 32, and 64 bit processors to deal with smaller chunks of data.

The 80x86 family, unlike many other processors, provides two distinct address spaces: one for memory and one for I/O. While the memory address busses on various 80x86 processors vary in size, the I/O address bus on all 80x86 CPUs is 16 bits wide. This allows the processor to address up to 65,536 different I/O *locations*. As it turns out, most devices (like the keyboard, printer, disk drives, etc.) require more than one I/O location. Nonetheless, 65,536 I/O locations are more than sufficient for most applications. The original IBM PC design only allowed the use of 1,024 of these.

THE MEMORY SUBSYSTEM

A typical 80x86 processor addresses a maximum of 2^n

different memory locations, where *n* is the number of bits on the address bus[1]. As you've seen already, 80x86 processors have 20, 24, 32, and 36 bit address busses (with 64 bits on the way).

Of course, the first question you should ask is, "What exactly is a memory location?" The 80x86 supports *byte addressable memory*. Therefore, the basic memory unit is a byte. So with 20, 24, 32, and 36 address lines, the 80x86 processors can address one megabyte, 16 megabytes, four gigabytes, and 64 gigabytes of memory, respectively.

Think of memory as a linear array of bytes. The address of the first byte is zero and the address of the last byte is 2^n-1. For an 8088 with a 20 bit address bus, the following pseudo-Pascal array declaration is a good approximation of memory:

Memory: array [0..1048575] of byte;

To execute the equivalent of the Pascal statement "Memory [125]:= 0;" the CPU places the value zero on the data bus, the address 125 on the address bus, and asserts the write line (since the CPU is writing data to memory).

To execute the equivalent of "CPU:= Memory [125];" the CPU places the address 125 on the address bus, asserts the read line (since the CPU is reading data from memory), and then reads the resulting data from the data bus.

The above discussion applies *only* when accessing a single byte in memory. So what happens when the processor accesses a word or a double word? Since memory consists of an array of bytes, how can we possibly deal with values larger than eight bits?

Different computer systems have different solutions to this problem. The 80x86 family deals with this problem by storing the L.O. byte of a word at the address specified and the H.O. byte at the next location. Therefore, a word consumes two consecutive memory addresses (as you would expect, since a word consists of two bytes). Similarly, a double word consumes four consecutive memory locations. The address for the double word is the address of its L.O. byte. The remaining three bytes follow this L.O. byte, with the H.O. byte appearing at the address of the double word *plus three.* Bytes, words, and double words may begin at *any* valid address in memory. We will soon see, however, that starting larger objects at an arbitrary address is not a good idea.

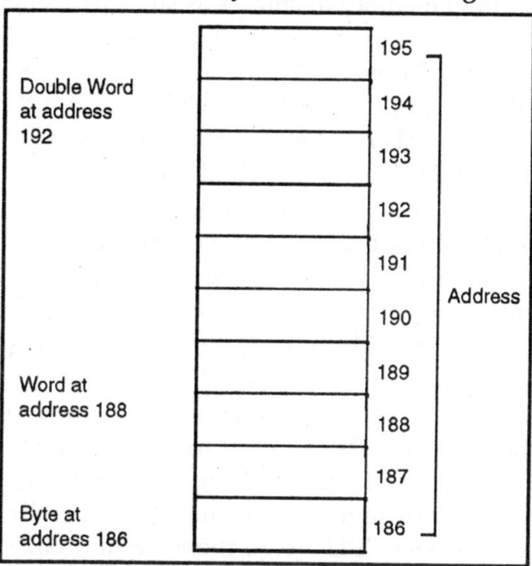

Fig. Byte, Word, and DWord Storage in Memory

Note that it is quite possible for byte, word, and double word values to overlap in memory. For example, in Figure you could have a word variable beginning at address 193, a byte variable at address 194, and a double word value beginning at address 192. These variables would all overlap.

A processor with an eight-bit bus (like the old 8088 CPU) can transfer eight bits of data at a time. Since each memory address corresponds to an eight bit byte, this turns out to be the most convenient arrangement (from the hardware perspective),.

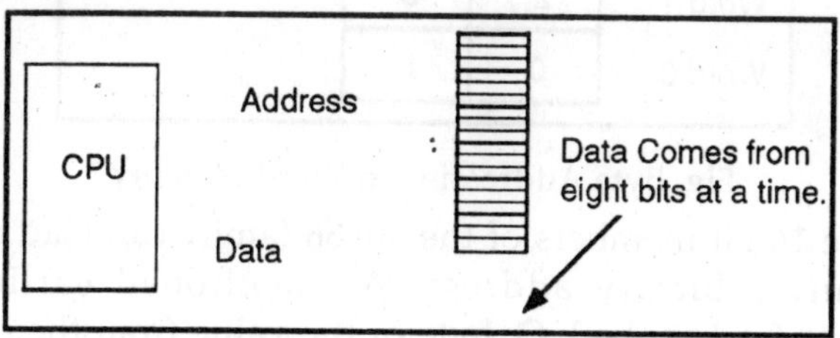

Fig. Eight-Bit CPU ↔ Memory Interface

The term "byte addressable memory array" means that the CPU can address memory in chunks as small as a single byte. It also means that this is the *smallest* unit of memory you can access at once with the processor. That is, if the processor wants to access a four bit value, it must read eight bits and then ignore the extra four bits. Also realise that byte addressability does not imply that the CPU can access eight bits on any arbitrary bit boundary. When you specify address 125 in memory, you get the entire eight bits at that address, nothing less, nothing more. Addresses are integers; you cannot, for example, specify address 125.5 to fetch fewer than eight bits.

CPUs with an eight-bit bus can manipulate word and double word values, even through their data bus is only eight bits wide. However, this requires multiple memory operations because these processors can only move eight bits of data at once. To load a word requires two memory operations; to load a double word requires four memory operations.

Some older x86 CPUs (e.g., the 8086 and 80286) have a 16 bit data bus. This allows these processors to access twice as much memory in the same amount of time as their eight bit brethren. These processors organize memory into two *banks*: an "even" bank and an "odd" bank figure illustrates the connection to the CPU (D0-D7 denotes the L.O. byte of the data bus, D8-D15 denotes the H.O. byte of the data bus):

	Even	Odd
Word 3	6	7
Word 2	4	5
Word 1	2	3
Word 0	0	1

Numbers in Cells represent the byte addresses

Fig. Byte Addressing in Word Memory

The 16 bit members of the 80x86 family can load a word from any arbitrary address. As mentioned earlier, the processor fetches the L.O. byte of the value from the address specified and the H.O. byte from the next consecutive address.

This creates a subtle problem if you look closely at the diagram above. What happens when you access a word on an odd address? Suppose you want to read a word from location 125. Okay, the L.O. byte of the word comes from location 125 and the H.O. word comes from location 126. What's the big deal? It turns out that there are two problems with this approach.

First, look again at Figure. Data bus lines eight through 15 (the H.O. byte) connect to the odd bank, and data bus lines zero through seven (the L.O. byte) connect to the even bank. Accessing memory location 125 will transfer data to the CPU on the H.O. byte of the data bus; yet we want this data in the L.O. byte! Fortunately, the 80x86 CPUs recognize this situation and automatically transfer the data on D8-D15 to the L.O. byte.

The second problem is even more obscure. When accessing words, we're really accessing two separate bytes, each of which has its own byte address. So the question arises, "What address appears on the address bus?" The 16 bit 80x86 CPUs always place even addresses on the bus. Even bytes always appear on data lines D0-D7 and the odd bytes always appear on data lines D8-D15.

If you access a word at an even address, the CPU can bring in the entire 16 bit chunk in one memory operation. Likewise, if you access a single byte, the CPU activates the appropriate bank (using a "byte enable" control line). If the byte appeared at an odd address, the CPU will automatically move it from the H.O. byte on the bus to the L.O. byte.

So what happens when the CPU accesses a *word* at an odd address, like the example given earlier? Well, the CPU cannot place the address 125 onto the address bus and read the 16 bits from memory. There are no odd addresses coming out of a 16 bit 80x86 CPU. The addresses are always even.

So if you try to put 125 on the address bus, this will put 124 on to the address bus. Were you to read the 16 bits at this address, you would get the word at addresses 124 (L.O. byte) and 125 (H.O. byte) - not what you'd expect. Accessing a word at an odd address requires two memory operations. First the CPU must read the byte at address 125, then it needs to read the byte at address 126. Finally, it needs to swap the positions of these bytes internally since both entered the CPU on the wrong half of the data bus. Fortunately, the 16 bit 80x86 CPUs hide these details from you. Your programmes can access words at *any* address and the CPU will properly access and swap (if necessary) the data in memory. However, to access a word at an odd address requires two memory operations (just like the 8088/80188). Therefore, accessing words at odd addresses on a 16 bit processor is slower than accessing words at even addresses. By carefully arranging how you use memory, you can improve the speed of your programme on these CPUs.

Accessing 32 bit quantities always takes at least two memory operations on the 16 bit processors. If you access a 32 bit quantity at an odd address, a 16-bit processor will require three memory operations to access the data. The 80x86 processors with a 32-bit data bus (e.g., the 80386 and 80486) use four banks of memory connected to the 32 bit data bus. The address placed on the address bus is always some multiple of four. Using various "byte enable" lines, the CPU can select which of the four bytes at that address the software wants to access.

As with the 16 bit processor, the CPU will automatically rearrange bytes as necessary. With a 32 bit memory interface, the 80x86 CPU can access any byte with one memory operation. If (address MOD 4) does not equal three, then a 32 bit CPU can access a word at that address using a single memory operation. However, if the remainder is three, then it will take two memory operations to access that word. This is the same problem encountered with the 16 bit processor, except it occurs half as often.

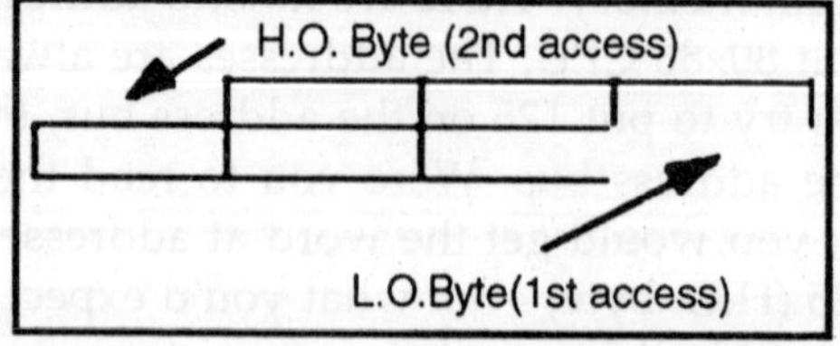

Fig. Accessing a Word at (Address mod 4) = 3.

A 32 bit CPU can access a double word in a single memory operation *if* the address of that value is evenly divisible by four. If not, the CPU will require two memory operations. Once again, the CPU handles all of this automatically. In terms of loading correct data the CPU handles everything for you. However, there is a performance benefit to proper data alignment. As a general rule you should always place word values at even addresses and double word values at addresses which are evenly divisible by four. This will speed up your programme.

The Pentium and later processors provide a 64-bit bit data bus and special cache memory that reduces the impact of non-aligned data access. Although there may still be a penalty for accessing data at an inappropriate address, modern x86 CPUs suffer from the problem.

THE I/O SUBSYSTEM

Besides the 20, 24, or 32 address lines which access memory, the 80x86 family provides a 16 bit I/O address bus. This gives the 80x86 CPUs two separate address spaces: one for memory and one for I/O operations. Lines on the control bus differentiate between memory and I/O addresses. Other than separate control lines and a smaller bus, I/O addressing behaves exactly like memory addressing. Memory and I/O devices both share the same data bus and the L.O. 16 lines on the address bus. There are three limitations to the I/O subsystem on the PC: first, the 80x86 CPUs require special instructions to access I/O devices; second, the designers of the PC used the "best" I/O locations for their own purposes, forcing third party developers to use less accessible locations; third, 80x86 systems can address no more than 65,536 (2^{16}) I/O addresses. When you consider that a typical video display card requires over eight megabytes of addressable locations, you can see a problem with the size of I/O bus. Fortunately, hardware designers can map their I/O devices into the memory address space as easily as they can the I/O address space. So by using the appropriate circuitry, they can make their I/O devices look just like memory. This is how, for example, display adapters on the PC work.

Chapter 8

Introduction to 8085

OVERVIEW

A microprocessor is an electronic device that reads instructions from memory, accepts binary data and provides output after processing data according to the instructions. You can say its function is just like human brain. Basically microprocessor consists of three important units: input unit, output unit and a memory unit.

8085 is a 8-bit microprocessor. Here the data is usually 8 bit and the address is 16 bit. Let's analyse the each and every components of 8085 microprocessor.

- Register section
- ALU
- The buses
- Timing & Control unit
- Register section

It consists of number of registers for storing dataand addresses.

It can be of two types:

- General purpose regi'sters
- Special purpose registers

General purpose registers are used for temporary storage of data or address during execution. They are B, C, D, E, H and L. They are all 8 bit registers. So, to store 16 bit data we have to form a register pair like: BC, DE or HL.

- *Special purpose registers*: The following registers come under this category and each performing a special function.

- *Accumulator (A)*: It is a 8 bit register which is used for storing the operands/data during execution.
- *Programme counter (PC):* It is a 16 bit register used to store the memory address of the next instruction to be executed.
- *Index register:* This is used for addressing index addressing mode.
- *Status register:* It stores the present status of the microprocessor after any arithmetic and logical operation. It records any occurrence of carry, auxiliary carry, sign, zero and odd/even parity.
- *Stack pointer:* It is a 16 bit register used to initialize the stack.
- *Instruction register:* It is a 8 bit register that stores the instruction fetched from memory
- *Arithmetic and Logical Unit (ALU):* It performs arithmetic and logical operations. Addition, subtraction, multiplication, division, AND, OR, XOR, NOT, shift and rotate operations are done by ALU.
- *The Buses:* It is the interface section for communication between processor and external devices.

There are 3 buses:

- *Address bus:* It carries the address of the instruction. It is 16 bit wide and unidirectional.
- *Data bus:* It carries data between external devices and processor. It is 8 bit wide and bidirectional.
- *Control bus:* It is used to send control signals to different units of microprocessor.

GENERAL DESCRIPTION

The Intel 8085 microprocessor is an NMOS 8-bit device. Sixteen address bits provide access to 65,536 bytes of 8 bits each. Eight bi-directional data lines provide access to a system data bus. Control is provided by a variety of lines which support memory and I/O interfacing, and a flexible interrupt system.

The 8085 provides an upward mobility in design from the 8080 by supporting all of the 8080's instruction set and interrupt capabilities. At the same time, it provides cleaner designs by virtue of a greater on-device component density, and by requiring only a 5 volt supply. In addition, the 8085 is available in two clock speeds.

The 8085 comes in two models, the 8085A and the 8085A-2. The 8085A expects a main clock frequency of 3 MHz, while the 8085A-2 expects a main clock frequency of 5 MHz. In both cases, the clock is a single phase square wave. This single clock is generated within the 8085 itself, requiring only a crystal externally. This eliminates the need for an external clock generator device. In all other respects, the A and A-2 devices are identical.

The 8085 supports the interrupt structure of the 8080, including the RST instruction and the eight vectors. It extends these by the addition of four more interrupts, each with their own pins, three of which are maskable, and which use vector areas between the existing ones of the 8080. The 8085 is adaptable for use with the 8259 Priority Interrupt Controller, a programmable device. It is possible, upon an interrupt from this device, to jam either a RST instruction onto the data lines, or a CALL instruction to any location in RAM directly.

The 8085 has two pins dedicated to the generation or reception of serial data. While these do not constitute a complete serial I/O system, they do allow the MP to send and receive serial bits, albeit with a large software overhead. The 8085 therefore finds itself useful as a complete control device for remote control applications.

The 8085 supports the entire 8080 instruction set. In addition, two new instructions are added. These instructions permit software control over the extended interrupt capabilities of the '85, by making the new interrupts both maskable and interrogatable. The masks can be set, examined, etc.. The same instructions also allow investigation of the serial input line, and generation of conditions on the serial output line.

Unlike the 8080 which had discrete pins for the address and data busses, the 8085 make use of multiplexing of the lower 8 bits of the address with the data bits on the same 8 pins. This requires that the external circuitry be able to catch and hold the A0-A7 lines for later use. The upper 8 bits of the address have their own pins, however. Three primary control bus lines allow the device to identify whether the cycle in progress is for RAM or I/O, and whether it is a Read or a Write. Two status pins are provided, to allow advance knowledge of certain events in multiprocessor applications.

The internal timing of the device makes use of machine cycles in which, in almost every case, a bus cycle is involved. Each machine cycle consists of several T-states, which are defined by the clock input signal. Thus, many clock cycles are needed to effect one complete instruction.

The 8085 has many new support devices to ease design work. These include the 8259 Programmable Interrupt controller, the 8202 Dynamic RAM controller, plus several new I/O devices with various amounts of RAM, ROM, parallel I/O, and timer-counters. The general approach was to make the device as compatible with the Multibus architecture as possible.

DATA FLOW

Locate the dataflow diagram in your reference manual. The dataflow of the 8085 is made up of the following units:

- A General Purpose Register Array, most of which is accessible by the programmer, and which forms the essential data manipulation ability of the system;
- An address generation system consisting of the Programme Counter, Stack Pointer, address latches, and incrementer/decrementer. Two additional 8-bit latches are provided. The first, labeled Address Buffer, provides the upper byte of an address to the system address bus in a straight-through manner. The second, labeled Data/Address Buffer, provides the lower byte of the address early in a machine cycle; it is used later in the cycle to provide or accept an 8-bit data byte from the internal data bus of the MP to the system data bus, or from the system data bus to the MP's data bus. This buffer therefore provides the AD0 - AD7 multiplexed address/data function mentioned above.

- A mathematical and logical subsystem composed of the Arithmetic Logic Unit (ALU) and asSOciated registers, which handle the math and logic functions of the machine;
- An Instruction Register and decoder system which interpret the programmer's instructions and implement them via nanocode;
- A timing and control package which provides the bodily functions of power and clock circuits, and handles the wait, interrupt, and hold functions of the system;
- An 8-bit internal data bus, which provides the data path between functional elements, and to the outside world via the Address/Data Buffer;
- Interrupt control interfacing which provides both the standard 8080 interrupt structure, and 4 new interrupts which are maskable under special programme controls, these last via the internal data bus;
- Two serial data lines, Serial Input Data and Serial Output Data, which feed the internal data bus directly, and are serviced as part of the interrupt control structure mentioned above.

The General Purpose Register Array contains the B, C, D, E, H, and L registers, each 8 bits wide. The B and C, D and E, and H and L registers may be grouped into 16-bit register pairs. The H&L register pair may be used to store indirect addresses. The array also contains the Programme Counter (PC) and Stack Pointer (SP). These 16-bit registers contain the address of the next instruction part to be fetched, and the address of the top of the stack, respectively.

The GPR array also includes an Address Latch/Incrementer-Decrementer circuit, to make the address next required on the system address bus available to it, and to increment or decrement addresses or register contents as required. The mathematical and logical function of the system are provided by an 8-bit Arithmetic-Logic Unit (ALU), which accepts two 8-bit arguments and generates an 8-bit result. It is fed by an Accumulator register and a Temporary register, both 8 bits wide; the result returns to the internal data bus for distribution. The ALU also has a Condition Flags register, for the storage of the conditions under which an operation ended, which may be used by following instructions. In all cases, the ALU, Accumulator, and Condition Flags function exactly as in the 8080. The Instruction Register and Instruction Decoder accept the incoming byte from the data bus during the first machine cycle of an instruction, and interpret it by controlling the internal reSOurces of the MP as SOurces and destinations for bits and bytes. The 8085 is nanoprogram-controlled.

Acting under the direction of the instructions, the Timing and Control section of the 8085 generates the necessary timing pulses to synchronize their execution. The 8085 has its own internal oscillator, which requires only an external crystal to generate the clocks. The internal workings of the '85 require only a single phase clock, with a 50% duty cycle, which minimizes system timing requirements. This clock is made available to the outside world to allow external functions to be synchronized to the MP's cycles.

READY

Wait functions are provided in the '85. If a memory circuit's response time is such that the MP will expect data before the RAM is ready to respond, the memory subsystem may request a Wait State (Tw) by pulling the Ready line low. This must be done prior to a certain point in the machine cycle. This function is important because the '85 is designed to work at 3 MHz, decreasing the time within which the RAM may respond.

The Timing and Control section of the '85 also provides several native signals, both inbound and outbound, which interface with the external world, and provide control signals and timing to the three-bus architecture. This makes way, then, for the multiplexing of the address and data on the AD0-AD7 lines. These lines include /Read, /Write, and I-O/M, which indicate whether the function to be performed is a input or an output, and whether it is addressed to memory or an I/O device; Address Latch Enable and two status lines so and

S1, which advise the external world of the status of each machine cycle of the 8085; Hold and Hold Acknowledge, which allow the external I/O to ask for and receive a DMA cycle; and Reset In and Out, which provide the reset.

The 8085 also supports the interrupt structure of the 8080, with the Interrupt and Interrupt Acknowledge lines. In the '85, however, these lines are made available to the internal data bus of the MP instead of being connected directly to the Timing and Control logic. The external circuits see the operation of them as the same, however. In addition, four more interrupts are available, also connected to the data bus inside the MP, but these are under special software control with two OP codes. The reason for the placement of the interrupts onto the data bus will be shown later.

Two I/O lines are provided on the '85 which allow a single bit to be tested or presented directly by the MP. The Serial Data In (SID) and Serial Data Out (SOD) lines may be sensed or driven under programme control via the same two instructions included for the new interrupt scheme. They allow the MP to treat them as either true serial data I/O, if programmed timing loops are included, or as simple single bit test or control ports for the sensing or control of external events.

INTERFACING THE 8085

A brief description of the signals between the 8085 and the outside world follows.

ADDRESS LINES A8 - A15

These tristate lines are outbound only. They provide the upper 8 bits of the 16-bit-wide address which identifies one unique 8-bit byte within the MP's address space, or the 8-bit address of an I/O device. Sixteen address lines provide an address space of 65,536 locations.

ADDRESS-DATA LINES AD0 - AD7

These tristate lines may by either inbound or outbound. They provide a multiplexing between the lower 8 bits of the 16-bit-wide address early in a machine cycle and 8 data bits later in the cycle. When containing addresses, these lines are outbound only; when containing data, they may be either inbound or outbound, depending upon the nature of the machine cycle. They also will contain the 8 bits of an I/O device address during an I/O operation.

ADDRESS LATCH ENABLE (ALE)

This signal appears outbound early in a machine cycle to advise the external circuitry that the AD0 - AD7 lines contain the lower 8 bits of a memory address. It should be used to clock a catch-and-hold circuit such as a 74LS245 or 74LS373, so that the full address will be available to the system for the rest of the machine cycle. The documentation states that the falling edge of ALE is the point at which the signals on the AD lines, as well as the so, S1, and I-O/M lines (below) will be stable and may be taken by the external circuitry.

STATUS LINES SO, S1, & I-O/M

These three status lines serve to indicate the general status of the processor with respect to what function the MP will perform during the machine cycle. The so and S1 lines are made available for circuits which need advanced warning of the ensuing operation, such as very slow RAM or other specialized devices. The system may not normally need to monitor these lines. The I-O/M line approximates in one line what the so and S1 lines do in two. It indicates whether the operation will be directed toward memory (line is low), or toward I/O (line is high). Refer to the manual for a full explanation.

READ & WRITE (/RD & /WR)

These lines indicate which direction the MP expects to pass data between itself and the external data bus. Read indicates that the MP is expecting data to be fed to it; Write indicates that the MP is going to send data away from itself. These lines also serve to time the event, as well as identify its direction.

READY

This is an input line which may be used as a signal from

external RAM that a wait state is needed, since the RAM is not able to provide the data or accept it in the time allowed by the MP. The negation of Ready, by being pulled low, will cause the 8085 to enter wait states.

HOLD & HOLD ACKNOWLEDGE (HOLD & HLDA)

These lines provide the 8085 with a DMA capability by allowing another processor on the same system buses to request control of the buses. Upon receipt of HOLD, the ' 85 will tristate its address, data, and certain control lines, then generate HLDA. This signals the other processor that it may proceed. The '85 will remain off the buses until HOLD is negated.

INTERRUPT & INTERRUPT ACKNOWLEDGE (INTR & INTA)

These lines provide a vectored interrupt capability to the 8085. Upon receipt of INTR, the '85 will complete the instruction in process, then generate INTA as it enters the next machine cycle. The interrupting device will jam a Restart (RST) instruction onto the data bus, which the '85 uses to locate an interrupt vector in low RAM.

RST 5.5, 6.5, 7.5

These three lines are additional interrupt lines which generate an automatic Restart, without jamming, to vectors in low RAM which are between those used by the normal INTR instruction.

The 5.5 line, for example, will cause an automatic restart to a 4-byte vector located between 5 and 6 of the normal vectors used by INTR. These lines have priority over the INTR line, and each other. They also have certain electrical characteristics for assertion, and may be masked off or on by software.

TRAP

This is an unmaskable interrupt with a fixed vector in low RAM.

RESET IN & RESET OUT

These lines provide for both MP and system reset. The reset circuitry in the 8224, used with the 8080, has been brought inside the MP. The RESET IN line is generated asynchronously by some sort of external circuit, such as an RC network or Reset switch. Upon receipt of this signal, the '85 will internally synchronize the Reset with the clock of the processor, then generate RESET OUT for other devices in the system.

X1 & X2

These two pins provide connection for an external frequency determining circuit to feed the 8085's clock. This is normally a crystal, although other resonant circuits may be used. X1 alone may be used as a single input from an external oscillator. The internal oscillator of the '85 will divide the frequency by two for the system clock.

CLOCK (CLK)

This line provides a system clock signal to external circuits which need to be in synchronization with the MP.

SERIAL INPUT DATA & SERIAL OUTPUT DATA (SID & SOD)

These two lines provide for a single serial input or output line to/from the 8085. These lines are brought into the device as D7, and may be tested or set by the Read Interrupt Mask (RIM) or Set Interrupt Mask (SIM) instructions. These two instructions also have control over the mask which controls the RST 5.5, 6.5, and 7.5, and TRAP, interrupts. The SID and SOD lines are simple single bit I/O lines; any timing required to provide external communication via them must be provided by the software.

VCC & VSS

These are the power connections for +5 volts and ground, respectively.

SYSTEM TIMING

Refer to the Reference Manual for diagrams and details

on the system timing. This will be a general discussion to point out the highlights and guide the student through the essential information. The instructor will augment it with discussions of the timing diagrams.

THE PROCESSOR CYCLE

The time required by the 8085 to fetch and execute one machine language instruction is defined as an Instruction Cycle. As in the 8080, the instructions may be of different complexities, with the result that the more complicated instructions take longer to execute. The 8085's method of instruction execution inside the MP is more organized, however, and so the time required to execute any instruction is more predictable and more regular.

Each instruction is divided into one to five Machine Cycles. Each machine cycle is essentially the result of the need, by the instruction being executed, to access the RAM. The shortest instruction would require just one machine cycle, in which the instruction itself is obtained from RAM.

The longest, of five machine cycles, would consist of five RAM accesses, the first to obtain the instruction byte itself, and the remaining four to be divided into fetching and saving other bytes. For example, cycles numbers 2 & 3 may be needed to fetch two more bytes of an address, while numbers 4 & 5 may be needed to save a 2-byte address somewhere else in RAM.

The type of machine cycle being executed is specified by the status lines I-O/M, S0, and S1, and the control lines /RD, /WR, and /INTA. These six lines can define seven different machine cycle types as follows. Refer to the chart in the manual which defines the bit patterns of each.

OP CODE FETCH

This is the first machine cycle of any instruction. It is defined with S0 and S1 asserted high, and I-O/M and /RD low. It is a read cycle from RAM to obtain an instruction byte.

MEMORY READ

This is a normal read cycle of any byte except the OP

code. It is defined with S0 and S1 set to 0, 1 respectively, and I-O/M and /RD low. It is a read cycle from RAM to obtain a data or address byte.

MEMORY WRITE

This is a normal write cycle to memory. It is defined with S0 and S1 set to 1, 0 respectively, and I-O/M and /WR low. It is a write cycle to RAM to store one byte in the specified address.

I/O READ

This is a normal read cycle from an I/O device. It is defined with S0 and S1 set to 0, 1 respectively, and with I-O/M high and /RD low. It is a read cycle which will bring one byte into the MP from the input device specified.

I/O WRITE

This is a normal write cycle to an I/O device. It is defined with S0 and S1 set to 1, 0 respectively, and with I-O/M high and /WR low. It is a write cycle which will send one byte outbound from the MP to the specified output device.

INTERRUPT ACKNOWLEDGE

This is a response to an interrupt request applied to the MP via the INTR line. It is defined with S0 and S1 set to 1, 1 respectively, I-O/M set high, and both /RD and /WR also high. The Interrupt Acknowledge pin is also held to a low asserted level. l It is neither a read nor write cycle, although the interrupting device will jam an interrupt vector onto the D0-D7 lines on the next machine cycle.

BUS IDLE

This is an idle cycle in which no specific bus activity is defined. It occurs under three differently defined conditions:

- *Double Add Instruction (DAD):* This instruction requires enough execution time to merit its own Idle cycle. It is defined with S0 and S1 set to 0, 1 respectively, I-O/M set low, and neither /RD nor /WR asserted (both high). Since neither a read nor a write are specified, no bus action takes place.

- *Acknowledge of Restart or Trap:* This idle cycle allows time for the '85 to cope with a RST or Trap interrupt request. All bits are held high.
- *Halt:* This idle cycle indicates that the MP has executed a Halt instruction. The I-O/M, /RD, and / WR lines are all tristated, which would allow them to be controlled by other devices. INTA is held inactive, but not tristated. The Hold line is really the proper one to use for DMA or multiple processors.

Each of the machine cycles defined above, during which an access of a RAM address or an I/O device is made (except the idle cycles), is further divided into T-states. Each T-state, for an '85 with a 3 MHz clock, will be about 333 nanoseconds in length. The first machine cycle, during which the OP code is being fetched, will be either 4 or 6 T-states in length.

Whether 4 or 6 T-states are used depends upon whether the instruction needs further information from RAM, or whether it can be executed to completion straight away If multiple accesses are needed, the cycle will be 4 states long; if the execution can run to completion, 6 states are required. (Remember that the '85 is running with a faster clock, so that less time per T-state is available.)

The number of T-states for the second and succeeding machine cycles will always be 3 for normal instructions. There are two exceptions to this general rule. The first exception is in response to the request for wait states from an external device which has pulled the Ready line low. This will cause the '85 to insert one or more Tw states between T2 and T3, as in the 8080.

The second exception is when the '85 is placed into the Hold condition in response to a signal from an outside device applied to the Hold line. This will be an indeterminate amount of time during which the external device will be performing a DMA function.

The documentation includes a small chart which specifies the actions of the major signals of the '85 during each of the 10 possible types of T-states.

It may be summarized as follows:

- *T1 State:* This state is the first of any machine cycle. The chart shows that S0-S1 lines, I-O/M, A8-A15, and AD0-AD7 contains whatever would be appropriate for the type of instruction being executed. (The "X" in the chart is defined as "unspecified", which translates to "whatever is normal".) The S0-S1 and I-O/M lines will define, at this early point in the machine cycle, whether the MP is attempting to address a RAM location or an I/O device. The address lines will identify the location or I/O device to be dealt with. The Address Latch Enable (ALE) line will allow some sort of external circuitry to catch and hold the contents of the AD0-AD7 lines to be used as the low byte of the address.
- Note that while the S0 and S1 lines may safely be ignored for general purposes, they are provided to allow the engineer to obtain an advanced warning of the type of function that will be specified during T2, i.e., a read or a write. An engineer can monitor this lines with circuitry of his own to generate his own "Early Read" or "Early Write" if he needs it for slow peripheral devices or devices.
- The /RD, /WR, and /INTA lines are all negated at this time. Since the AD0-AD7 lines are being used to present an address byte, it would be inappropriate to move data on the data bus; besides, it's too early to do so. It's also too early for /INTA. ALE, however, is asserted, since this is the time that the AD0-AD7 contents will contain the lower address byte, which must be caught and held outside the '85 for use by the following T-states.
- *T2 State:* The chart indicates that all lines except ALE (which will be inactive for the rest of the machine cycle) will assume the proper level for the type of instruction in progress. The address lines retain the bit pattern selecting one byte from RAM or an I/O device; the AD0-AD7 lines will now prepare to either

accept or present a data byte (they are in a state of transition during T2); I-O/M and the S0, S1 lines are still displaying the original settings of T1. Either /RD or /WR will assert during T2, to indicate the nature of the data transaction. /INTA will assert at T2 if an interrupt cycle has started.

- *Wait State:* If the Ready line was negated during T2, a Tw is inserted to allow the external circuitry more time to prepare for data transmission. A specific point in T2 is defined, after which a late negation of Ready will not cause the Tw to be inserted. This corresponds to the same actions in the 8080 device. All signals set up during T2 will remain constant during Tw.
- *T3 State:* All lines set up during T2 will remain the same in T3, except the AD0-AD7 lines, which will be conducting data either into or out of the 8085. At the end of T3, the /RD or /WR line will negate to indicate the end of the active function. This will cause the data byte standing on AD0-AD7 to disappear.
- *T4 - T6 States:* These states are required for time to permit the 8085 to continue processing internally. No bus actions are required. The S0 & S1 lines are both asserted, while I-O/M is negated, which specifies that the '85 is involved in an 0P code fetch. Since T4 through T6 will exist only on the first machine cycle of an instruction, this corresponds correctly with the Machine Cycle chart. The AD0-AD7 lines are tristated; the A8-A15 retain their original setting; the /RD, /WR, and INTA lines are all negated.

In addition to the T-states described above, the chart also indicates the conditions during states involved in Resets, Halts, and Holds. It must be kept in mind that during any of these, the MP clocks are still running, and the '85 is alive inside; it has simply shut itself off the buses to allow external events to occur.

These states tristate the address, AD, I-O/M, /RD, and /WR lines to allow external devices to control them. The other lines are held at inactive levels except the S0 & S1 lines, which do indicate what type of machine cycle the system is in, i.e., whether it is a Reset, Hold, or Halt.

TIMING DIAGRAMS

Locate the figure in the Intel documentation labeled 8085A Basic System Timing. This diagram illustrates the events in an instruction of three machine cycles. The M1 cycle is four states long, and the events at each state are shown. Notice particularly the operation of the AD0-AD7 lines, which provide the lower address byte during T1, followed by data during the later part of T2 and all of T3.

Observe that the ALE line corresponds to the presentation of this low address byte. Note also that in a machine cycle in which data is going to be read, the AD lines actually capture the incoming byte during the middle of T3, and may drift around in the later part of T2. Compare this to the case of a write, in which the '85 presents the data byte to be written early in T2, and holds it constant until the end of T3.

Several other timing diagrams are included in the documentation which illustrate the details of each different cycle that the '85 can perform. These all conform nicely to the Basic System Timing diagram, with the addition of wait states, and of specific lines to perform specific functions. The Instructor will discuss these with you.

HOLD AND HALT STATES

The 8085 has provisions for the execution of a Halt instruction, which causes the system to go into T-halt states. During this time, the '85 is simply waiting for something to occur. There are three ways out of a Halt: A Reset, a Hold Request, and an enabled interrupt.

If a Hold Request occurs during a Halt, the '85 will honour it by going into T-hold cycles as long as the Hold line remains asserted; it will return to the halt condition when Hold negates.

If an interrupt occurs during a halt, the MP will go into an interrupt cycle if the interrupt was enabled; it will be ignored if it was not enabled. An enabled interrupt during a hold state will have to wait until the hold clears before being given control of the system. Two diagrams are included in the documentation to indicate the various combinations of hold, halt, and interrupts.

INSTRUCTION SET

The instruction set of the 8085 is identical to that of the 8080, with the exception of the addition of two instructions, RIM and SIM.

The definitions of the OP codes, how they work, the operation of the condition flags, addressing modes, and the use of the H and L register pair for indirect addressing are all identical between the two processors.

The Intel documentation shows many symbols used to describe the functions and relations of parts of instructions. These include the use of lower case letters, especially the "r", to indicate a register, "rp" to indicate a register pair, "addr" to indicate an address, "data" to indicate an 8-bit data byte, "data 16" to indicate a 16-bit data word, "rh" and "rl" to indicate the high-order register and the low-order register of a register pair, respectively, and the use of some upper case, such as "PC" for programme counter and "SP" for stack pointer.

Many graphics symbols are used, and the instructor will now discuss them with you at length, using the documentation as reference. Be sure you understand them before proceeding.

FLAG REGISTER

The Status Flags of the 8080 and 8085 are single bits which indicate the logical conditions that existed as a result of the execution of the instruction just completed. This allows instructions following to act accordingly, such as a branch as a result of two values comparing equal. The flags are:

Zero Flag: This flag is set to a 1 by the instruction just ending if the A Register contains a result of all 0's. Besides the obvious mathematical applications, this is useful in determining equality in a compare operation (a value subtracted from a second value with an answer of 0), or in logical AND or OR operations where the result left the A Register with no bit set to a 1 (the AND was not satisfied). If any bits were left set to a 1 in the A Register, the flag will be reset to a 0 condition.

Sign Flag: This flag is set to a 1 by the instruction just ending if the leftmost, or highest order, bit of the A Register is set to a 1. The leftmost bit of a byte in signed arithmetic is the sign bit, and will be 0 if the value in the lower seven bits is positive, and 1 if the value is negative.

Parity Flag: This flag is set to a 1 by the instruction just ending if the A Register is left with an even number of bits set on, i.e., in even parity. If the number of bits in the A Register is odd, the bit is left off. This may be useful in I/O operations with serial devices, or anyplace that error checking is to be done.

Carry Flag: This flag is set to a 1 by the instruction just ending if a carry out of the leftmost bit occurred during the execution of the instruction. An example would be the addition of two 8-bit numbers whose sum was 9 bits long.

The 9th bit would be lost, yielding an erroneous answer if the carry bit was not captured and held by this flag. This flag is also set if a borrow occurred during a subtraction or a compare operation.

AUXILIARY CARRY FLAG

This flag is set to a 1 by the instruction just ending if a carry occurred from bit 3 to bit 4 of the A Register during the instruction's execution. Because of the relationships of decimal in pure BCD to hexadecimal coding, it is possible to bring BCD values directly into the A Register and perform mathematical operations on them.

The result, however, will be as if two hex characters are being processed. If the result must be returned to the programme as BCD rather than as hex, the Decimal Adjust Accumulator (DAA) instruction can make that translation; the Auxiliary Carry Flag is provided to assist in this operation.

INSTRUCTION ORGANIZATION

The 8085's instructions are made up of bytes. In microprocessor parlance, a byte is described as 8 contiguous binary bits treated as a unit. The least significant bit is on the right, and is labeled Bit 0. The most significant bit is on the left, and is Bit 7.

Thus, the machine coding is "origin zero", unless noted otherwise. Note also that there is no parity bit, or provision for it, as would be found in larger systems.

The 8085's instructions are either one, two, or three bytes long. In all cases, the first byte contains the essential information, such as the OP code. The second and third bytes, if included, provide operand information that won't fit in the first byte.

A close look at the first byte of each instruction will reveal a very great similarity between the 8085's instruction format and that of the PDP11 system by DEC. In many instances, the description of the instructions in the Intel documentation specifies that certain bits of the first byte (#2,1,0) be designated as the "source" operand, and others (#5,4,3) as the "destination" operand.

In this manner, all of the major functional units available to the programmer are encoded into three bits, according to the chart below:

DDD or SSS	Register Name
111	A
000	B
001	C
010	D
011	E
100	H
101	L

Similarly, the registers may be defined as register pairs, and two bits within the first byte may then be used to define these:

RP Bits	Register Pair
00	B-C
01	D-E
10	H-L
11	SP

The similarity between PDP11 and 8085 instruction sets is interesting, but by no means rigid. Many differences exist, primarily due to the difference between the 8- and 16-bit architectures.

ADDRESSING MODES

The 8085 provides four different modes for addressing data, either in its registers or in memory. These are described below:

DIRECT MODE

This mode creates instructions three bytes long. The first byte contains the operation to be performed. The second and third bytes contain the address in memory where the data byte may be found.

Thus, the instruction directly specifies the absolute location of the data. Note that the second byte of the instruction contains the low order byte of the address, while the third byte contains the high order byte of the address. This illustrates the inverse addressing of the device.

REGISTER MODE

This mode results in single-byte instructions. The byte contains bits which specify a register or register pair in which the data is located.

REGISTER INDIRECT MODE

This mode results in single-byte instructions. The byte contains bits which specify a register pair, which in turn contains the address of the data in memory. Thus, the instruction indirectly specifies the address of the data by referring to a register pair for the absolute address. Note that the high order byte of the address is stored in the leftmost register of the pair, while the low order byte of the address is stored in the rightmost register of the pair. The address 3000H, therefore, would be stored in the HL register pair as 30 in H, and 00 in L.

IMMEDIATE MODE

This mode results in a two or three byte instruction. The first byte contains the instruction itself. The second and third bytes contain the immediate data, either as a single 8-bit value, or as a 16-bit value. If the 16-bit value is used, the bytes are reversed as discussed previously, with the second byte containing the low order byte, and the third byte containing the high order byte.

BRANCH INSTRUCTION TYPES

Normal execution of instructions is in a straight line. Branch instructions are available to alter the course of execution flow.

These instructions can specify the address of the next instruction to be executed, if it is not the one immediately following the branch, in two ways:

DIRECT BRANCH

In this mode, the branch contains the address to be used, if the branch occurs, as two bytes following the instruction byte. The second byte contains the low order byte, while the third byte contains the high order byte.

REGISTER INDIRECT BRANCH

In this mode, the branch specifies a register pair which will contain the address for the branch. This address must obviously be set up prior to the branch occurring.

The register pair contains the high order byte of the address in the first, or right-most register of the pair, and the low order byte of the address in the second, or left-most register of the pair, in order to maintain alignment with the general addressing scheme. The Intel documentation divides the 8085's instruction set into five groups. These are the Data Transfer Group, Arithmetic Group, Logical Group, Branch Group, and a Machine Control-I/O Group.

These will now be discussed individually, with specific instructions mentioned for illustration in these notes. The entire set will be reviewed by the instructor as this section progresses.

DATA TRANSFER

This group of instructions provides the 8085 with the ability to move data around inside the RAM, between the RAM and the registers of the MP, and between registers within the MP.

They are important because a good deal of moving must be done to offset the fact that in an 8-bit byte, there is insufficient room to define the operands as specifically as is done, for example, in the PDP11. These instructions do not affect the condition codes. A few comments on the OP code groups follow:

MOV GROUP

These three instructions (MOV r1,r2, MOV r,M, and MOV M,r) are the general means of moving data between memory and registers. They move one byte with each execution.

The second and third examples illustrate the use of the Register Indirect mode of addressing, in which the H&L registers of the MP contain an address, and the data is moved to or from that address. This saves space, in that the instruction is only one byte long. It requires, however, that the H&L registers be previously set up with the address required.

The letter "M", when appearing as an operand in this description, specifies Register Indirect mode with H&L as the register to contain the address. No other register pair is used as such.

MVI GROUP

These two instructions (MVI r,data, and MVI M,data)

provide a means of loading a byte immediately into a register or a memory address. Note that the Register Indirect mode again is evident.

The immediate data is stored as a byte directly below the instruction byte.

LXI INSTRUCTION

This single instruction (LXI rp,data 16) provides a means of loading any register pair with a two-byte value. The second byte l of the instruction is loaded into the leftmost, or low-order, register of the pair, while the third byte is loaded into the rightmost, or high order, register of the pair.

LDA & STA

The Load Accumulator Direct (LDA) and the Store Accumulator Direct (STA) instructions provide a means of moving a byte between the accumulator and a RAM address. This may also be done with the MOV OP code, but only indirectly, that is, with the help of the H&L registers. The address of the byte to be loaded or stored follows the instruction, again with the inverse addressing.

LHLD & SHLD

The Load H&L Direct (LHLD) and Store H&L Direct (SHLD) instructions provide a means of moving two bytes between the HL register pair and a RAM address. Since the H&L register pair is heavily used in the Register Indirect mode, these instructions provide a quick means of loading the two bytes of an address into the pair in only one instruction.

The two bytes following the instruction contain an address in RAM, again low-order in byte 2, and high-order in byte 3.

For the LHLD, this address points to a single byte, which is obtained and loaded into the L register. The second byte from RAM is obtained from the address one higher than the RAM byte, and loaded into the H register. The SHLD simply stores as above, instead of loads.

LDAX & STAX

The Load Accumulator Indirect (LDAX) and Store Accumulator Indirect (STAX) instructions provide a means of moving data between the U accumulator and a memory location indirectly, with the RAM address contained in either the BC or DE register pair.

This is not the same as the MOV, which uses only the HL register pair. This instruction permits the accumulator to access groups of data bytes, as may be necessary with long precision arithmetic. Obviously, the BC or DE pair must be previously loaded with the address desired.

XCHG INSTRUCTION

The Exchange (XCHG) instruction permits the HL register pair's contents to be exchanged with the DE register pair's contents.

This allows an address to be built in the DE pair, then, when ready, to be transferred at once to the HL pair. This would be advantageous in complex data handling.

ARITHMETIC GROUP

This group provides the 8085 with mathematical ability to manipulate 8-bit data, and, by judicious use of the condition codes, to manipulate larger values. The A register (Accumulator) can perform true adds, subtracts, and compares.

The other registers can only increment or decrement by 1. Unless otherwise indicated, all the condition code flags are affected.

ADD INSTRUCTIONS

The Add Register (ADD r) and Add Memory (ADD M) instructions add the byte specified, either in a register or in the address contained by the H&L registers, into the accumulator. They assume that the accumulator already has in it the other value to participate in the add. The sum will remain in the accumulator. If the answer resulted in a ninth bit, it is stored in the Carry flag of the PSW.

ADD WITH CARRY

The Add Register with Carry (ADC r) and Add Memory with Carry (ADC M) instructions will add the specified byte, either in a register or in the address contained by the H&L registers, AND the value of the Carry bit, into the accumulator.

By including the carry bit in the operation, mathematical operations on values longer than 8 bits are possible. As above, the first value must already be loaded in the A register prior to execution of these instructions. The sum remains in the accumulator. If the answer resulted in a ninth bit, it is stored in the Carry flag.

ADD IMMEDIATES

The Add Immediate (ADI) and Add Immediate with Carry (ACI) instructions provide a means of adding a fixed value into the accumulator.

These instructions assume that an initial value has already been loaded into the accumulator. The immediate data is provided by the second byte of the instruction. The ACI instruction adds the immediate value and the value of the Carry flag, while the ADI does not take the Carry flag into account.

The sum remains in the accumulator. If the answer resulted in a ninth bit, it is stored in the Carry flag.

SUBTRACT INSTRUCTIONS

The Subtract Register (SUB r) and the Subtract Memory (SUB M) instructions subtract the specified byte, in a register or in the address contained by the H&L registers, from the contents of the accumulator. The accumulator must have the first value already loaded , prior to the execution of the instructions.

The subtract is accomplished by the complement-and-add technique, in which the two's complement of the specified value is computed first, and then added to the contents of the A register. The Carry flag will be set to a 1 if a borrow was required during the subtraction.

SUBTRACT WITH BORROW

The Subtract Register with Borrow (SBB r) and the Subtract Memory with Borrow (SBB M) instructions will subtract the specified byte, either in a register or in the address contained in the H&L registers, and the value of the Carry flag, from the contents of the A register.

The first value must be loaded into the A register prior to the execution of the instructions. The subtract is accomplished by the complement-and-add technique. The Carry flag will be set to a 1 if a borrow was required during the subtraction.

SUBTRACT IMMEDIATES

The Subtract Immediate (SUI data) and Subtract Immediate with Borrow (SBI data) instructions provide a means of subtracting a fixed value from the contents of the accumulator. The immediate value is provided by the second byte of the instruction. The first value must be loaded into the accumulator prior to the execution of the instructions. The subtract is accomplished by the complement-and-add technique.

The SBI instruction will subtract both the immediate value and the contents of the Carry flag from the A register, while the SUI does not take the Carry flag into account. The Carry flag will be set at the end of the instruction if , a borrow was required during execution.

INCREMENT INSTRUCTIONS

The Increment Register (INR r) and Increment Memory (INR M) instructions provide a quick means of adding one to the contents of a register or memory location. These instructions allow the programmer to create counting routines and reiterations. Note that the Carry flag is not affected by these instructions.

DECREMENT INSTRUCTIONS

The Decrement Register (DCR r) and Decrement Memory (DCR M) instructions provide a quick means of subtracting one from the contents of a register or a memory location. These instructions allow the programmer to create counting routines and reiterations. Note that the Carry flag is not affected by these instructions.

REGISTER PAIR INSTRUCTIONS

The Increment Register Pair (INX rp) and Decrement Register Pair (DCX rp) instructions provide a means of adding to, or subtracting from, a 16-bit value contained in a register pair.

In the INX instruction, this means that the carry from the sum of the low order byte of the pair and the one will be added into the upper byte automatically. In the DCX instruction, this means that a borrow from the high-order byte, if required, will be allowed into the low-order byte, if the subtraction of one from the low-order byte demands it. Note that none of the flags are affected.

DOUBLE ADD

The Add Register Pair to H&L (DAD rp) instruction adds a 16 bit value already existing in the BC or DE register pair into the 16-bit value contained in the H&L registers. The sum remains in the H&L registers.

The Carry flag will be set if a carry occurred out of the high order byte; a carry from low- to high-order bytes within the add is taken into account automatically. This instruction allows a fixed index-like value to be added to the H&L registers for Register Indirect mode.

DECIMAL ADJUST

The Decimal Adjust Accumulator (DAA) instruction converts the 8-bit value in the A register, which normally is assumed to be two 4bit hexadecimal values, into two 4-bit BCD values.

This allows the programmer to accept input data as BCD, process it in the accumulator using essentially hexadecimal arithmetic, and then convert the result back into BCD. This may be done by virtue of the fact that the ten numbers of

BCD (0 to 9) are coded in binary exactly as are the first ten of the sixteen numbers of binary coded hexadecimal. i.e., adding 38_{10} and 38_{16} are exactly the same.

The conversion be may accomplished by the use of the Auxiliary Carry flag. If the contents of the low-order four bits of the A register is >9, or if the AC flag is set, a value of 6 is added to these bits.

Then the high-order four bits of the A register are examined; again, if they contain a value >9, or if the Carry flag is on, a 6 is added to them. The Carry flag, of course, indicates that the hexadecimal value of the byte before the instruction, when translated to BCD, is too large to fit in one byte.

LOGICAL GROUP

This group of instructions provides the decision-making ability of the 8085, and includes some logically oriented utility instructions as well.

By using these instructions, the condition flags may be **set** so that they can be tested by Jump-on-condition instructions. Unless otherwise noted, all the condition codes are affected. A few notes follow:

AND INSTRUCTIONS

The And Register (ANA r) and And Memory (ANA M) instructions perform a logical And function between the specified byte, either in a register or in the address contained in the H&L registers, and the contents of the accumulator. The accumulator must first be loaded with an initial value.

The And function occurs on a bit-by-bit basis. The low order bit of the specified byte is Anded with the low order bit of the A register; if both the bit from the outside byte AND the bit from the A register are a 1, the bit in the A register is left as a 1. If either the bit position of the outside byte or the bit position in the A register, or both, contained 0's, that bit position in the A register is reset to 0.

Identical actions occur on the other seven bit positions at the same time. The result, left in the accumulator, is a bit pattern which indicates, with 1's left on, in which positions of the bytes both the A register and the outside byte contained 1's. This is valuable for testing the conditions of specific bits within a byte, and reacting accordingly. All condition flags are involved, but the Carry flag is always cleared by an And.

AND IMMEDIATE

The And Immediate (ANI data) instruction allows the programmer to match the byte in the accumulator with a fixed mask byte, contained in the second byte of the instruction. The A register must first be loaded with the byte to be tested. The Anding function occurs exactly as shown above. All condition flags are involved, but the Carry flag is cleared.

OR INSTRUCTIONS

The Or Register (ORA r) and Or Memory (ORA M) instructions perform inclusive Or's between the specified byte, either in a register or in the address contained in the H&L registers, and the contents of the accumulator. The A register must be loaded with the first , value prior to the execution of these instructions.

The Or function occurs on a bit-by-bit basis. The low order bit of the outside byte is Ored with the low order bit of the A register; if either the bit from the outside byte OR the bit from the A register is a 1, or both, that bit position is set to a 1 in the A register.

If neither bit position from the outside bit or the A register is a 1, a 0 is loaded into that bit position of the A register. (Note that this satisfies the "one, the other, or both" requirements of an inclusive Or.) Identical operations occur on the other seven bit positions of the bytes. The result, left in the accumulator, is a bit pattern in which a 1 exists in any bit position in which either of the bytes also had a bit set. All condition flags are affected, but the Carry and Auxiliary Carry flags are always cleared.

OR IMMEDIATE

The Or Immediate (ORI data) instruction allows the

programmer to match the contents of the accumulator against a fixed mask byte which is contained in the second byte of the instruction. The Or function occurs on a bit-by-bit basis, exactly as shown above. The first byte must be loaded into the A register prior to execution of the instruction. All condition flags are affected, but the Carry and Auxiliary Carry flags are always cleared.

EXCLUSIVE OR INSTRUCTIONS

The Exclusive Or Register (XRA r) and D Exclusive Or Memory (XRA M) instructions perform exclusive Or functions between a specified byte, either in a register or in a byte contained in the address in the H&L register, and the contents of the accumulator.

The A register must be loaded with the first byte prior to the execution of the instruction. The Exclusive Or occurs on a bit-by-bit basis. The low order bit of the outside byte is XOred with the low bit of the accumulator; if the bit in the outside byte is a 1 and the position in the A register is a 0, or if the bit in the outside byte is a 0 and the position in the A register is a 1, a 1 is set into that bit in the A register.

If the bits are either both 1's or both 0's, the bit position is reset in the A register. (Note that this agrees with the "one, the other, but not both, and not neither" parameters of an Exclusive Or.)

Identical operations occur on the other bit positions of the bytes at the same time. The results are left in the accumulator, which contains a bit pattern with 1's set where there was a 1 in either the A register or the outside byte, and 0's set where there was either 0's in both bytes or 1's in both bytes, in the same bit position. All condition flags are affected, but the Carry and Auxiliary Carry flags are always cleared.

EXCLUSIVE OR IMMEDIATE

The Exclusive Or Immediate (XRI data) instruction allows the programmer to perform an Exclusive Or between a mask byte stored as the second byte of the instruction and the contents of the accumulator. The first byte must be loaded into the A register prior to the execution of the instruction. The Exclusive Or function occurs on a bit-by-bit basis exactly as outlined above. All the condition flags are affected, but the Carry and Auxiliary Carry flags are cleared.

COMPARE INSTRUCTIONS

The Compare Register (CMP r) and Compare Memory (CMP M) instructions compare the contents of the specified byte, either in a register or in the address contained in the H&L registers, to the contents of the accumulator. This is accomplished by subtracting the outside byte from the contents of the accumulator.

The contents of the accumulator remain unchanged, and the actual answer of subtraction is lost. The condition flags are all affected, and are set to indicate the conditions of the lost answer.

Particularly, the Zero flag, if set on, will indicate that the two values compared are equal, since the result of subtracting one from the other is zero. Also, the Carry flag will be set if the value in the A reg is smaller than the outside byte. If neither the Z nor the C flags are left on, the value in the A register is larger than the outside byte.

COMPARE IMMEDIATE

The Compare Immediate (CPI data) instruction compares the contents of the accumulator to a fixed value provided by the second byte of the instruction. The first value must be loaded into the A register prior to the execution of the instruction.

The function occurs by a subtraction with lost answer, as described above. The contents of the A register are left unchanged.

ROTATE INSTRUCTIONS

The Rotate Left (RLC) and Rotate Right (RRC) instructions rotate the accumulator's contents one bit position left or right, respectively. In the RLC, all the bits move one position to the left; the high order bit which is shifted out of the A register is moved around to the low order bit position. It is also moved to the Carry flag. In the RRC, all the bits move one position to the right; the bit shifted out of the low order position of the A register is moved around to the high order position.

It is also moved to the Carry flag. Thus, the Carry flag in either case indicates whether a bit was shifted out of the accumulator. Only the Carry flag is affected by these instructions.

ROTATE THROUGH CARRYS

The Rotate Left through Carry (RAL) and the Rotate Right through Carry (RAR) instructions rotate the accumulator's contents one bit position left or right, respectively.

Unlike the rotates above, however, these instructions use the Carry flag as a ninth bit in the circle. In the RAL, the bits in the A register are shifted left one position; the high order bit moved to the Carry flag; the Carry flag is moved to the low order position of the A register. In the RAR, the bits in the A register are shifted right one position; the low order bit is moved to the Carry flag; the Carry flag is moved to the high order position of the A register. Only the Carry flag is affected.

COMPLEMENT ACCUMULATOR

The Complement Accumulator (CMA) instruction provides a 1's complement of the 8 bits in the A register, i.e., the 1's are set to 0's, and the 0's are set to 1's. A two's complement may be effected by following the CMA with an INR A instruction. No condition flags are affected.

CARRY INSTRUCTIONS

The Complement Carry (CMC) and Set Carry (STC) instructions allow direct control of the Carry flag by the programmer. The CMC will change the flag from 1 to 0, or 0 to

1, depending upon its initial condition. The STC forces the flag to a 1, regardless of its previous state. No other flags are affected.

BRANCH

This group of instructions permits the programmer to alter the flow of programme execution from a normal straight line. There are two major types of these instructions in the 8085. The first type is the Jump, in which the flow is altered with no intention of returning to the place where the Jump occurred.

The second type is the Call, which provides linking, via the system stack, to save the address of the next instruction following the Call, proceed to a subordinate routine, and return to the saved address when that routine is completed. Further, both Jumps and Calls may be conditional or unconditional.

An unconditional Jump or Call causes the function to be executed absolutely. The conditional Jump or Call causes the function to be executed if the conditions specified are met. In the first byte of these instructions, three bits labeled CCC will contain a code which specifies the conditions to be tested.

These may be specified by the programmer in assembly language by putting together a mnemonic composed of a J, for Jump, or a C, J for Call, followed by one or two more characters which specify the conditions to be tested. The breakdown follows:

Mnemonic	Condition	CCC Bits
NZ	Not Zero (Z=0)	000
Z	Zero (Z=1)	001
NC	Not Carry (C=0)	010
C	Carry (C=1)	011
PO	Parity Odd (P=0)	100
PE	Parity Even (P=1)	101
P	Plus (S=0)	110
M	Minus (S=1)	111

JUMP INSTRUCTIONS

The Jump (JMP addr) and Jump Conditional (Jxx addr) instructions allow programme flow to be altered by loading the contents of the two bytes following the instruction to be loaded into the Programme Counter.

The next instruction to be fetched, therefore, will the first of the new routine. The JMP instruction is unconditional; the Jump occurs absolutely. The Jxx instruction will alter programme flow if the conditions specified by the "xx" bits are true; otherwise, programme flow remains in a straight line. No condition codes are affected.

CALL INSTRUCTIONS

The Call (CALL addr) and Call Conditional (Cxx addr) instructions allow linkage to permit a subroutine to be invoked, with the address of the next sequential instruction saved for later reference.

The Call will move the high byte of the PC into the address pointed to by the Stack Pointer minus 1, and the low byte of the PC into the address below that. The SP is then decremented by two, to update it to the new stack position. The two bytes following the Call instruction will then be moved to the PC, with the second byte of the instruction containing the low order byte of the address, and the third byte of the instruction containing the high order byte of the address.

Thus, the address of the instruction following the Call is saved on the system stack, and the address of the first instruction of the subroutine is fetched next. The Call Conditional executes exactly the same way, providing that the conditions specified by the CCC bits are true. None of the flags are affected.

RETURN INSTRUCTIONS

The Return (RET) and Return Conditional (Rxx) instructions provide a means, at the end of a subroutine, of resuming programme execution at the instruction following the Call instruction which invoked the subroutine. These instructions are placed at the end of the subroutine, not in the body of the main programme. When encountered, the Return will move the byte pointed to by the Stack Pointer into the lower byte of the PC, the next byte higher in RAM to the higher byte of PC, and add 2 to the contents of SP.

Thus, the address of the instruction following the Call, previously saved on the stack, is now in PC, and will be fetched next.

Also, the stack pointer is updated accordingly. The Return Conditional executes exactly the same way, providing that the conditions specified by the CCC bits are true. None of the flags are affected.

RESTART

The Restart (RST n) instruction provides part of the vectored interrupt system by which any one of eight different levels of interrupt may stop the execution of the programme currently in progress, save the address of the next instruction onto the stack, and then jump to any one of eight different locations in low core, depending upon the contents of the bits marked NNN in the instruction. Thus, as many as eight different external events, i.e. I/O devices, etc., may ask for service; the place where the programme left off is saved; and one of eight different interrupt handling routines may be entered, which correspond to the level of the interrupt.

JUMP INDIRECT

The Jump H&L Indirect (PCHL) instruction moves the contents of the H&L registers, assumed to be a valid address, into the Programme Counter. The contents of H&L must be previously built, and may be assembled by other parts of the programme to the advantage of the writer. The original contents of the PC are destroyed, so this is a one-way jump.

MACHINE CONTROL

This group is a collection of miscellaneous instructions which control bodily functions of the MP, or provide utilities. Explanations follow:

PUSH AND POP

The Push Register Pair (PUSH rp) and Pop Register Pair (POP rp) instructions allow programmers to manipulate the system stack. The Push will place the contents of the BC, DE, or HL register pairs onto the stack, and update the SP accordingly.

The Pop instruction will return the last two items on the stack to the specified register pair, and update the SP. The condition flags are not affected; the SP register pair may not be specified, for obvious reasons.

PSW INSTRUCTIONS

The Push Processor Status Word (PUSH PSW) and the Pop Processor Status Word (POP PSW) instructions will allow the programmer to save the contents of the A register and of the condition flags on the stack, or to retrieve them from the stack. The Processor Status Word (PSW) of the 8085 is defined as a "Flag Byte" which contains the condition flag bits in a specific sequence: SZ0AC0P1C

In addition, the contents of the A register is also saved as part of the PSW. When the PUSH PSW is encountered, the contents of the A register is pushed onto the stack first, followed by the Flag byte.

The SP is then updated. When the POP is executed, the Flag byte is retrieved first, and the bits are loaded into their proper flip-flops. The A register is then loaded with the next byte retrieved. This allows programmers to save conditions at the beginning of subroutines so that the execution of the instructions within the routines will not alter the conditions under which the original programme was operating.

EXCHANGE STACK TOP

The Exchange Stack Top with H&L (XTHL) instruction causes the contents of the H&L registers to be exchanged with the two bytes which are currently on the top of the system stack. These will be the last two bytes pushed. It is a two-way instruction; the stack receives the original contents of

H&L, while H&L receives the two bytes from the stack. The contents of SP remain unchanged. No flags are affected.

MOVE H&L TO SP

The Move H&L Register to Stack Pointer (SPHL) instruction will directly move the contents of the H&L registers into the Stack Pointer; the original contents of SP are destroyed. This may be used to permit multiple stacks to exist at one time in the system. No flags are affected.

I/O INSTRUCTIONS

The Input (IN port) and Output (OUT port) instructions allow the MP to communicate with the outside world. In both cases, the address byte of the device to be used is contained in the byte following the instruction. This byte is presented at once to both the upper and lower bytes of the A0-A15 address lines. In the case of IN, the byte accepted on the D0-D7 data lines by the MP is placed in the A register. For the OUT, the byte to be sent on the data lines is placed in the A register prior to execution of the instruction. No flags are affected.

INTERRUPT INSTRUCTIONS

The Enable Interrupts (EI) and Disable Interrupts (DI) instructions allow the MP to permit or deny interrupts under programme control. For the EI, the interrupts will be enabled following the completion of the next instruction following the EI. This allows at least one more instruction, perhaps a RET or JMP, to be executed before the MP allows itself to again be interrupted. For the DI, the interrupts are disabled immediately. No flags are affected.

HALT AND NO-OP

The Halt (HLT) and No-Operation (NOP) instructions serve general utility purposes. The Halt will stop the processor from further execution; it can be restarted again only by an interrupt. A reset signal applied to the MP will abort the Halt. The MP may enter a Hold state, as the result of another device wanting the bus, from a Halt, but will return to the Halt state when the Hold is canceled. The NOP is simply a one-byte long place holder, which is passed through automatically without any data motion or action of any kind. It is used primarily as a programmer's aid in saving space within language programmes for later use.

The Read Interrupt Mask (RIM) and Set Interrupt Mask (SIM) instructions are used to service both the extended interrupt system of the '85 and the Serial Input Data (SID) and Serial Output Data (SOD) pins on the device. While these items are both serviced by the same instructions, they are not electrically or logically related, and should not be confused. The Interrupt Mask is a group of bits which can be accessed by these two instructions via the accumulator. A discussion of the two instructions follows.

READ INTERRUPT MASK (RIM)

This instruction permits the system to examine the interrupt mask by loading into the A register a byte which defines the condition of the mask bits for the maskable interrupts, the condition of the interrupts pending for the maskable interrupts, the condition of the Interrupt Enable flag, and the condition of the Serial Input Data (SID) pin on the MP. The format is:

D7	D6	D5	D4	D3	D2	D1	D0
SID	I7.5	I6.5	I5.5	IE	M7.5	M6.5	M5.5

INTERRUPT MASK BITS D0, D1, D2

These bits indicate whether the interrupts for vectors 5.5, 6.5, and 7.5 are masked on or off. The bits are set to a 1 for disabled, and 0 for enabled. These bits allow the programme to examine the mask and obtain the current status of it. It is a valuable tool, since one programme section may not necessarily know what a second section is doing or expecting.

Interrupt Enable Bit D3: This bit corresponds to the Interrupts Enabled, flip-flop in the 8080. It is set or reset by the Enable Interrupts or Disable Interrupts OP codes in the same manner as in the 8080. The interrupts involved are the standard 8 vectored interrupts, and it has no effect on those special to the 8085. However, in the case of a Trap interrupt (unmaskable), the status of bit 3 may be lost, so that Intel suggests that a RIM be executed as part of the Trap service routine to preserve the condition of the Interrupts Enabled flag prior to the occurrence of Trap. The flag is not affected by the other special interrupts.

Interrupts Pending Bits D4, D5, D6: These bits indicate what interrupts have occurred since the last time that specific interrupt was serviced. If interrupts 5.5 or 6.5 are masked off by bits D0 or D1, bits D4 and D5 will not be set. Bit D6, which corresponds to the 7.5 interrupt, will be set on to indicate that an interrupt was requested, even if it was masked off. *Serial Input Data Bit D7:* This bit provides the condition of the SID pin.

It will be 1 if the pin is high, and 0 if it is low. The software examining this bit must have total ability to deal with whatever it finds there. The pin provides only a voltage level that exists at the time of the RIM execution.

When the RIM instruction is executed, the status of all the lines indicated are sampled, and the resulting bit pattern is placed in the A register. The instruction simply provides these conditions for display; it has no affect on the bits themselves. The bits in the A register may then be examined directly by logical instructions, or moved to a register or memory location for safekeeping.

Set Interrupt Mask (SIM): This instruction is the reverse of the RIM. While the RIM simply reads the status of various lines, the SIM sets various bits to form masks or generate output data via the SOD line.

The conditions that the programmer wishes to set up must be set into the A register exactly as desired first, then the SIM Instruction is executed.

The SIM will take the bit pattern it finds in the A register and loads it into the masks in the following format:

D7	D6	D5	D4	D3	D2	D1	D0
SOD	S0E	X	R7.5	MSE	M7.5	M6.5	M5.5

RST MASKS BITS D0, D1, D2: These bits are the interrupt masks for the 5.5, 6.5, and 7.5 interrupts brought into the '85 on their own pins. The bits are 0 to enable and 1 to disable the interrupts.

If bits D0 or D1 are disabled (set to 1), a signal applied to their respective pins cause no action. If D0 or D1 are set to 0 (enabled), their respective bits will be visible via the RIM instruction, and the call to the interrupt vector will occur. In the case of bit D2 for masking the 7.5 interrupt, the RIM instruction will indicate that a 7.5 interrupt is pending, but an automatic call will not occur.

Mask Set Enable Bit D3: This bit permits bits D0, D1, and D2 to be changed. If a SIM is executed with this bit low, the condition of the mask bits will not change. If a SIM is executed with this bit set high, the mask bits will take on the same arrangement as those given in the lower bits of the A register. This permits accessing of the mask byte to deal with the interrupts without affecting SOD.

Rst 7.5 Reset Bit D4: This bit permits the SIM instruction to reset the interrupt pending flag indicated by bit D6 in the RIM instruction byte. Since the 7.5 interrupt is handled somewhat more importantly than the 5.5 and 6.5, it can indicate that it is pending via the RIM instruction even though it is masked off. This bit allows that pending request to be reset individually under programme control.

Undefined Bit D5: This bit is unused.

Sod Enable Bit D6: This bit works in conjunction with bit D7. If it is set to 1 when the SIM is executed, the condition of bit D7, high or low, is electrically loaded into the SOD latch, and in turn appears on the SOD pin of the '85. If bit D6 is low, the SIM's execution has no affect on the bit D7. This, like bit D3, allows executing SIMs to service either interrupts or the serial I/O without affecting the other.

Serial Output Data Bit D7: This bit contains the voltage level (+5 volts = 1, 0 volts = 0) which should appear at the SOD pin of the '85. If the SIM instruction is executed and bit D6 is set to 1 (enabled), the level contained by D7 is forwarded to the SOD latch, which will in turn cause it to appear on the

SOD pin. If bit D6 is low, the SIM instruction will have no affect on bit D7. The /RESET IN line affects the flags of the interrupt masks. First, the RST 7.5 latch which catches the rising edge of the 7.5 flip-flop and holds it for a RIM instruction is reset. Next, all three mask bits are set to a 1, which will disable all interrupts.

Lastly, the SOD latch is reset to a 0. These will effectively allow the new instructions following the Reset to take full control of the MP, without interrupts causing immediate problems.

ADDITIONAL INFORMATION

This xhapter details several interesting items to round out the 8085 discussion. These include the Reset function, the expanded interrupt facilities, the SID and SOD lines, and additional support devices.

RESET SYSTEM

The 8085 generates its own Reset function upon receipt of an asynchronous /RESET IN signal from an external source. This signal is probably generated from two sources, a Reset switch of some kind accessible to the operator, and a Power-on Reset circuit which causes a reset when power is applied to system.

Receipt of /RESET IN is latched by an internal flip-flop at the rising edge of the next clock pulse (low asserted). At the beginning of the state following the latch of /RESET IN, RESET OUT is generated to the outside world, and the MP enters T-reset cycles. These cycles continue until the /RESET IN line is released. The release is sensed at the rising edge of the next clock pulse. This, in turn, allows the rising edge of the clock pulse following to enter a T1 state for the first instruction after reset.

The /RESET IN line should be held low for at least three T-states worth of time, to allow the '85 to fully synchronize itself and accomplish its tasks of resetting certain flip-flops and registers. Remember that the MP is very much alive during reset, and that it must have time in Reset mode to accomplish these tasks. The documentation mentions that certain of the control lines are tristated during reset, so that pull-up resistors are essential.

When the /RESET IN line goes high, the MP will place the contents of the PC onto the address bus, and enter T1 of the M1 cycle for the next instruction.

The PC was reset to all zeroes during the Reset cycle; therefore, the address appearing on the A0-A15 lines will be 0000H.

The Reset cycle does not affect the contents of any register except PC, or the arrangement of the condition flags. The Intel documentation indicates that the occurrence of Reset is essentially asynchronous with respect to the execution of the programme in process.

Therefore, the results of a Reset are undetermined, and not guaranteed.

The Reset cycle will reset, or turn off, the following items:

- Programme Counter
- Instruction Register
- Interrupt Enable FF
- RST 7.5 FF
- Trap FF
- SOD FF
- Machine State FF's
- Machine Cycle FF's
- Hold Internal FF
- Interrupt Internal FF
- Ready FF

The following items are turned on, or set, by the Reset cycle:

- RST 5.5 Mask
- RST 6.5 Mask
- RST 7.5 Mask

Those items turned off, as listed above, will cause the MP to essentially become iSOlated from the possibilities of interrupts or any exterior interference until the new programme, whatever was at 0000H, is underway.

Turning on the mask bits effects the same thing, as these are on (set to 1) to disable the interrupts.

INTERRUPT FACILITIES

The 8085 contains three levels of interrupt capabilities. The first is essentially identical to that of the 8080 which technique it fully supports. The second technique involves the direct input pins 5.5, 6.5, and 7.5.

These are maskable hardware interrupts. The third is Trap, which has its own pin and is non-maskable. Each will be discussed in detail.

8080 TYPE INTERRUPTS

The 8085 has facilities for servicing interrupts similar to the 8080. The functional items required are an Interrupt Request (INTR) pin, an Interrupt Acknowledge (INTA) pin, an Interrupt Enable (INTE) pin, eight interrupt vectors in low RAM, and the Restart instruction. These perform in the same way as the 8080 interrupt system.

Here is a brief review:

- A programme is running normally in the system. The 8214 Priority Interrupt Controller or similar circuit has its compare mask set to some priority level. The Interrupt Enable bit has been set on by some previous routine, enabling interrupts.
- A device wishes to interrupt the system. It raises its own line which connects directly to the 8214. The 8214 compares this request with the current status of the system. If the new request is higher in priority than the existing (if any), the interrupt will be allowed. If not, the interrupt will be latched for later use, but no further action is taken.
- The Interrupts Enabled line exiting the 8085 is high, indicating that interrupts are permitted. The 8214 raises the Interrupt line, which causes the MP to finish the current instruction, and then enter an interrupt service cycle. The MP generates the Interrupts Acknowledge line at the beginning of this cycle to permit the 8214 to proceed.
- Upon receipt of the INTA line, the 8214 along with

an 8212 octal latch or similar circuit, generates a Restart instruction which it jams onto the data bus at T3 of the interrupt service cycle. The MP receives this, and removes from it the three-bit modulo-8 vector, which it then multiplies by 8 to find the vector in low RAM. This vector contains one or more instructions which can service the device causing the interrupt.

- The execution of the Restart instruction causes the address of the next normal instruction to be executed, obtained from PC, to be placed onto the stack. The next machine cycle will be the M1 of the instruction located in the vector in low RAM. This instruction can now guide the MP to the routine to service the interrupt.
- At the end of the interrupt service routine, a Return (RTN) instruction will cause the popping of the address off the stack which was of the next instruction to be serviced if the interrupt had not occurred.

The system now finds itself back where it came from. There are three possible variations to the above scenario. First, unlike the 8080, the 8085 will permit the interrupt as described above as long as no other interrupts are pending which are of greater importance. These, of course, are the 5.5, 6.5, 7.5, and Trap. If any of these are pending, they will be serviced first.

Secondly, while the 8214 was the original device to service interrupts on the 8080 system, the 8085 can work with the 8259A Programmable Interrupt Controller as well. This is a more complex device, programmable as to how it handles interrupts, and stackable to two levels, providing as many as 64 levels of interrupt for the '85.

The 8259A, moreover, generates Call instructions as well as Restarts. This means that a Call may be jammed onto the data bus during T3 of the interrupt cycle, instead of Restart.

While the Restart provides a vector to eight different places in low RAM, depending upon the modulo-8 bits it contains, the Call contains a full two-byte-wide address, which can effectively vector the MP to any-place within the 64K RAM address space.

This obviously provides a vastly extended ability to handle interrupts more efficiently. The third item to be aware of is that the Interrupt Enable flip-flop of the 8080 is now observable as the IE bit #3 of the byte obtained by executing the RIM instruction.

It hitherto has not been available, and its status must be remembered by the programmer. Now the bit may be checked with the RIM instruction, to aid in programming.

MASKABLE INTERRUPTS

Three maskable interrupts are provided in the 8085, each with their own pins. They are named RST 5.5, RST 6.5, and RST 7.5, respectively.

To see where these names come from, study this chart:

Name	Address
RST 0	00H
RST 1	08H
RST 2	10H
RST 3	18H
RST 4	20H
TRAP	24H
RST 5	28H
REST 5.5	2CH
RST 6	30H
RST 6.5	34H
RST 7	38H
RST 7.5	3CH

Note in the chart that the items in light face are those with which we are already familiar. They are the normal vectors for the Restart instructions 0 through 7, as created by the 8214. They are 8 bytes apart, which is ample room for such jumps as are needled to obtain the interrupt servicing routines. Now look at the bold face items. These items have vector areas which are between the original vectors in RAM. 12he 5.5, for instance, is half way between the RST 5 and the RST 6 vectors, hence the ".5". If all the vectors were in use, those located above address 20H would each have only four bytes in which to locate and jump to the interrupt service routine. This should be enough room, however, if used wisely. Note also that the Trap interrupt is located at the 4.5 point in the vectors.

The 5.5, 6.5, and 7.5 vectors have several items in common. First, they each have their own pin directly into the 8085. These pins will accept asynchronous interrupt requests without the need for any sort of external priority interrupt device. Secondly, these interrupts are individually maskable. This is accomplished via the Set Interrupt Mask instruction. This instruction allows bits to be set or cleared which will permit or deny an interrupt on one of these lines to force the '85 into an interrupt service cycle.

When an input is received on one of these lines and its respective mask bit is enabled (set to 0), the processor will finish the current machine cycle, then enter a interrupt service cycle in which an automatic jam inside the MP will vector it to 2CH, 34H, or 3CH for 5.5, 6.5, or 7.5 respectively. Those locations will assumedly have been previously set to contain directions to the interrupt servicing routines.

The RST 5.5 and RST 6.5 interrupts are "level sensitive" This means that the device wishing to interrupt will apply a steady high level to the appropriate pin and hold it there until the 8085 gets around to responding. When the '85 recognizes the applied high level, it will permit the interrupt to be serviced in the next machine cycle. The mask bits set by the SIM instruction will directly determine what the RIM instruction sees with respect to the 5.5 and 6.5 interrupt pending bits.

If the mask bits are set high (to a 1), these interrupts are masked off. This means that a following RIM will not see them as pending. If the mask bits are set to 0 (enabled), a RIM will see the true condition in bits 4 and 5 of the mask byte. The

RST 7.5 interrupt is "edge sensitive". This means that a pulse applied to this pin, requesting an interrupt, can come and go before the processor gets around to servicing it. This is possible because, unlike the 5.5 and 6.5, the 7.5 has a flip-flop just inside its pin which instantly registers the fact that an interrupt request, albeit short, was applied to the device.

This flip-flop provides a bit which is read in RIM instruction as bit 6. This bit will indicate an interrupt pending if a quick pulse is applied to pin 7.5, even though bit 2 of the SIM instruction, the 7.5 mask bit, is turned on (disabled). Bit 2 of SIM byte, therefore, acts differently as a mask bit than does bits 0 and 1 for 5.5 and 6.5.

Whereas bits 0 and 1 will mask off all indication of action on pins 5.5 and 6.5, bit 2 will allow the indication of a 7.5 interrupt pending, but will prevent the actual servicing of the 7.5 vector unless the mask is enabled for it. In this way, even though the mask set by the SIM prevents the MP from servicing a 7.5 interrupt, the fact that such an interrupt did occur, captured by the flip-flop, is indicated to whatever routine next executes a RIM instruction. While the normal interrupt and 5.5 and 6.5 interrupts' enable bits are reset when these are serviced, the 7.5 interrupt flip-flop must be turned off individually.

This may be accomplished by actually responding to the interrupt, just like the other interrupts above; by having the 8085 receiving a /RESET IN, which would also reset the whole system; or by executing a SIM instruction in which bit 4 of the SIM byte is set on. This bit 4 is the "Reset RST 7.5" bit, and will reset the flip-flop if it is on when a SIM is executed.

NON-MASKABLE INTERRUPT

The Trap instruction is a non-maskable interrupt provision for the 8085. There is no mask bit related to it, and no control bits of any kind. It is used for interrupts of a catastrophic nature, such as the impending doom of a power failure. It is essentially an edge-sensitive input, since its pin connects directly inside the '85 to a flip-flop to capture the fact that a request was made.

However, the inside circuitry around the flip-flop requires that although the flip-flop is set, the asserted level be continually applied thereafter until the processor enters the service cycle. This is shown in a diagram in the documentation. The Trap, therefore, is called both edge-sensitive and level sensitive as well.

The order of priority for all of the interrupts of the 8085, from least important to most important, are the Restart 0 through Restart 7, RST 5.5, RST 6.5, RST 7.5, and finally the Trap. Remember that through the use of the 8214, the RST 0 through 7 interrupts are also prioritized, with 0 as the least important and 7 as the most important. Collectively, the 8085 has a complete set of interrupt capabilities that should serve every need.

SERIAL INTERFACING

The 8085 is equipped with two pins which provide for sending and receiving of serial data. Actually, the pins simply accept or generate a voltage level out according to programme control. Whether or not the timing of the highs and lows on these pins constitute real serial-by-bit data or not is determined by the programming and other components involved and surrounding the '85.

Accepting single-bit serial data into the 8085 is accomplished by the use of the Serial Input Data (SID) line. A voltage from an outside source is applied directly to this pin. It may be sampled at any time by executing a RIM instruction. Upon completion of the RIM, bit 7 of the A register will contain either a 1 or 0, indicating the conditions existing on the SID pin at the time of the instruction's execution.

The arrival of a bit on SID or the change of the level applied to it between high and low in no way effects the interrupt system. No interrupts are generated, nor is any electrical indication of the activity on SID made in any way. Only the execution of a RIM, at the time desired by the programme, will indicate the condition of the SID pin. Generating single-bit serial data out of the 8085 is accomplished by the use of the Serial Output Data (SOD) line.

This pin has placed upon it a voltage high or low that is determined by the SOD flip-flop. This flip flop, in turn, is controlled by bits 6 and 7 of the interrupt mask byte loaded via the SIM instruction.

If bit 7 is high and a SIM is executed, the SOD flip-flop is set high, and SOD pin will be high accordingly. If bit 7 of the mask byte is low and a SIM is executed, the SOD flip-flop is reset low, and pin contains a low output. Bit 6 of the mask byte acts as a permissive toggle.

The contents of bit 7 will be transferred to the flip-flop if bit 6 is high. If bit 6 is low, the SIM instruction will have no affect on the SOD flip-flop. This permits independent execution of SIMs to service either SOD or interrupts without affecting the other.

It is obvious that the SID and SOD controls are relatively dumb, and that sort of signals appear or are accepted by them are under control of the programme to a great extent. This is important if a serial data transmission is in progress and interrupts must be serviced at the same time.

SUPPORT DEVICES FOR THE 8085

At the time of introduction of the 8085, several additional support devices were introduced to enable the '85 to be adapted to a great variety ofE system organizations. A few are listed here. The student is encouraged to look them up in the documentation and review their usage characteristics.

- *8155 Works In A Drawer:* (For lack of a better description.) This device provides several items of general use for a small '85-based control environment. It includes 256 bytes of RAM, two 8-bit wide parallel ports, one 6-bit wide parallel port (usually used as control lines for the other two ports), and an interval timer. The timer is programmable, and the ports may be used for input, output, or both. The device accepts standard 8085 electrical interface lines and operates on a single 5 volt supply.
- *8755 EPROM With I/O:* This device provides 2Ks worth of 8-bit bytes of UV-erasable EPROM, and two

8-bit-wide bi-directional parallel I/O ports. It uses the 8085 electrical interface, and a 5 volt supply.

- *8259 Programmable Interrupt Controller:* This is later device which interfaces with several processors, including the 8085 and the 16-bit 8086. It handles 8 vectored interrupts by itself, and is cascadable to a total of 64 interrupts by adding additional 8259's to each of the first one's input lines. It requires initialization bytes to be sent to it before it can perform, and these bytes can tailor its operation to a variety of conditions. It requires a single 5 volt supply.

Index